T0330439

Knowledge, Beliefs and Economics

Knowledge, Beliefs and Economics

Edited by

Richard Arena

Professor of Economics, DEMOS–GREDEG/
Centre National de la Recherche Scientifique (CNRS),
University of Nice-Sophia Antipolis, France

and

Agnès Festré

Associate Professor of Economics, DEMOS–GREDEG/
Centre National de la Recherche Scientifique (CNRS),
University of Nice-Sophia Antipolis, France

Edward Elgar

Cheltenham, UK • Northampton, MA, USA

Published by
Edward Elgar Publishing Limited
Glensanda House
Montpellier Parade
Cheltenham
Glos GL50 1UA
UK

Edward Elgar Publishing, Inc.
136 West Street
Suite 202
Northampton
Massachusetts 01060
USA

A catalogue record for this book
is available from the British Library

Library of Congress Cataloguing in Publication Data

Knowledge, beliefs and economics/edited by Richard Arena and Agnès Festré.
    p. cm.
    'This book is the translation of an extended version of a special issue of *Revue d'économie politique* (*Connaissance et croyances en économie*, vol. 5, 2002)' — Acknowledgments.
    Includes bibliographical references and index.
    1. Economics. 2. Economics—Study and teaching. 3. Economists. I. Arena, R. (Richard). II. Festré, Agnès, 1969–   . III. *Revue d'économie politique*.
HB71.K56   2006
330—dc22

                        2005057707

ISBN-13: 978 1 84376 405 2
ISBN-10: 1 84376 405 9

Printed and bound in Great Britain by MPG Books Ltd, Bodmin, Cornwall

Contents

List of contributors   vii
Acknowledgments   ix

1 Introduction   1
   Richard Arena and Agnès Festré

PART I   KNOWLEDGE AND BELIEFS IN THE HISTORY OF
         ECONOMIC ANALYSIS: MARSHALLIANS,
         AUSTRIANS AND WALRASIANS

2 Expectations, uncertainty and beliefs in Marshallian and
   post-Marshallian analyses of economic systems   11
   Brian J. Loasby

3 Knowledge and beliefs in economics: the case of the Austrian
   tradition   35
   Richard Arena and Agnès Festré

4 General equilibrium, co-ordination and multiplicity on spot
   markets   59
   Roger Guesnerie

PART II   KNOWLEDGE AND BELIEFS IN GAME THEORY

5 Justifications of game theoretic equilibrium notions   83
   Bernard Walliser

6 Game theory and players' beliefs on the play   107
   Christian Schmidt

PART III   BELIEFS AND DECISION THEORY

7 Beliefs and dynamic consistency   137
   Jean-Marc Tallon and Jean-Christophe Vergnaud

8 Utility or rationality? Restricted or general rationality?   155
   Raymond Boudon

v

PART IV   KNOWLEDGE, BELIEFS AND COGNITIVE
          ECONOMICS

 9 The cognitive turning point in economics: social beliefs and
    conventions   181
    André Orléan

10 A cognitive approach to individual learning: some experimental
    results   203
    Marco Novarese and Salvatore Rizzello

PART V   AGENTS, COMMUNITIES AND COLLECTIVE
         BELIEFS

11 Consumer communities, self-organization and beliefs   223
    Stéphane Ngo-Maï and Alain Raybaut

12 Informal communication, collective beliefs and corporate
    culture: a conception of the organization as a 'community
    of communities'   239
    Patrick Cohendet and Morad Diani

Index   267

Contributors

Richard Arena, DEMOS–GREDEG/Centre National de la Recherche Scientifique (CNRS)/University of Nice-Sophia Antipolis, France.

Raymond Boudon, Académie des sciences morales et politiques, Paris, France.

Patrick Cohendet, BETA/Centre National de la Recherche Scientifique (CNRS)/University of Strasbourg I, France.

Morad Diani, BETA/Centre National de la Recherche Scientifique (CNRS)/University of Strasbourg I, France.

Agnès Festré, DEMOS–GREDEG/Centre National de la Recherche Scientifique (CNRS)/University of Nice-Sophia Antipolis, France.

Brian J. Loasby, Department of Economics, University of Stirling, United Kingdom.

Roger Guesnerie, Collège de France and Ecole des Hautes Etudes en Sciences Sociales (EHESS), Paris, France.

Stéphane Ngo-Maï, DEMOS–GREDEG/Centre National de la Recherche Scientifique (CNRS)/University of Nice-Sophia Antipolis, France.

Marco Novarese, Centre for Cognitive Economics, Università del Piemonte Orientale, Italy.

André Orléan, Centre National de la Recherche Scientifique (CNRS) and Ecole des Hautes Etudes en Sciences Sociales (EHESS), Paris, France.

Alain Raybaut, DEMOS–GREDEG/Centre National de la Recherche Scientifique (CNRS), Sophia Antipolis, France.

Salvatore Rizzello, Centre for Cognitive Economics, Università del Piemonte Orientale, Italy.

Christian Schmidt, LESOD/University of Paris-Dauphine, France.

Jean-Marc Tallon, EUREQua/Centre National de la Recherche Scientifique (CNRS), Paris, France.

Jean-Christophe Vergnaud, EUREQua/Centre National de la Recherche Scientifique (CNRS), Paris, France.

Bernard Walliser, Ecole Nationale des Ponts et Chaussées and Ecole des Hautes Etudes en Sciences Sociales (EHESS), Paris, France.

Acknowledgements

This book is the translation of an extended version of a special issue of *Revue d'économie politique* (*Connaissance et croyances en économie*, vol. 5, 2002).

The editor would like to thank Gilbert Abraham-Frois for his generous support and help during the preparation of the special issue of *Revue d'économie politique* and his permission for the translation of some of the papers in this volume; all the authors of the papers included in this book, not only for their contribution to it but also for the fruitful discussions which took place on several occasions during the preparation of the special issue and this volume.

Finally, this volume would not have had the slightest chance of completion without the help of Marianna Vintiadis, who not only translated several papers from French and revised all the contributions of the volume, but also helped the co-editors to avoid various wrong meanings and ill-founded arguments.

1. Introduction

Richard Arena and Agnès Festré

The role played by the notion of belief in modern economics is somewhat paradoxical. On the one hand, it is clearly and increasingly gaining prominence in most fields of contemporary analysis, such as decision theory, price theory, finance, game theory, information theory, sunspot theory, economics of the mind and organization theory. On the other hand, this popularity stands in stark contrast to the lack of precision that characterizes the concept of belief within economics. The paradox could be easily dismissed by arguing that belief shares the fate of many other concepts encountered in modern economic analysis: the more they are used, the less precise they are. The reasons for this tendency are certainly complex and we shall not attempt to tackle them here. Suffice it to say that a more general and systematic reflection on the role of beliefs in economics still needs to be carried out, especially given that by doing so our knowledge of many economic phenomena and their interactive mechanisms would certainly increase.

It is by no mere accident that beliefs have come to occupy an increasingly prominent place in modern economics. This is the result of the influence of three current strains of modern economic thought, all affecting our representation of economic agents and of economic forms of rationality.

The progressive decline of the General Equilibrium research programme substantially changed the idea of economic equilibrium that prevailed among economists during the first two decades following the Second World War. Until the 1970s, economists assimilated the micro-coordination issue into the problem of the co-ordination of individual agents in interacting markets through a unique central co-ordination mechanism (the well-known 'tâtonnement' process – see, for instance, Arrow and Hahn, Chapter 11, especially pp. 264–70). As the General Equilibrium agenda came to be replaced by a research programme based on the theories of games and information the landscape changed. Strategies came into the picture and these had to be based on mutual and rational knowledge and beliefs. Briefly speaking, a new view of micro-coordination emerged, which was no longer forced to rely on the analytical assumption of centralized markets. However, the introduction of this new view was confronted with a difficulty, which both Morgenstern (1935) and Hayek (1937) had already emphasized in the interwar years. Given that agents interact in all economic systems their decisions are at least partially based on the forecasts they are able to make in relation to the expected behaviour of other agents. Now, if we accept the assumption that these decisions and forecasts must be rational, a logical problem arises. In order to display rational micro-behaviours, agents must acquire some knowledge of the beliefs and information of other economic agents. However, it is clear that part of this information and beliefs also depends on their own knowledge and beliefs. A problem of logical circularity thus arises, which game theory tried to solve.

While all these developments were taking place, substantial work was also being carried out in an attempt to better understand the processes leading to equilibrium. This work gave rise to the competing ideas of 'eductive' and 'evolutionary' processes (see the contributions of Guesnerie and Walliser in this volume). Eductive processes are processes in which an equilibrium state stems solely from the reasoning of hyper-intelligent players who share a common knowledge of the game structure and of their rationality (see the introductory part of Walliser's contribution to this volume). By contrast, evolutionary processes are those in which an equilibrium state results from the convergence of a learning or an evolutionary process followed by players with bounded rationality but mindful of previous play (ibid.). Evolutionary mechanisms have many variations. Despite this diversity, they all share a form of rationality which is radically different from the one featured in eductive models. Evolutionary models exclude a 'strong' form of rationality, which allows agents to have direct access – i.e. through purely mental means and independently of any form of social interaction – to the common knowledge of the structure of the economic system and of the rationality of other agents. In fact, 'evolutionary' decisions take into account beliefs founded only on the knowledge of past individual actions and observed forms of social interaction. This means that agents contribute to the generation of inter-individual evolutionary mechanisms which they ignored *ex ante*. However, this type of individual learning does not imply a strong knowledge of the strategic neighbourhood of agents and most importantly it does not require knowledge of the overall consequences such mechanisms have on the whole economic system.

The increasing attention paid to the notion of agent heterogeneity also substantially contributed to the emergence of the notion of belief in economic theory. We are all very well aware of the theoretical limits imposed by the treatment of agents and individual rationality in General Equilibrium theory with complete markets or by the use of the idea of a representative agent. These limits clearly derive from the assumption of agent homogeneity.

Various attempts have been made to relax it, putting various forms of heterogeneity in its place. For instance, the pioneering works of Radner and Hahn, mentioned by Guesnerie in this volume, used information to characterize the heterogeneity of individual agents in different situations. They showed how different individual information sets and different micro forecast structures allowed for the characterization of agent 'specificities' in relation to, but quite independently of, their particular preferences and initial endowments. Agent heterogeneity based on information specificities is commonplace within game theory: agents differ depending on the nature of their knowledge and the structure of their beliefs.

The assumption of agent heterogeneity is not, however, the result of modern analytical developments. General Equilibrium and game theory only revived an assumption that has been present in economic theory for a long time. For instance, as Loasby in this volume shows, Alfred Marshall insisted on the temporal variability of the nature and economic preferences of men as well as the variety of their types of knowledge. Orléan's chapter in this volume also shows how Keynes emphasized the diversity of agent beliefs and expectations in financial markets and studied how this diversity could be reduced through the emergence of market conventions. Finally, as Arena and Festré note in their chapter, the Austrian tradition delved deeply into the fundamental heterogeneity of agents' subjective beliefs and knowledge as well as the contrast between 'innovative' and 'imitative' types of behaviour.

The increasing presence of the concept of belief in contemporary economics is also due to the recent simultaneous but distinct rise of the theory of 'knowledge-based economies' and of the 'economics of the mind'. The former focuses on the role played by the concept of tacit knowledge in innovation processes or entrepreneurial decisions. We are all very well aware of the way in which this concept is connected to the structure of knowledge and beliefs of the different agents and communities within particular firms (see also the chapters by Cohendet and Diani, Loasby, and Ngo-Maï and Raybaut in this volume).

'Economics of the mind' provides a new kind of explanation of decision making, the formation of rules and market interaction. First, it shows how decision making cannot be limited to the field of expected utility theory, as Boudon sets out in this volume. Secondly, the degree of confidence of agents in their own beliefs and therefore belief updating also require serious consideration – as the contribution of Tallon and Vergnaud shows. Thirdly, a convergent pre-existing path does not predefine rule formation, as Novarese and Rizzello argue. Finally, market interaction cannot be reduced to the study of the properties of equilibrium states but implies an analysis of the relationship between individual behaviour, beliefs and market organization, as stressed in the contributions of Orléan and of Ngo-Maï and Raybaut in this volume.

As we just noted, the concept of beliefs plays an increasingly important role in the recent advances of economics and especially of game theory (see, for instance, the contributions of both Schmidt and Tallon and Vergnaud in this volume). These advances must not hide however that it is also crucial to identify the main analytical problems that the introduction of this concept has brought along.

The first problem that arises is the compatibility between economic rationality and a serious attempt to take individual beliefs into account. Even if economic rationality cannot be reduced to its instrumental dimension, it is clear that, very often, this first problem is reduced to the question of the compatibility between the existence of beliefs and the theory of the rational choice. If one takes this reductionist approach, the main problem following the introduction of the concept of beliefs in economics can be identified with the search of the logical conditions necessary to define rational and consistent beliefs.

The requirement of instrumental rationality implies a strict separation of the spheres of the preference system, of the rules of the game and of the scheme of beliefs. The usual preference system must remain unchanged after the inclusion of the influence of individual beliefs on the process of economic choices. Technically, agents must still have a preference ordering because it is only when preferences are ordered that agents will be able to begin to form beliefs about how different actions can satisfy their preferences in different degrees. The rules of the game must be defined perfectly independently of both the preference system and the scheme of beliefs. In order to fulfil this condition, individuals are assumed to know the rules of the game perfectly, i.e., they are assumed to know all the possible actions and how these combine to yield particular pay-offs for each agent. In the context of game theory, this assumption obviously implies the notion of common knowledge. Individual motives for choosing specific actions must also be independent from the rules of the game, which structure the set of possible actions.

The requirement of consistency implies a characterization of the scheme of beliefs that allows the formation of an equilibrium ensuring the compatibility of different individual schemes. One of the first consequences of this requirement is the definition of the concept of belief within economic theory. For instance, as noted by Guesnerie in this volume, the requirement of consistency in the tradition of General Equilibrium theory implies the assimilation of individual beliefs to pure probabilistic expectations on future prices. In the same way, Walliser's distinction between 'structural', 'factual' and 'strategic' beliefs appears to be a prerequisite of the condition of consistency. Clearly, this first problem disappears if we decide to drop the theory of rational choice and tackle the consistency requirement in a different way. This however does not imply that new problems will not emerge.

The second problem is related to what Hargreaves Heap and Varoufakis (2004) call the notion of 'consistent alignment of beliefs', which, according to them, 'means that no instrumentally rational person can expect another similarly rational person who has the same information to develop different thought processes' (ibid., p. 28). From this standpoint, 'your beliefs about what your opponent will do are consistently aligned in the sense that if you actually knew what her plans were, you would not want to change your beliefs about those plans. And if she knew your plans, she would not want to change the beliefs she holds about you and which support her own planned actions' (ibid., p. 28). This notion implies the reduction of all agent reasonableness to strict instrumental rationality. It contradicts Boudon's argument (in this volume), which supports the idea that there exist rational beliefs that are not founded on the search for self-interest, that are not consequentialist and that do not require a cost–benefit calculation. It also obviously contrasts with pragmatist views that see beliefs as the establishment of a certain habit determining the way in which agents will act when appropriately stimulated. This definition implies that the various individual habits related to different individual beliefs can correspond to various 'good reasons'.

A third problem concerns the relations between the individual and the collective dimensions of beliefs. According to standard economic theory, it is clear that all social relations, institutions or structures derive from interactions between initially and *ex-ante* asocial agents. From this standpoint, collective magnitudes or structures do not exist as such but are only the result of the aggregation of microeconomic magnitudes: Guesnerie and Walliser's contributions stress this particular feature of modern mainstream economic theory. Although this is the predominant conception, others are conceivable. Orléan's and Ngo-Maï and Raybaut's chapters share the idea that there exist collective beliefs which cannot be reduced to pure shared beliefs. This viewpoint always presupposes some autonomy of social entities vis-à-vis microeconomic behaviours. An interesting example is provided by 'team thinking': in this case, collective intentionality (see, for instance, Gilbert 1989 and Tuomela 1995) replaces individual intentionality and some behavioural autonomy is attributed to the team considered as a whole. Another example is provided by Keynes' typology of beliefs (see Arena 2004). In the *Treatise on Probability*, certain beliefs are assimilated to pure knowledge. They correspond to cases in which the 'weight' of argument is related to the maximum 'degree of rational beliefs'. Rational beliefs are tantamount to probabilistic beliefs; they correspond to the situation in which the weight of argument is associated to an intermediate 'degree'. Now, non-rational beliefs correspond to *collective* or conventional beliefs. In this last case, the weight of argument tends to zero and real knowledge is replaced by *collective* beliefs elaborated thanks to the interaction between agents. These beliefs are the result of a social convention, which creates what can be called collective knowledge.

As described earlier, the compatibility between the rational theory of choice and the introduction of beliefs presupposes the independence of preference sets, schemes of beliefs and rules of the game. Recent developments in the new field of 'psychological games' (Hargreaves Heap and Varoufakis 2004, Chapter 7) suggest that this independence could be abandoned (see also Schmidt's contribution in this volume). From this standpoint, beliefs could be directly related to and constitute the agents' preferences, a position that could imply the abandonment of the strict separation of preferences from the rules of the game. Alternatively, it could also be possible to start from some social practices or shared rules (as Hargreaves Heap and Varoufakis (2004) remind us, Wittgenstein related them to what he called 'forms of life') and derive preferences and rules mutually and simultaneously from them. In this context, the agents' perception of their preferences is ill-defined before the game is played and instrumental rationality must be defined after the characterization of prevailing norms of behaviour, as it appears in Novarese and Rizzello's chapter in this volume. This route is new to game theory and only appears in its most advanced developments (see the contribution of Schmidt in this volume).

However, its way had already been paved by older approaches. For instance, pragmatist thinkers in the social sciences related individual and collective beliefs directly to social rules. A good example can be found in Peirce's process of 'fixation of beliefs'. Most of the methods he described in order to determine agent beliefs (the 'method of tenacity', the method of 'authority' and the '*a priori* method', see Peirce [1897] 1966, pp. 101–12) generate beliefs which can be true or false, instrumentally rational or non-rational. However, they allow the elimination of what Peirce called states of doubt (Peirce [1897] 1966, pp. 98–101) and the discomfort that is associated with them. The last method of fixation of beliefs analysed by Peirce is the 'scientific method'. This method clearly differs from the first three in that the fixation of beliefs is no longer a purely human endeavour, in the sense that the ideas that are fixed are ultimately determined by what we wish to believe. Therefore, it proceeds from the recognition that nature does not accommodate itself to agents' beliefs but that agents' beliefs must accommodate themselves to nature. In other words, according to this last method, as Peirce would have it, preferences and beliefs are, to a large extent, constituted by social rules and practices. Another example could be provided by the second Wittgenstein who, in his *Philosophical Investigations*, criticizes the idea of a strict separation of action from shared rules. Shared rules limit what can be done but it makes no sense to think of them as distinct from actions since they are also enabling. Rules cannot be understood independently of the actions which exemplify them. Actions and belief structures are, therefore, mutually constituted in the agents' practices of a given society or a given economy.

These insights show how much work still needs to be done. A serious investigation of beliefs within economics seems to imply the need for a multidisciplinary approach. This is why this book includes contributions related to various disciplines such as mathematical economics, history of economic thought, economic analysis, experimental economics, sociology, social philosophy and economic methodology. We hope it will be interpreted more as an incentive to further research on the role of knowledge and beliefs in economics than as a final assessment of what has already been done.

REFERENCES

Arena, R. (2004), 'On the relation between individual and collective beliefs: a comparison between Keynes and Hayek's economic theories', in L.R. Wray and M. Forstater (eds), *Contemporary Post Keynesian Analysis*, Cheltenham: Edward Elgar, pp. 249–66.

Arrow, K. and Hahn, F. (1971), *General Competitive Analysis*, San Francisco: Holeden-Day and Edinburgh: Oliver and Boyd.

Gilbert, M. (1989), *On Social Facts*, London: Routledge.

Hargreaves Heap, S. and Varoufakis Y. (2004), *Game Theory: A Critical Text*, 2nd edn, London and New York: Routledge.

Hayek, F. von (1937), 'Economics and knowledge', presidential address delivered before the London Economic Club, 10 November 1936, *Economica* (new series, **4**).

Morgenstern, O. (1935), 'Perfect foresight and economic equilibrium', *Zeitschrift für Nationalokonomie*, reprinted in A. Schotter (ed.), *Selected Economic Writings of Oskar Morgenstern*, New York: New York University Press (1976), pp. 169–83.

Peirce, C.S. ([1897] 1966), 'The fixation of beliefs', in P. Wiener (ed.), *C. Peirce, Selecting Writings (Values in a Universe of Chance)*, New York: Dover Publications.

Tuomela, R. (1995), *The Importance of Us: A Philosophical Study of Basic Social Notions*, Standford: Standford University Press.

Wittgenstein, L. (2001), *Philosofische Untersuchungen – Philosophical Investigation*, Oxford: Blackwell.

PART I

Knowledge and Beliefs in the History
of Economic Analysis: Marshallians,
Austrians and Walrasians

2. Expectations, uncertainty and beliefs in Marshallian and post-Marshallian analyses of economic systems

Brian J. Loasby

2.1 MAKING SENSE

Economies are complex systems, composed of many levels of partially interacting subsystems; and so they are necessarily beyond the detailed comprehension of any single brain within that system (Hayek 1952, p. 185). In seeking to understand them we are therefore obliged to resort to simplifications, omissions, aggregations of heterogenous elements which are treated as homogenous, and formulations that are false but manageable. We have to make sense of the world by creating representations; and it is a representation, not the presumed reality, that is the subject of both our theoretical manipulations and the decision processes of economic agents. In this chapter we shall consider the work of a group of economists who were particularly concerned that their analysis should adequately represent the economic systems and economic processes – including the cognitive processes of economic agents – that they were trying to understand.

It is reasonable to try to adjust the particular combination of simplifications, shortcuts and admitted falsehoods that constitute a representation to the particular purposes or problems that we have in mind. Moreover, continued reliance on a particular kind of representation is necessary for progress in any scientific or productive endeavour, and this representation must be shared by those contributing to this endeavour, as Thomas Kuhn (1962, 1970) pointed out. However, it is essential not to confuse any representation with the truth that it purports to represent; the partial truths that may be attained by using any representation should therefore be exposed to further investigation before being used as a basis for policy or for any economic activity. Most firms whose business depends on scientific or technological proficiency respect this principle; that is why their research and development is mainly development. Politicians pressed to take decisive and immediate action often neglect it; that explains many policy failures. Even if all necessary precautions are taken, from time to time it may be desirable to make substantial changes to the representations that are applied to particular fields of knowledge, as Kuhn also emphasized.

This fallibilist approach to knowledge is strikingly at odds with the established mode of economic theorizing, in which 'rational choices' are derived from the perceived consequences of the available alternatives. Expectations are therefore fundamental; but although 'rationality' may be interpreted as requiring no more than the correct alignment of choice with perceptions, the standard assumption in economic analysis is that these perceptions are accurate. Most economists are very reluctant to treat expectations as problematic, and so collapse knowledge, expectations and beliefs into a 'correct model'. This practice simplifies the analysis of equilibria, and is in turn supported by it, for in rational choice models equilibrium implies that there are no unexploited gains from trade, and therefore no possibility of 'knowing better'.

In many pieces of analysis, including the foundational textbook analyses of consumers' choice and the firm's choices of product mix, input combinations, output and price, the possibility set is simply assumed to be precisely defined, usually with no warning that such an assumption is being made. Such analyses can be extended to include a range of outcomes for each alternative by defining probabilities over this range, and these probabilities may even be deemed to be 'subjective'. This extension allows economists to deny that they always assume perfect knowledge; but in treating the resulting equilibrium as valid they are implicitly assuming perfect knowledge of probability distributions. Although the formal analysis is unaffected by calling probabilities 'subjective' rather than 'objective', its status in prediction, in supporting equilibrium, or in advising decision-makers is very different: it introduces the possibility of error without considering either the consequences of error or any means of mitigating those consequences. We may be unable to dispense with beliefs as guides to action; but it is the beginning of wisdom not to confuse belief with certainty. The next step in wisdom is to consider whether an economic system (and a social and political system) which is prone to such errors has, or can be provided with, means for coping with this propensity to err.

The potential to cope with error, to modify beliefs, and to improve knowledge was a major element in the search for the principles of a viable civil society which motivated Adam Smith's work and provided the context for his economics. The economists to be considered in this chapter took up some of Smith's principal ideas, though sometimes unconsciously. To appreciate their ways of thinking, it is important to avoid treating correct expectations as the base case, uncertainty as a variant, and beliefs as the unanalysed source of subjective probabilities. Instead one should start at the other end, with ignorance as the base case; the problem is then how to reduce that ignorance – or, more positively, how to increase knowledge, though never achieving absolute certainty. This, incidentally, is a perspective much closer than that of mainstream economics to both the philosophy of knowledge and some current ideas in neurobiology; and it has the advantage of allowing us to conceive of novelty as a product of the system rather than as an exogenous shock, and therefore to develop a growth theory in which growth is truly endogenous.

2.2 MARSHALL

2.2.1 Marshall's Problem of Knowledge

Though the origins of theories do not provide sufficient grounds for judging their value, an understanding of origins is sometimes a great help in understanding why theories take the form that they do; and to understand the significance of expectations, uncertainty and beliefs in Marshall's economics it is necessary to go back to his early years as a Fellow of St John's College, Cambridge, when his status as Second Wrangler in the Mathematics Tripos gave him a great deal of freedom in what he should study and what he should teach.

For Marshall these were troubled years, of which Groenewegen (1995) provides a comprehensive account. Marshall had been brought up by his father in the demonstrable truths of evangelical Christianity, and had chosen at Cambridge to immerse himself in the demonstrated truths of mathematics. The privileged status of mathematics at Cambridge was attributed to its power of deriving empirical knowledge by pure axiomatic reasoning – most notably in the theorems of Euclid, which were deemed to constitute the only conceivable geometry; and it was quite widely argued that something like axiomatic proof was attainable for Christianity (Groenewegen 1995, p. 116). However, before Marshall arrived in Cambridge, Henry Mansel, a distinguished theologian and philosopher, had argued in a series of lectures that the truths of religion were impossible to prove; they rested on faith. These lectures provoked a double debate, about the validity of Mansel's argument and the implications of accepting it. Marshall discovered this debate after completing his degree, when his own religious beliefs were wavering, and he realized its significance, not only for religious belief but also for the status of axiomatic reasoning. He noted, for example, that

John Stuart Mill's dismissal of any axiomatic basis for Christian truth seemed incompatible with the unquestioned power of Euclidean geometry to deliver necessary truths about the universe (Butler 1991, p. 276). Then in late 1869 or early 1870, Marshall's closest friend, Clifford, introduced him to non-Euclidean geometry (Butler 1991, p. 282), which demonstrated that axiomatic reasoning could not be relied on to ensure the empirical truth of its conclusions; and both of the major sources of certainty in Marshall's life were undermined.

Marshall might have derived a similar sceptical conclusion from David Hume, but there is no evidence that he did. Nevertheless, even before his acquaintance with non-Euclidean geometry, his deep uneasiness about the possibility of attaining true knowledge had prompted a reaction similar to Hume's: since there was no route to assured empirical truth, it was better to turn to the question of how people developed particular beliefs. The key was to be found not in axiomatics but psychology. For some years, Marshall contemplated a specialization in psychology, and at the end of his life wondered whether he had been right to prefer economics; and if we read Marshall with this strongly motivated early interest in mind, it is not difficult to identify substantial psychological elements in his writing, as Raffaelli (2003) has done. Moreover, this interest coincided with the impact of Charles Darwin's ideas, and so Marshall's psychology is evolutionary. What people come to know (or to believe they know) is the consequence of trial and error in a particular environment; thus, different environments tend to lead to different knowledge. An enquiry into the growth of knowledge entails a fundamental shift of analytical attention from proof to process; for economists it implies a requirement for theories which are 'in time', not just theories in which time is a parameter. (For a superb exposition of this issue, see Hicks [1976] 1982.)

The most substantial evidence of Marshall's conception of evolutionary psychology is a paper called 'Ye machine' (Marshall 1994), written for a Cambridge discussion group; this is the most elaborate model to be found anywhere in his writings. He envisages a machine which is capable of registering impressions from its environment and performing various actions in response, under guidance from a control system which links 'ideas' of impressions to 'ideas' of actions. There is no initial operating programme for this control system, but once the machine is set in motion a sequence begins of ideas of impression – ideas of action – ideas of subsequent impression; and if the latter is favourable the initial impression becomes linked to the apparently successful action. Over time, such a machine may develop a range of closely connected ideas of impressions and actions, which we might now call routines; these routines are not the result of anticipatory choice but of environmental selection among actions which, by Marshall's intentional specification of his model, cannot originate in consequential reasoning. To be precise – and this may sometimes be very important, though Marshall does not say so – selection depends on the environment as it is perceived by the machine. In the elaboration of his model this environment contains other machines that operate on similar principles, but because of differences in initial perceptions and initial actions and the selective reinforcement of what appears to work they may develop different connections. Thus, a population of machines constructed to a uniform design may generate the variety which is essential for any evolutionary process.

Marshall continues his evolutionary sequence by postulating the emergence of a second level of control. Impressions which have not been linked to any satisfactory action can now be referred to this higher level, which may generate the idea of a novel action and associate it with the idea of an impression of its effects. This linkage of ideas is then transferred to the lower level, where (if apparently successful in practice) it forms a new routine. The second level thus introduces expectations, which cannot be deduced from evidence but may be influenced by experience; and so the variations generated at this level, which are still subject to selection at the practical level, are not random but oriented to problems – in contrast to modern Neo-Darwinian principles of variety generation.

This formulation allows Marshall to bypass the philosophical issue of free-will versus determinism. It also has substantial virtues as an evolutionary model which conforms to a basic economic principle: certain regularities of behaviour are selected and reinforced by their success in extracting benefit from their environment at low cost in mental energy. The second level requires the prior development of the first as an effective survival mechanism and subsequently as a problem-generator; with this precondition it becomes an important source of potential improvement in the machine's performance, achieved at low cost in mental energy by the separation of levels. The additional effort of generating and checking novel ideas is undertaken only when the existing set of routines has proved inadequate, and does not disturb those elements in the set which appear to work well; any improvements in performance are stored at the lower level, and thus cease to require active supervision. It is an efficient mechanism for making local adjustments, a precursor of Marshall's partial equilibrium analysis. In modern economics, even when information is assumed to be scarce, cognition is not; for Marshall this was never an acceptable assumption.

2.2.2 Marshall's Method

Marshall's encounter with the problem of knowledge had lasting effects on his views of the appropriate method of doing economics. His assertion that '[k]nowledge is our most powerful engine of production' (Marshall 1920, p. 138) implies that the knowledge available to any person or organization at any time is inevitably incomplete; but he never sought to develop the economics of uncertainty in its usual modern sense as an extension of rational choice, because he never regarded optimization on the basis of perfect knowledge as a credible reference model, as such modern treatments do. On the contrary, his 'machine' begins by knowing nothing, and creates knowledge which is always subject to refutation. Neither evidence nor the strictest application of formal reasoning can exclude this possibility; equilibrium is therefore always provisional – though it may sometimes be durable.

Rather than the economics of uncertainty, Marshall focused on the uncertainty of economics. The implications of non-Euclidean geometry were profound, and their relevance for economics were impressed on Marshall (1961, p. 521) by his discovery that, despite the initial appeal of Cournot's analytical method, its application to increasing returns led directly to empirical falsehood. The applicability of axiomatic reasoning depends crucially on the premises; and when reasoning about anything as complex as an economy it is impossible to ensure that all the necessary premises have been correctly specified or even recognized. Long chains of reasoning should therefore be avoided, and theory, though indispensable in organizing thought, was 'a very small part of economics proper: and by itself sometimes even – well, not a very good occupation of time'; much the greater part was 'a wide and thorough study of facts', which for Marshall were to be found both in documents and by direct experience (Whitaker 1996, vol. II, p. 393).

Instead of seeking to reduce his exposition to a theoretical core, Marshall strove to keep it as realistic as possible. This was not simply a rhetorical preference: the theoretical core could not be relied on unless it could be shown to fit reality. His use of equilibrium is the most striking illustration. Schumpeter (1934, p. 80) asserted that it was the slow emergence of routine, and not rationality, which made Walrasian equilibrium an acceptable fiction, but saw no need to study this emergence; his focus was on the importance of disruptive entrepreneurship as the generator of change. However, as Raffaelli (2003, pp. 43–7) argues, for Marshall equilibrium was the end-state of a process, and should not be used as a theoretical concept unless some adequate account of this process and its setting could be supplied. This adequate account, in Marshall's view, must be related to a partial, not a general, equilibrium; and Marshall's partial equilibrium is dynamics in disguise (Dardi 2002). Indeed, Marshall told J.B. Clark that 'my *statical* state is a mere phase in my dynamical state' (Whitaker 1996, vol. II, p. 419); and in the Preface to the fifth edition of the *Principles* he wrote that 'while a *description* of structure need not concern itself with causes or *forces*, an *explanation* of structure must deal with the forces that brought that structure into existence; and therefore it must be in the physical sense of the term "dynamical"' (Marshall 1961, p. 48).

It may be claimed that it was because Marshall was even more impressed than Walras by the manifold interdependencies of economic phenomena that he demurred from Walras' concept of general equilibrium as the principal basis of analysis. Walras tried to encapsulate all interdependencies in a single perspective, which was later to be extended by Arrow and Debreu. However, even with these extensions the general equilibrium model is incomplete, and yet is not capable of generating any satisfactory general account of how such an equilibrium is to be attained (a problem to which we shall return). Marshall preferred to work with a multi-layered concept of equilibrium, in which the layers related both to different time-periods of activity and different groups of actors. This accorded with his general advice that complex problems must be first broken up for analysis, before these analytical components can be assembled into a coherent structure; it also reflected the need for agents to find a stable basis on which to reach their own decisions. A Marshallian equilibrium represents a balance of forces that allows people to rely on established routines and relationships; a disturbance of this balance stimulates a search for new actions, which if successful will generate new routines (as in his psychological model). However, in undertaking this search people must continue to rely on the continued adequacy of many established practices and assumptions: *ceteris paribus* is a necessary basis not only for the analysis of change but for the orderly conduct of change. What is impossible is to respond to a variation in any of the established parameters by recalculating the optimal configuration of all activities; yet this is precisely what the general equilibrium model requires. It is almost a trivial conclusion from this argument that perfect competition is not a credible setting for these adjustment processes; continuing contacts between economic agents are needed to provide both knowledge and reassurance. To this point we shall return more than once.

Hicks ([1976] 1982, pp. 285–6) points out the implications of this difference in method in consumer theory, where the replacement of marginal utility by an ordinal preference system

> was not so clear an advance as is usually supposed. ... The marginal utility of money, on which Marshall relies, is much more than the mere Lagrange multiplier, the role to which it has been degraded. It is the means by which the consumer is enabled to make his separate decisions, and to make them fairly rationally, without being obliged to take the trouble to weigh all conceivable alternatives.

Not only does Marshall's formulation provide a basis for believing that people will usually be able to make reasoned decisions of the kind that will support equilibrium; it also suggests that reasonable consumer behaviour will be disrupted 'when all prices, or nearly all prices, have broken loose from their moorings'. The routine trivialization of the costs of inflation as 'shoe-leather costs' by many economists would have been much harder to sustain if Marshall's consumer theory, along with other applications of Marshall's method, had not been discarded.

2.2.3   The Growth of Knowledge

From method we turn to content, indicating how Marshall's conception of the human mind is reflected in his account of the working of the economic system that he knew; in doing so, we shall be drawing substantially on the work of Raffaelli (2001, 2003). Marshall's primary reason for preferring economics to psychology was the 'increasing urgency of economic studies, as a means towards human well-being ... not so much in relation to growth as to the quality of life' (Whitaker 1996, vol. II, p. 285); and the obverse of the problem of uncertainty was the possibility of expanding knowledge. Better knowledge was a primary source not only of increased productivity, as mainstream economists have rediscovered, but also of better patterns of consumption, which is still neglected. For Marshall, preference functions, like production functions, were a product of the economic system.

Raffaelli argues that it was because Marshall was both so concerned with improving the quality of life for most people and impressed with the effects of the economic system on this quality, and especially on individual character, that he was not prepared to follow John Stuart Mill's prescription that economists should deduce the necessary general laws of economic activity and leave to psychologists the study of individual variations and their consequences. Economics was 'on the one side a study of wealth; and on the other, and more important side, part of the study of man ... man's character has been moulded ... by the way in which he uses his faculties in his work, by the thoughts and the feelings which it suggests, and by the relations to his associates at work' (Marshall 1920, pp. 1–2). Marshall therefore gave particular attention to the effects of economic organization on the use of talents and the development of character, which he believed were aspects of the same process; and since progress depended on variation the differences between individuals should not be suppressed either in economic analysis or in economic systems.

The implications for demand analysis are clear. Though at any instant the pattern of demand may be taken as data (even if the data are not always easy to establish), 'each new step upwards is to be regarded as the development of new activities giving rise to new wants, rather than of new wants giving rise to new activities' (Marshall 1920, p. 61). Therefore the study of activities must precede the study of wants; and so, in a volume on foundations, Book IV (on the relationships between organization and productive knowledge) is much more substantial than Book III (on wants). Marshall's analysis of the development of wants is not the least important casualty of his failure to produce the second volume, which was an essential part of his original plan.

It seems highly plausible that Marshall's model of the 'machine', the evolved skills of which were shaped by its particular environment, made it easy for him to appreciate the link between Darwinian variation and Smith's division of labour as evolutionary mechanisms; and his exploration of the potential of his 'machine' explicitly included such aspects of character as the willingness to forgo immediate advantage for greater but later gains. Though Marshall seems never to have read Smith's ([1795] 1980) psychological theory of scientific development, presented in his *History of Astronomy* (in which the division of labour appears as an extension of this theory), he had a similar conception of progress, in both productivity and character, that rested on the human ability to make sense by making patterns, rather than on logical skills. Therefore the simplifying assumption of 'economic man' (not yet refined into a model of the rational optimizer) was not adequate, though Marshall recognized the necessity for a general presumption that people would prefer a larger gain to a smaller – as these alternatives were perceived. This qualification led him to recognize the contribution of skills in perception, in consumption as well as production, as a source of human progress, which was his fundamental motivation. By the time that he came to economics, Marshall already had a different model of how the mind works: it was an organized system of connections, developed through interactions between internal structure and external phenomena and events.

Marshall's model of the mind reflected both the operational constraints and the productive potential of human mental processes and of any organizational structure that was intended to make use of them; and it was based on the universal scarcity of cognition, which in most standard economics is the only resource which is never assumed to be scarce. Long before the 'planning debate' Marshall had already identified the limitations of human cognition and the consequent necessary dispersion of knowledge as the crucial weaknesses of socialist schemes. Science itself, the activity most crucially dependent on cognitive skills, is undertaken by a dispersed community that relies on a wide-ranging *ceteris paribus* clause in order to focus on closely-defined problems, which it attempts to reduce to repetitive patterns (Ziman 2000); and the enterprising business man must, likewise, be selective in his focus and rely on many established regularities in order to devise and implement new patterns. The growth of knowledge is always at the margin.

Marshall's recognition of this is exemplified by his 'principle of substitution', which is a guide to selective experimentation against a baseline of established practices (Loasby 1990), as in scientific procedures. In summarizing the qualities required of 'the manufacturer who makes goods not to meet special orders but for the general market', Marshall links ' a thorough knowledge of *things* in his own trade' with 'the power of forecasting the broad movements of production and consumption, of seeing where there is an opportunity for supplying a new commodity that will meet a real want or improving the plan of producing an old commodity' and also with the encouragement of 'whatever enterprise and power of origination' his employees may possess (Marshall 1920, pp. 297–8). Innovation requires both imagination and existing procedures, each of which is represented by a level in the 'brain' of Marshall's 'machine'.

When many people or many organizations pursue this sequence of creativity against a background of routines, leading to new routines which provide a more advanced basis for further creativity, their somewhat differently-organized mental structures (the product of different histories) generate a variety of products and processes to be winnowed by competition. Unlike biological variety, however, this economic variety is the product of freedom as well as chance; and the selection among this variety depends on its compatibility with existing patterns, and to some extent on conscious choices. The dialectics of evolution are presented by Marshall in his discussion of custom:

> If custom had been absolutely rigid, it would have been an unmixed evil. ... However it did not crush out of everyone the desire to humour his own fancy, or his love of novelty, or his inclination to save trouble by a rather better adjustment of implements to the work done: and ... the solidity of custom has rendered the supreme service of perpetuating any such change as found general approval. (Marshall 1919, p. 197)

This 'limited but effective control over natural development by forecasting the future and preparing the way for the next step' (Marshall 1920, p. 248) may be reasonably compared with Darwin's recognition of the significant success of artificial breeding. In both, purposeful though fallible activities, the results of human selection, are subject to the selection processes of the wider environment, and the favoured activities become embodied in routines. The overall result of this process, Marshall believed, was a tendency, emphasized by Herbert Spencer, towards ever greater differentiation of function, matched by closer co-ordination (Marshall 1920, p. 241). This closer co-ordination was exhibited in the various forms of organization that aid the utilization and expansion of knowledge, which for Marshall were joint products of the human mind and the systems which it supported.

2.2.4   Organization

Since human action is directed by the human brain, the successful organization of human activity must respect the particular powers and limitations of the brain; and Marshall's treatment of organization matches his early model of mental activity (Raffaelli 2001). That may well be why he suggested that organization might be recognized, alongside land, labour, and capital, as a fourth factor of production (Marshall 1920, p. 139). Indeed, Marshall's discussion of organization begins in Chapter 9 of the *Principles* with an account (corresponding to his early model) of the multi-level structure of the brain, in which conscious attention is reserved for problem-solving or the introduction of novelty; the application of solutions or the repetition of new actions 'develops new connections between different parts of the brain' (Marshall 1920, p. 252), which gradually take over the maintenance of these activities, leaving the conscious brain free for new initiatives, including those which utilize these now-automatic connections. The process is illustrated by learning to skate; acquired skills no longer require thought, which may then be devoted to devising and controlling particular sequences of skating (Marshall 1920, p. 251). Order makes room for creativity, which is stabilized in a new order which combines newly-established expectations and beliefs into a patterned performance.

All this applies to organized groups of humans. Directed action within a group relies on pre-existing routines within which no choices, in the normal sense, are exercised; but if directed action fails to achieve its objective, the recognition of failure leads either to a modification of existing routines or to experimentation resulting in new routines. Thus knowledge that is already organized into routines facilitates the creation of new knowledge – especially that which builds on the old; and new knowledge which is corroborated by apparently successful application is consolidated into new routines. It is not then surprising that experimentation should be at one or other of the margins of knowledge; and these margins will differ according to the past history of the growth of knowledge within each organization, because this history influences beliefs about the capabilities of that organization and where they might be most effectively applied. The generation of variety is a natural consequence; and this may be considered an effective response to the underlying and pervasive uncertainty about the likely directions of progress.

Moreover, since individual learning is embodied in new connections within the brain, we may expect organizational change to be an essential factor in economic development; and so it was for Marshall: '[T]he part which man plays [in production] shows a tendency to increasing return. The *law of increasing return* may be worded thus:- An increase of labour and capital leads generally to improved organization, which increases the efficiency of the work of labour and capital' (Marshall 1920, p. 318). Increasing return is not a property of any production function, but the outcome of a cognitive process in which new productive arrangements are created. Indeed, it is a phenomenon of the human brain itself; for in the brain as in the economy, the increasing return is to be attributed not to the elements but to the organization of more productive connections between them.

Among the difficulties that naturally arise from this conception of progress is that of finding an appropriate balance between order and creativity. Marshall saw this as a particular problem with large firms, in which routines are prime supporters of organizational coherence, and especially dangerous because of the valid claims that large firms could achieve greater efficiency through more carefully-planned and larger-scale routines: the means of achieving this efficiency may repress 'elasticity and initiative' (Marshall 1919, p. 324), and therefore the changes in mental and formal organization that aid knowledge. Moreover, larger firms necessarily imply fewer firms, and therefore a reduction in variety. In standard economics fewer firms may reduce welfare because they reduce allocative efficiency; that they may reduce welfare because they reduce the range of experiments is not compatible with the assumptions that are necessary to sustain the standard analyses of rational choice equilibria. This, however, is a direct implication of Marshall's theoretical system, in which economies of scale should not be confused with increasing returns.

It is perhaps because of this double threat to initiative and variety that Marshall was so impressed with the virtues of an industrial district, which seemed to ensure the 'automatic organization' (Marshall 1919, p. 600) of highly specialized activities while facilitating both the generation and the active discussion of novel ideas, including ideas for constructing new patterns of relationships between firms. In view of the more recent history of many British industrial districts, it is worth recording Marshall's warning (1919, pp. 135–7) that a network of well-proven routines could impede a major reordering of productive systems, which would then be undertaken by newcomers. Confidently-held expectations provide the assurance to act, but this confidence may prevent the timely revision of those expectations.

The industrial district organizes most of the external knowledge on which each firm within it relies. However, Marshall insisted that every firm required some form of external organization: a set of linkages to customers, suppliers and (perhaps indirectly through trade associations and trade journals) to other firms in the same trade. The development of an appropriate and reliable set of linkages is necessarily a lengthy business (Marshall 1920, p. 500), and requires much conscious attention before it can be taken sufficiently for granted to provide the expectations on which both regular business and experimentation can be based. (Remember that the two are closely linked.) Atomistic competition will not suffice.

2.2.5 Equilibrium

Marshall sought to explain how human action, in a context of human organization and market relations, generated economic progress. This seemed to require a definition of 'normal' that was explicitly differentiated from 'competitive' (Marshall 1920, pp. 347–8), and a range of partial equilibria, with expectations considered in corresponding time perspectives and organizational contexts. Moreover, as noted earlier, Marshall believed that the use of equilibrium theorizing was questionable, and even misleading, without some account of equilibration in contemporary economies. Because the knowledge of each person is incomplete, especially when the total amount of knowledge in the economy is being continually expanded by the joint effects of the division of labour and the 'tendency to variation in any trade' (Marshall 1920, p. 355), and also because the ability of the human brain to process knowledge is severely restricted, any account of movement towards equilibrium must rely on local interpretation of local knowledge.

The standard practice of deriving equilibria directly from the basic data of the model – goods, preferences, and production sets – requires knowledge to be relevantly complete. Probability distributions are admissible, and even asymmetric information, if the asymmetries are themselves known; but the data must allow closure if proof of equilibrium, or of multiple equilibria, is to be possible. In Marshall's system, however, knowledge is never complete, for that would exclude the possibility of generating new knowledge. On the other hand every agent has a history, which has left that agent with a cluster of productive and decision-making skills, including a set of expectations which provide a baseline for conscious thought, and a cluster of connections to other agents and to institutions which may be expected to guide behaviour within groups. Not least among these institutions is the current set of prices, which depend on the use of money as a unit of account (the significance of which Hicks eventually recognized, as we have seen). From the agents' perspective, therefore, what economists see as the equilibration problem is not a task to be solved *de novo*, but always a question of adjustment – which may be difficult – from an established position. Moreover, this established position has a history, although the interpretation of that history may vary across agents. Thus, the problem of finding a new equilibrium configuration is precisely the problem of finding new knowledge about the prices and quantities that are appropriate in the new situation. What makes both problems soluble in principle, most of the time, is the familiarity of the setting. Marshall's principle of continuity links movement with stability, a combination that is essential to Darwinian evolution.

In Book V of the *Principles* the most elaborate demonstration of the importance of a familiar setting in reaching equilibrium is provided in Marshall's treatment of temporary equilibrium (Marshall 1920, pp. 332–6); this is appropriate because the most localized adjustments provide the most secure basis for expectations. He begins in what is now orthodox fashion, by deducing the equilibrium price from supply and demand curves, but then, noting that out-of-equilibrium transactions might lead to a different price, enquires whether this is a likely outcome. Taking as his setting the corn market in a country town, he argues that in a local and regular market the traders will be equally-matched and well-informed; their expectations will be derived from appropriate experience and normally compatible enough to lead to a price close to that which might be calculated by an omniscient analyst.

Short-run prices are also affected by the history of repeated transactions between buyer and seller, and the expectation that these will continue. This leads to the prediction, contrary to modern theory, that short-run prices, even in times of depressed trade, will 'be generally very much above' short-run cost (Marshall 1920, p. 374); this is a consequence of the continuing relationships that contribute to each party's 'external organization'. His presentation of long-run equilibrium is less well supported by an examination of the setting, perhaps because the long run allows for much greater changes in relationships and in expectations. Indeed, the creation of an external organization that guides short-run decisions is specified by Marshall as a long-run phenomenon. Overall, we may conclude that the analysis of Book IV logically precedes Book V not only because it deals with supply but also because it provides the institutional and cognitive setting for explaining the formation of prices – which has never been satisfactorily explained within a Walrasian system.

That this setting may sometimes be inadequate to ensure full employment is noted by Marshall (1920, pp. 710–12) in a few paragraphs carried over from *Economics of Industry*, written with his wife and published in 1879. Equilibration depends on beliefs, and it will fail if confidence is lacking. The human brain cannot invariably imagine a plausible new course of action when familiar routines no longer work; and when a cluster of familiar routines, based on established relationships, seems inadequate, businessmen may simply not know what to do, and so do nothing. (This was Schumpeter's (1934) explanation for the depression which, he claimed, followed radical innovation.) It is significant that Marshall described this situation as 'commercial disorganization'; the structure is inadequate to support expectations. *Ceteris paribus* no longer applies. This is not a Walrasian concept; it does, however, hint at Keynes' explanation of unemployment.

In Quéré's (2000, p. 59) words, 'relationships among producers and consumers are fairly particular in the sense that they require specific and mutual knowledge between the partners involved'; the consequence is an interfirm organization of knowledge which makes 'feasible an evolution of productive activities'. Such an evolution may be necessary for an individual businessman to maintain his position, for though he 'has a plant, an organization, and a business connection, which put him in a position of advantage for his special work ... others can easily equip themselves in like manner' (Marshall 1919, p. 196); since these are Marshall's words, it is hardly necessary to add 'given time'. This is the kind of competition, Darwinian though not neo-Darwinian, which is a major instrument of economic progress. It does not meet the requirements of perfect competition, or of rational choice as that is now defined. Instead of perfect knowledge, even perfect knowledge of probability distributions, it relies on created knowledge, assumptions that are not explicitly recognized unless something goes wrong, and fallible beliefs which may need to be revised – perhaps by newcomers – in order to conceive productive opportunities, some of which will prove, often in an amended form, to be genuine.

2.3   POST-MARSHALLIANS

Within the space constraints of this chapter, consideration of post-Marshallians cannot be more than indicative, and we must leave aside two fascinating questions for historians of economic thought: why was the development of economic theory in the twentieth century so little influenced by those ideas of Marshall which have been discussed that, until recently, the category of 'post-Marshallian economics' would have had no discernable meaning, and why are there now perceptible, though modest, Marshallian influences in economics (Loasby 2002)? Some significant influences, especially on Keynes, are entirely omitted.

2.3.1   Allyn Young

Marshall's central concern in economics is precisely defined by the title of Allyn Young's paper 'Increasing returns and economic progress' (Young 1928). The core of Young's exposition is the intimate connection between the division of labour as the prime instrument for the growth of knowledge, which Adam Smith had identified and Marshall had adopted, and Marshall's own distinctive insistence on the importance of diverse forms of organization as aids to knowledge. This diversity allows labour to be divided, and also co-ordinated, in a variety of ways, thus providing different foci of attention and different combinations of stability and enterprise, corresponding to the variation within species and the emergence of new species in biological evolution. Young extended Marshall's analysis by combining an emphasis on 'the progressive division and specialization of industries [as] an essential part of the process by which increasing returns are realised' with the crucial importance of 'the persisting search for markets' (Young 1928, p. 539) in which to apply new knowledge and to supply new environments for the continued growth of knowledge.

That this is an extension, rather than a novel element, is clear when we recall Marshall's (1920, p. 318) definition of his law of increasing return as leading to greater productivity through changes in organization as a consequence of increased inputs – a sequential relationship which is not a property of a conventionally defined production function but a process of respecifying productive relationships – and his unique emphasis on the need for each firm to build an external organization. However, Young's own respecification of Marshall's link between the organization of production and the organization of markets is sufficient to shift the focus of attention, and Young claimed that such a shift required a change in the theoretical structure: 'No analysis of the forces making for equilibrium ... will illumine this field, for movements away from equilibrium ... are characteristic of it' (Young 1928, p. 528). Thus, Marshall's conception of equilibrium as the end-point of a process is called into question – though not necessarily Marshall's 'evolutionary pattern *innovation/standardization*' (Raffaelli 2003, p. 103). Young shares Marshall's background assumption of pervasive uncertainty, which both treat not primarily as a threat but as an incentive to devise better arrangements for discovering new knowledge, which changes expectations and creates new opportunities for improvements in the quality of life.

2.3.2   Philip Andrews

Allyn Young died before he could develop his initiative, and no one followed it up. Growth was not a prominent topic in the interwar years, and microeconomics turned towards allocative efficiency and the associated topic of market failure, using a framework which increasingly approximated optimization on the basis of knowledge that was relatively complete, but extended it to include imperfect competition. In this framework increasing returns were degraded into simple economies of scale and necessarily became a major threat to welfare, as Samuelson ([1967] 1972, p. 39) later insisted, or alternatively to the continued relevance of 'competitive theory', as Hicks (1939, pp. 83–5) perceived. This theoretical turn stimulated the Oxford Economists' Research Group's enquiry into businessmen's decision making; and it was the evidence from this enquiry that businessmen did not behave in accordance with the assumptions of the new theory which provoked Philip Andrews, one of the Group's members, encouraged by another member, Douglas McGregor (who also deserves recognition as a post-Marshallian), to look to Marshall for help in explaining the contrast between the new theories and business practice.

Like Young, Andrews (1964) came to distrust what he called 'equilibriumistic' theorizing, but the context for his alternative, perhaps conditioned by the contemporary condition of much British industry, was not growth but a steady state. However, what kept this state reasonably steady, according to Andrews (1949, 1951), was not the falling demand curve for each individual firm, which was the most striking novelty in the market theory of the 1930s. Andrews rejected this concept on Marshall's (1919, p. 196) argument that a manufacturer's special advantages give him no lasting protection from the competition of other firms with similar capabilities. He then argued that the internal organization of each firm (which, in contrast to Marshall's treatment, had no conceptual existence in what was, nevertheless, called 'the theory of the firm') provided incentives for managers to gain promotion by the quality of their decision making, in reducing costs and exploiting any complacency in rival firms. This combination of external constraint and internal incentive, he believed, would generally maintain overall stability while slowly improving practice, both in established businesses and in actual and potential rivals. As with Marshall, expectations are based on experience and experimentation is at the margin of knowledge.

2.3.3 George Richardson

Like Andrews, George Richardson (1953) turned to Marshall for guidance in resolving a conflict between standard theory and the practicalities of a functioning economic system; but his initial focus was on the implications for policy, and his reference point was not business practice but the foundational assumptions of the theory on which welfare economics was based. In his very first article, he began with Hayek's (1937) argument that economic performance depended on the utilization of dispersed knowledge, which could never be made available for a comprehensive allocation of resources, and then invoked Frank Knight's (1921) distinction between risk and uncertainty, and his definition of the latter as a condition in which there was insufficient evidence of probabilities, and often even of the range of possible outcomes, to allow the specification of any choice algorithm that could be shown to be correct. In conditions of Knightian uncertainty, efficient allocation could not be ensured by objective procedures, because the premises for reasoning were always problematic.

Richardson believed that such situations were very common, not least when significant decisions were required, and agreed with Knight that the skills which tended to lead to good decisions were very unevenly distributed, both between individuals and, for each individual, across classes of decisions. Consequently, the standard definition of the economic problem as the identification and achievement of an efficient allocation of resources was not adequate; there was also the problem of selecting those who were to be provisionally entrusted with parts of this allocation, and also the sorting problem of deciding which parts should be entrusted to whom. It was clear that this second pair of problems could not be resolved by strictly rational choice; attention should therefore be directed to the implications of various selection environments. For the first time in this survey, we find that the primary focus is on uncertainty, rather than its obverse, the growth of knowledge; but though Richardson recognized the connection with Marshall's industrial analysis, he made no reference to the possible association between selection and an evolutionary process.

Richardson (1959, 1960) subsequently turned to the contradiction inherent in the concept of perfect competition: it provided no basis on which an individual could respond rationally to an external change that invalidated the established equilibrium configuration for a particular commodity, since a rational response required knowledge of everyone else's response; and in a world of anonymous agents, without a benevolent auctioneer, such knowledge was beyond discovery. Richardson's solution drew on the limitations that are imposed on each agent by differentiated skills, the importance of time in making and implementing plans, and established relationships between agents, which simultaneously provide information and impose constraints on action, thus providing a credible basis for expectations. This is consciously related to Marshall's explanation, and therefore resembles Andrews's. (That Richardson and Andrews, though both at Oxford in the 1950s, nevertheless had little contact may seem scarcely credible to those who are not aware of the institutional peculiarities of Oxford University and the patterns of behaviour that these peculiarities tend to encourage.) Richardson (1960, p. 105) went on to consider how the set of commodities itself may be enlarged, and found, as Marshall had done, a crucial role for imagination.

Richardson (1972) later extended the concept of differentiated capabilities, which as we have seen had been introduced in his first publication, from decision making (where it is crucial to Knight's linked explanations of entrepreneurship and profit) to productive skills; and the degrees of similarity and complementarity between skills were then used to provide a framework for the explanation of industrial organization. This is now the leading contender to transaction-cost and principal–agent theories, and is distinguished from them by emphasizing the advantages of alternative organizational arrangements for promoting knowledge, rather than mitigating opportunistic threats.

2.3.4   Edith Penrose

Richardson's analysis of capabilities was explicitly related to Edith Penrose's (1959) *Theory of the Growth of the Firm*, which is thoroughly Marshallian. However, it is unconsciously so, because (as she subsequently explained) her orthodox economics training included Marshall among the neoclassicals, his particular contribution being then specified as his time-period analysis, not his treatment of knowledge and organization in an evolutionary setting. Nevertheless, in defining the firm as 'a pool of resources the utilization of which is organized in an administrative framework', Penrose (1959, p. 149) draws attention to the effects of organization both on the uses to which existing knowledge is put and on the directions in which further knowledge is sought. In the introduction to the third edition, she emphasized the need in her theory for a firm with 'insides' in order to provide a basis for emerging and continuing differences between firms (Penrose 1995, p. xi).

Uncertainty – the essential incompleteness of knowledge – is the precondition of enterprise; expectations are revised on the basis of experience, experimentation occurs at the margin, and it is often prompted by results which are unexpected – whether better, worse, or merely different. Neither new knowledge nor apparently attractive courses of action can be derived from initial data; links between resources and productive services are not defined by a production function of unspecified provenance but supplied by fallible conjectures, and further conjectures are required to link these services to profitable opportunities. Since '*entrepreneurs are fully aware of this*', the search for knowledge is 'so much a part of the normal operations and thinking of businessmen' that it must be an essential part of the theory of the firm (Penrose 1959, p. 77).

Because Penrose's objective was to explain the process by which some firms could grow, and to identify the characteristics of the firm as an organization which made such growth possible and shaped its course – nothing of which, as she pointed out, was supplied by the standard theory of the firm – she did not go on to consider how the interaction between firms, including the respecification of administrative frameworks on which Young had focused, could be used in a broader explanation of economic progress; for example, her discussion of the shaping of demand (Penrose 1959, pp. 80–81) is not linked to Young's (1928, p. 539) search for markets. She thus never raises issues for which evolutionary concepts might be relevant, though the connection receives due attention in her introduction to the third edition

(Penrose 1995). Nor does she raise the issues of co-ordination with which Marshall, Andrews, and Richardson tried to deal; indeed, she seeks to clear the ground for her theory by arguing that growth and resource allocation are distinct issues, better assigned to different theoretical systems – a strategy, we may note, that was also adopted by Schumpeter (1934) in his *Theory of Economic Development*. However, since Penrose followed Marshall, and so differed sharply from Schumpeter, in showing how the management of existing systems – the supposed domain of allocation theory – could lead directly to the enhancement of capabilities, and then by imagination to innovation, whether this strategy of separation is still the best is an open question; it will not be tackled here.

2.3.5   George Shackle

Though it is right that George Shackle's work should be associated first with that of Keynes, this association has overshadowed his close affinity with Marshall. The strongest link with Keynes is provided by the pervasiveness and consequences of the problems caused by uncertainty, especially in decisions that require a long time horizon; but Shackle also insisted that without uncertainty life would be unremittingly dismal. 'For the view of the "all is solvable and foreseeable" school is fatalism; the reverse of hope, the opposite of freedom' (Shackle 1966, p. 133) and 'When all life's questions are answered for any one of us, life will surely have ceased to hold for him any interest or purpose' (Shackle 1953, p. 1). Shackle recognized that for Marshall, as we have seen much earlier, equilibrium was the end state of a process, and that this conception of equilibrium was 'Marshall's own and declared fiction, for it is a state that *would* be attained if the very endeavour to reach it did not reveal fresh possibilities, give fresh command of resources, and prepare the way for inevitable, natural, organic further change' (Shackle 1965, p. 36).

We may observe that the occurrence of any 'favourable surprise' is fatal to the project of demonstrating convergence to a general equilibrium; but to exclude the possibility of favourable surprises, and especially the favourable surprises (along with many surprises that are less welcome) that may be created in a non-random though unpredictable fashion by the imagination, is to exclude the possibility of progress by intelligent action. Moreover, as the reference above to 'life's questions' indicates, it was not only material progress that uncertainty made possible; Shackle was no less concerned than Marshall with the improvement of character, and with the impact of economic organization on the possibilities of such improvement. Expectations and beliefs are neither natural givens nor the product of deductive reasoning, but nor are they generated by a random process. They are created by making new connections from some parts of what presently passes for the knowledge of the individual who is formulating a new expectation or belief. It may be impossible to complete the list of possible connections from an existing mental state (indeed it may be impossible to be precise about the structure of this mental state); and this list is certainly a relatively small sub-set of the connections that might be made from the existing mental states of a larger population – even from a larger population of people who are engaged in similar activities. That is how the variety is generated within a specialism; the variety across specialisms is correspondingly greater.

2.4 CONCLUSION

In this chapter we have been particularly concerned to emphasize the differences in the treatment of expectations, uncertainty and beliefs between this group of economists and the treatments usually offered in standard economics. There are also, of course, many similarities, and direct agreements, between 'Marshallian' and standard economics. However, it is perhaps more important to draw attention to the resemblances between these concepts and analyses and those of other less orthodox groups of economists, and in particular to note the growing awareness of their relevance for an understanding of economies as evolving systems, which is a focus of increasing interest. The nature of human cognition, which was Marshall's starting point, and the relationship between the organization of the human mind and the organization of economic activity, and between both of these and the development of knowledge and capabilities offer prospects for the integration of ideas and for new ventures.

We may conclude by reminding ourselves that choice is what economics is about, and choice is inherent in the practice of economics. George Shackle (1972) wrote a superb book on the choices that have been made within economics, and the consequences of these choices, and in his concluding chapter he provides a fitting commentary on the role of expectations, uncertainty and beliefs among economists:

Economic theory has concerned itself with the sources and consequences of conduct, and has sought in this field what can be conceived as rational, what can be expressed as proportion, what is publicly and unanimously agreed, and what belongs within bounds defined by the notion of exchange in an inclusive sense. For these choices it has strong incentives. (Shackle 1972, p. 443)

He then summarizes these incentives, and throughout the book he has given examples of the impressive achievements that have resulted. However, the inevitability of opportunity costs never drops out of sight; and he continues as follows:

> The attractions of such a programme are evident and compelling. The cost resides in what, by its nature, it is obliged to neglect or even implicitly to declare unimportant. ... the most serious of those exclusions ... is the brushing aside of the question, a unity though requiring three terms to express it, of time, knowledge, novelty. ... theory has chosen rationality, whole and unimpaired. And thus it has cut itself off from the most ascendant and superb of human faculties. Imagination, the source of novelty, the basis of men's claim, if they have one, to be makers and not mere executants of history, is exempted by its nature from the governance of given and delimited premises. (Shackle 1972, pp. 443–4)

REFERENCES

Andrews, Philip W.S. (1949), *Manufacturing Business*, London: Macmillan.

Andrews, Philip W.S. (1951), 'Industrial analysis in economics – with especial reference to Marshallian doctrine', in Thomas S. Wilson and Philip W.S. Andrews (eds), *Oxford Studies in the Price Mechanism*, Oxford: Clarendon Press, pp. 139–72.

Andrews, Philip W.S. (1964), *On Competition in Economic Theory*, London: Macmillan and New York: St Martin's Press.

Butler, Robert W. (1991), 'The historical context of the early Marshallian work', *Quaderni di Storia dell'Economia Politica*, **IX** (2–3), 269–88.

Dardi, Marco (2002), 'Alfred Marshall's partial equilibrium: dynamics in disguise', in Richard Arena and Michel Quéré (eds), *The Economics of Alfred Marshall*, Basingstoke: Palgrave, pp. 84–112.

Groenewegen, Peter (1995), *A Soaring Eagle: Alfred Marshall 1842–1924*, Aldershot, UK and Brookfield, VT: Edward Elgar.

Hayek, Friedrich A. (1937), 'Economics and knowledge', *Economica*, N.S. **4**, 33–54.

Hayek, Friedrich A. (1952), *The Sensory Order*, Chicago: University of Chicago Press.

Hicks, John R. (1939), *Value and Capital*, Oxford: Oxford University Press.

Hicks, John R. ([1982] 1976), 'Time in economics', in A.M. Tang, F.M Westfield and J.S. Worley (eds), *Evolution, Welfare and Time in Economics*, reprinted in *Collected Essays in Economic Theory, Volume II: Money, Interest and Wages*, Oxford: Basil Blackwell, pp. 282–300.

Knight, Frank H. (1921), *Risk, Uncertainty and Profit*, Boston: Houghton Mifflin.

Kuhn, Thomas S. (1962, 1970), *The Structure of Scientific Revolution*, 1st and 2nd edns, Chicago: University of Chicago Press.

Loasby, Brian J. (1990), 'Firms, markets and the principle of continuity', in John K. Whitaker (ed.), *Centenary Essays on Alfred Marshall*, Cambridge: Cambridge University Press, pp. 108–26.

Loasby, Brian J. (2002), 'Content and method: an epistemic perspective on some historical episodes', *European Journal of the History of Economic Thought*, **9** (1), 72–95.

Marshall, Alfred (1919), *Industry and Trade*, London: Macmillan.

Marshall, Alfred (1920), *Principles of Economics*, 8th edn, London: Macmillan.

Marshall, Alfred (1961), *Principles of Economics*, 9th (variorum) edn, vol. 2, London: Macmillan.

Marshall, Alfred (1994), 'Ye machine', *Research in the History of Economic Thought and Methodology, Archival Supplement 4*, Greenwich, CT: JAI Press, pp. 116–32.

Penrose, Edith T. (1959), *The Theory of the Growth of the Firm*, Oxford: Basil Blackwell.

Penrose, Edith T. (1995), *The Theory of the Growth of the Firm*, 3rd edn, Oxford: Clarendon Press.

Quéré, Michel (2000), 'Competition as a process: insights from the Marshallian perspective', in Jackie Krafft (ed.), *The Process of Competition*, Cheltenham, UK and Northampton, MA: Edward Elgar, pp. 49–64.

Raffaelli, Tiziano (2001), 'Marshall on mind and society: neurophysiological models applied to industrial and business organization', *European Journal of the History of Economic Thought*, **8** (2), 208–29.

Raffaelli, Tiziano (2003), *Marshall's Evolutionary Economics*, London and New York: Routledge.

Richardson, George B. (1953), 'Imperfect knowledge and economic efficiency', *Oxford Economic Papers*, **5** (2), 136–56. Reprinted in Richardson, George B. (1998), *The Economics of Imperfect Knowledge*, Oxford: Clarendon Press, pp. 1–21.

Richardson, George B. (1959), 'Equilibrium, expectations and information', *Economic Journal*, **69** (274), 223–37. Reprinted in Richardson (1998), pp. 66–80.

Richardson, George B. (1960), *Information and Investment*, 2nd edn 1990, Oxford: Oxford University Press.

Richardson, George B. (1972), 'The organisation of industry', *Economic Journal*, **82** (327), 883–96. Reprinted in Richardson (1998), pp. 143–56.

Samuelson, Paul A. ([1967] 1972) 'The monopolistic competition revolution', in R.E. Kuenne (ed.), *Monopolistic Competition Theory: Studies in Impact*, New York: John Wiley, pp. 105–38. Reprinted in Robert K. Merton (ed.), *The Collected Scientific Papers of Paul A. Samuelson*, vol. 2, Cambridge, MA and London: MIT Press, pp. 18–51. (Reference is to this reprint.)

Schumpeter, Joseph A. (1934), *The Theory of Economic Development*, Cambridge, MA: Harvard University Press.

Shackle, George L.S. (1953), 'Economics and sincerity', *Oxford Economic Papers*, **1** (1), 1–19.

Shackle, George L.S. (1965), *A Scheme of Economic Theory*, Cambridge: Cambridge University Press.

Shackle, George L.S. (1966), *The Nature of Economic Thought: Selected Papers 1955–64*, Cambridge: Cambridge University Press.

Shackle, George L.S. (1972), *Epistemics and Economics*, Cambridge University Press.

Smith, Adam (1795), 'The principles which lead and direct philosophical enquiries: illustrated by the history of astronomy', in *Essays on Philosophical Subjects*, reprinted in William P.D. Wightman (ed.) (1980), *Glasgow Edition of the Works and Correspondence of Adam Smith*, Vol. 3, Oxford: Oxford University Press.

Whitaker, John K. (1996), *The Correspondence of Alfred Marshall Economist*, 3 volumes, Cambridge: Cambridge University Press.

Young, Allyn (1928), 'Increasing returns and economic progress', *Economic Journal*, **38** (152), 523–42.

Ziman, John M. (2000), *Real Science*, Cambridge: Cambridge University Press.

3. Knowledge and beliefs in economics: the case of the Austrian tradition

Richard Arena and Agnès Festré

3.1 INTRODUCTION

The Austrians contributed to the analysis of the impact of individual knowledge and beliefs on economic activity more than any other school in the history of economic thought. This statement should not surprise the reader. The founding fathers of this school are strongly associated with a subjectivist conception of economics, in which cognitive capacities and the level of information of individual agents play an essential role in the explanation of their decision-making processes. They also spent a significant amount of time researching topics that are of the utmost importance to anyone interested in the role played by knowledge and beliefs in economics: Menger dedicated a lot of attention to the problem of the emergence of institutions and behavioural rules and placed great emphasis on the role played by the process of diffusion of beliefs within this context; Böhm-Bawerk dealt with the frontiers of pure economic theory and was interested in the impact of power and social relations on economic activity (Böhm-Bawerk 1914). As for Wieser, he built a real economic sociology approach and underlined the influence of organizational and social interactions in this context.

In this chapter, we shall concentrate on the second generation of Austrian economists, in particular on the contributions of von Mises, Hayek and Schumpeter who, despite developing very different approaches, shared many features of the intellectual vein of the founding fathers of the School.

At first sight, the subjectivist stance of most Austrian authors suggests that they attached importance to the role of individual beliefs in economic activity. It also suggests that these economists were reluctant to deal with social norms or collective beliefs. We will, however, show that their approaches are more complex than might appear at first sight. On the one hand, von Mises, Hayek and Schumpeter had divergent views of individual decision-making processes. On the other hand, and insofar as they advocated methodological individualism, they had to tackle the problem of inter-individual co-ordination. The ways they solved this problem differed substantially and did not always exclude, as we shall see, a recourse to collective beliefs or social rules in their analyses. In short, our reading of the contributions of von Mises, Hayek and Schumpeter is an attempt at a more thorough analysis of the role of individual and collective beliefs in the working of markets. It also allows us to see how a strictly subjectivist approach to economic behaviour and rationality can come up against serious problems relating to inter-individual co-ordination. To mention but a few:

- How are we to describe the nature of the state (or states) of the economy that results from individual agents' choices through direct or indirect interactions?
- Does this state (or these states) imply a prior agreement on collective beliefs by individual agents?
- How should social optimality issues be dealt with?

These types of questions will be guiding our reading of the three Austrian authors considered in this chapter.

3.2   LUDWIG VON MISES: APRIORISM AND INDIVIDUAL BELIEFS

Ludwig von Mises undoubtedly holds a special place in the second generation of the Austrian School. First, he is generally thought of as the eldest representative of this generation, since he was the first to bring about changes to the message delivered by the founding fathers of the Vienna School. Secondly, he played a fundamental role in the creation of the modern 'American' version of this School. Finally, von Mises is very often associated with the defence of radical subjectivism. This is very pertinent to the issue at hand. We shall, therefore, first examine the analytical consequences this defence implies.

3.2.1   Decision and Human Action in von Mises

As suggested by the title of his fundamental 1949 work, *Human Action: A Treatise of Economics*, von Mises starts from the notion of 'human action', which he takes as the basic unit of his analysis, and defines 'purposeful behaviour' as a 'will put into operation and transformed into an agency', the purpose of which consists in 'a person's conscious adjustment to the state of the universe that determines his life' (von Mises [1949] 1996, p. 11), or, to be more precise, in 'the satisfaction of the acting man's desire' (ibid., p. 14). This conception of human action from which von Mises tries to build a general theory – praxeology – derives from the Kantian philosophic tradition. In this perspective, von Mises considers that logical reasoning is the main engine of human activity (von Mises [1962] 1979, p. 44). It means, for the author, that the 'category' of human action is part of the structure of the mind itself. To put it differently, any argumentation based on *a priori* true assertions and on a sequence of well-formulated logical stages leads to absolutely certain conclusions.

This constitutes the first foundation of von Mises' 'apriorist' approach. However, this methodological principle is not sufficient to characterize his approach. On the one hand, according to von Mises, every economic and social fact can be reduced to a theoretical statement. On the other hand, these statements cannot be 'tested' empirically or be the subject of confirmation or falsification procedures. The only two criteria of truth accepted by the author are the internal logical coherence of a statement and its applicability in given historical situations. This apriorist conception therefore implies the refusal of an analysis of beliefs and human behaviour which would privilege their content or their empirical meaning. Praxeology concerns human action, 'irrespective of all environmental, accidental, and individual circumstances of the concrete acts. Its cognition is purely formal and general without reference to the particular features of the actual case' (ibid., p. 32). It also deals with the 'ultimate category' constituted by 'the logical structure of human mind' (ibid., p. 34). It is in this sense that von Mises notes that the 'fundamental logical relations are the indispensable prerequisite of perception, apperception and experience' (ibid., p. 34).

However, von Mises' apriorism does not exclude subjectivism. Indeed, he writes:

[N]obody is in a position to substitute his own value judgments for those of the acting individual, it is vain to pass judgment on other people's aims and volitions. (Ibid., p. 19)

This subjectivism does not, however, adapt to unconscious determinants of the decision process. Von Mises, as already emphasized, conceives of human action as deliberate behaviour or conscious adaptation.

3.2.2 Human Action and Individual Beliefs

Von Mises' subjectivism implies the existence of individual beliefs exclusive to every agent. He thus encounters the problem of co-ordination between autonomous decisions and actions of actors (von Mises [1949] 1996, p. 55). This problem is all the more crucial as, for our author:

> society is nothing but the combination of individuals for cooperative effort. It exists nowhere else than in the actions of individual men. It is a delusion to search for it outside the actions of individuals. To speak of a society's autonomous and independent existence is a metaphor which can easily lead to crass errors. (Ibid., p. 143)

Von Mises' apriorism, however, moderates his subjectivist individualism. In fact, two principles govern the logical structure that is common to everyone: the principle of causality and the principle of teleology (ibid., p. 25). These two principles play an essential role in von Mises' analysis of the co-ordination of individual beliefs.

3.2.3   From Individual Beliefs to Inter-individual Co-ordination

In order to solve the problem of the compatibility between the subjectivist approach to individual beliefs and market co-ordination, von Mises starts from the idea of introspection:

> it is beyond doubt that the principle according to which an *Ego* deals with every human being as if the other were a thinking and acting being like himself has evidenced its usefulness both in mundane life and in scientific research. It cannot be denied that it works. (Ibid., p. 24; cf. von Mises [1962] 1979, p. 72)

This idea is simple. Given that, for von Mises 'it is impossible for the human mind to conceive a mode of action whose categories would differ from the categories which determine our own actions (von Mises [1949] 1996, p. 29), agents, by introspection, can redraw the logical principles governing the ways of thinking of their allies or competitors. This is obviously only possible because it is assumed that every agent is endowed *a priori* with the same reasoning capacities. These are capacities 'common to all man' (ibid., p. 35).

In this context, introspection is only meaningful if it is combined with 'observation'. In fact, although the logical categories of causality and teleology are given *a priori*, this is not the case for the scale of values or wants of the agents. In von Mises' terms, this 'manifests itself only in the reality of action', by means of observed behaviour (ibid., p. 95).

In other words, von Mises, in line with his constant preoccupation to carefully separate the field of psychology from the one of economic analysis, rejects the possibility of interpreting this behaviour psychologically.

So, if agents can communicate by going beyond their strictly subjective universes, this is neither because they share the same cognitive capacities (in the sense of the Hayekian possibilities of appropriation of the reality by the brain), nor because they have similar psychological profiles. It is because their mind reveals the same logical structure.

This logical structure leads agents to analyse real phenomena, albeit imperfectly, by using similar schemes, such as those implied by the principles of teleology and causality. However, the agents' knowledge is inevitably imperfect. In fact, agent behaviour is not governed by strictly deterministic laws. Besides, the principles of teleology and causality are not sufficient to allow instant foresight of the future or the behaviour of other individuals. Thus, experience and observation enter the scene. Causality is revealed to agents only through the search for the 'regularity and the "law"' of observed phenomena (ibid., p. 22).

The apriorist hypothesis of the universality of the logical categories which characterize the common structure of human minds thus constitutes, for von Mises, the necessary condition for the communication of beliefs between agents and for the understanding of individual expectations. If this condition is necessary, it is however far from sufficient.

3.2.4 The Processes of Division of Individual Beliefs

Although von Mises champions radical subjectivist individualism, he does not endorse the contractualist explanation of the transition from the Natural State, where man was isolated, to the Social State, where man enters into connection with other people. For von Mises it is inconceivable to suppose that man can live 'in abstracto' (von Mises [1949] 1996, p. 46). Man is always located within a socio-cultural context which influences his subjective choices. Far from being unimportant, this influence can be determining for certain agents.

All 'common men' do is adapt the ideas and beliefs they inherit from the past and/or from their environment. From this point of view, the description von Mises provides is striking – the common man:

> does not himself create his ideas; he borrows them from other people. His ideology is what his environment enjoins upon him [...] Common man does not speculate about the great problems. With regard to them, he relies upon other people's authority, he behaves as 'every decent fellow must behave', he is like a sheep in the herd. (Ibid., p. 46)

These 'common men' are to be distinguished from those that von Mises calls the 'promoters'. They are seen as 'pacemakers', 'who have more initiative, more venturesomeness, and a quicker eye than the crowd' (ibid., p. 255). The promoter is, above all, a pioneer and this is why von Mises also calls him the 'creative genius' (ibid., p. 139). His incentive 'is not the desire to bring about a result, but the act of producing it' (ibid., p. 139). The promoters correspond to 'a general characteristic of human nature' (ibid., p. 269) and that is why, as in Schumpeter, they exist in most societies, at different times or in different activities (ibid., pp. 255). In the context of market economies, these promoters appear predominantly, according to von Mises, as entrepreneurs.

The distinction between 'promoters' or 'creators' and 'ordinary men' is important. First, it is a feature of the Austrian economic tradition inherited from Menger and Wieser (Arena and Gloria-Palermo 2001). Secondly, it allows us, according to von Mises, to explain the sharing, or rather the diffusion, of new individual beliefs via a social process of imitation. So, common men follow 'habits' or routines, which they modify only if they are convinced that the promoters will improve their well-being (von Mises [1949] 1996, p. 47). In this sense, the individual beliefs of common men are indeed shared individual beliefs; but, for von Mises, they can never be autonomous collective beliefs of individuals, as in Durkheim, for example (ibid., pp. 42–3).

The radical anti-holism of von Mises allows us to understand why his conception of the diffusion or the sharing of individual beliefs is related to imitation: if several agents agree to adopt the specific beliefs of a particular individual, it does not mean that they stop exercising individual choices:

> They can either all act together in accord, or one of them may act for them all. In the latter case the consideration of the others consists in their bringing about the situation which makes one man's action effective for them too. (Ibid., p. 44)

This approach, in terms of shared individual beliefs, appears coherent. Von Mises makes use of it in order to analyse the functioning of the market. The latter is not 'a place', 'a thing', or a 'collective entity' (ibid., p. 257), it is a 'process' in which 'value judgments' are compatible with individual beliefs (ibid.). Promoter-entrepreneurs play a leading role in this framework because they 'take the lead': they are 'the shrewder individuals [who] appreciate conditions more correctly than the less intelligent and therefore succeed better in their actions' (ibid., p. 328). Their attentiveness and speculative behaviour focused on the discovery of new opportunities are critical (ibid., p. 329), especially since, in the long run, they can only submit themselves to the 'sovereignty of the consumers' (ibid., p. 269).

Despite his views on the functioning of the market, von Mises did not go on to an operational analysis. If one can credit the author for a stimulating approach to the role of the promoter-entrepreneurs, his ideas on the ways markets are organized did not lead to an auction theory. Although von Mises suggests that prices convey efficient signals that lead to equilibrium between production and exchange, he fails to explain how entrepreneurial activity leads to prices and why they 'tell the producers what to produce, how to produce and in what quantity' (ibid., p. 258). The omnipotence and the equilibrating character of the market are not proved rigorously and, unfortunately, von Mises' radical condemnation of the use of mathematics in economics cannot reassure the reader about this point (see, for instance, ibid., pp. 350–58). Moreover, it should be pointed out that von Mises' analysis of the process of diffusion of individual beliefs is not restricted to the role of the promoters since, in the last resort, the 'sovereignty of consumers' constitutes the prime mover of the market process (ibid., p. 269).

Another factor explaining the sharing of individual beliefs is the 'catallactic function of money'. Von Mises explicitly draws a parallel between money and the promoter, noting that 'the notion of money [similarly to the notion of the entrepreneur-promoter] also defies a rigid praxeological definition' (ibid., p. 255).

First of all, a currency is not an *a priori* medium of exchange but a 'tool of action' because 'prices in currency are the only vehicle of economic calculation' (ibid., p. 201) and 'monetary calculation is the guiding star of action' (ibid., p. 210).

Moreover, monetary prices allow the comparison between alternative uses of resources over time, i.e., intertemporal calculation. The key function of money is to provide individuals with a scale against which to assess the future consequences of their present actions. Money thus allows the introduction of the dimension of evaluation prior to human action, namely, the appreciation or anticipation by individuals of alternative ways of removing the uneasiness they feel (ibid., p. 224).

Secondly, money gives rise to an objective dimension through the notion of purchasing power. This is passed on to individuals and serves as a guide for action. According to von Mises, this does not mean that monetary calculation can be used for 'any consideration which does not look at things from the point of view of individuals', such as the statistical forecast of aggregate economic magnitudes or the calculation of collective projects (ibid., p. 230). On the other hand, the specific function of money as a generalized medium of exchange confers on it an objective dimension.

Von Mises first indicates that money is to be distinguished from other economic goods in the sense that its subjective value depends on an objective economic characteristic: its purchasing power. Contrary to the value of any other economic good, the purchasing power of money cannot be influenced by non-economic factors such as technology or the psychology of individuals (von Mises [1924] 1981, p. 118). Consequently, it is not necessary to base the purchasing power of money on the existence of a demand for money as an instrument of exchange or for its use for industrial purposes:

> That component of money's purchasing power which is an outcome of the services it renders as a medium of exchange *is entirely explained by reference to these specific monetary services and the demand they create.* (von Mises [1949] 1996, p. 409, our emphasis)

This passage illustrates the self-referential and conventional character of currency. In particular, the self-referential nature of money becomes clear when we consider that money would cease to exist were individuals to lose memory of purchasing power:

> It is the fact that radically distinguishes the determination of the purchasing power of money from the determination of the mutual exchange rates between the various vendible goods and services. ... Knowledge about past prices is for the buyer merely a means to reap a consumer's surplus. If he were not intent upon this goal, he could, if need be, arrange his purchases without any familiarity with the market prices of the immediate past, which are popularly called present prices. He could make value judgments without appraisal. ... *But if knowledge about money's purchasing power were to fade away, the process of development of indirect exchange and media of exchange would have to start anew.* (Ibid., p. 411, our emphasis)

Although the analysis of the role of money proposed by von Mises is worth considering, it does not provide a rigorous analysis of the *formation* of the monetary prices of commodities. All we can say is that it is left as a possible line of research.

On the whole, von Mises' approach does not provide a satisfactory analysis of the impact of individual beliefs and shared individual beliefs on the functioning of a market economy. However, it highlights some of the difficulties confronting a strictly subjectivist approach to beliefs.

3.3   FRIEDRICH VON HAYEK: INDIVIDUAL BELIEFS AND KNOWLEDGE OF THE SOCIETY

Among the important economists of the twentieth century, Hayek is undisputedly the one who contributed the most to the analysis of the role of knowledge in economic activity. The scope of his epistemological thought remains unmatched in this field. No wonder, therefore, that Hayek belongs to the group of Austrian economists who tried to connect individual beliefs, social knowledge and the functioning of market economies. In order to better justify Hayek's presence in this section, we must first turn to his conception of knowledge.

3.3.1 Hayek's Conception of Knowledge

One can find Hayek's best definition of knowledge in his 1960 work entitled *The Constitution of Liberty*:

> The growth of knowledge and the growth of civilization are the same only if we interpret knowledge to include all human adaptations to environment in which past experience has been incorporated. Not all knowledge in this sense is part of our intellect, nor is our intellect the whole of our knowledge. Our habits and skills, our emotional attitudes, our tools, and our institutions – all are in this sense adaptations to past experience which have grown up by selective elimination of less suitable contact. They are as much an indispensable foundation of successful actions as is our conscious knowledge. (Hayek 1960, p. 26)

This passage provides a good illustration of the reasons that lead Hayek to believe that individual knowledge involves more than simply 'explicit and conscious knowledge' (ibid., p. 25). Fleetwood (1997, pp. 164–6) compellingly argues that Hayek's broad conception of knowledge includes three main forms of knowledge: general explicit knowledge, local explicit knowledge (ibid., p. 165) and tacit and unconscious knowledge. This last form of knowledge is essential to Hayek's analysis. It also illustrates a fundamental difference between Hayek and the approach adopted by von Mises. While von Mises' apriorism led him to consider exclusively conscious individual forms of beliefs and knowledge, Hayek's methodological choice paves the way for a broader conception of knowledge.

In fact, tacit knowledge refers to a form of knowledge that is accessible directly: unlike local and general explicit forms of knowledge, it does not require the preliminary definition of an objective to be deliberately learnt. It is fully 'absorbed', day after day, through the social interaction common to every individual from early childhood. It is not assimilated through formal institutions but instead by the repeated resort to rules of social conduct, the role or even meaning of which is not necessarily understood. The originality of Hayek's conception of tacit knowledge lies in its extensibility. More precisely, the behavioural rules that underlie tacit knowledge in Hayek's approach are not limited to practical and basic forms of behaviour. They can also relate to elaborate cultural traditions or professional routines.

More generally, Hayek's conception of knowledge must be understood in relation to his subjectivist methodology, which essentially rests on two justifications.

The first, which is *cognitive*, is found in *The Sensory Order* (1952). In this book, Hayek champions the idea that the brain functions in a connectionist way, so that the point of departure of mental representations is not the physical order of things, as 'scientistic objectivism', to use Hayek's expression (cf. Hayek 1952a, Chapter V), would have it, 'but the product of abstractions which the mind must possess in order to be capable of experiencing that richness of the particular [of the reality]' (Hayek 1978, p. 44). The conscious experiences that individuals regard as relatively concrete and primary and which they attribute to the intrinsic properties of the physical order 'are the product of a superimposition of many "classifications" of the events perceived according to their significance in many respects' (ibid., p. 36). There are thus as many subjective forms of knowledge as there are individual 'nervous systems', i.e., as there are heterogeneous agents.

The second justification for Hayekian subjectivism is found in what Hayek calls the 'social division of knowledge'. For Hayek, as a civilization develops, the knowledge of its society becomes more complex and specialist. However, no individual agent can have access to such knowledge alone. This is *dispersed* within society and each of the individuals constituting it can have access only to a very small part of the social knowledge and, in particular, to the processes by which social and economic activity is regulated and reproduced globally.

It is against the background of these two justifications that we are to understand the very wide conception of knowledge Hayek developed. In this perspective, the existence of tacit knowledge does not constitute a phenomenon to be analysed in itself. Instead, it represents one of the essential forms of dispersed knowledge, which is difficult to disseminate in society and which Hayek endeavours to characterize.

3.3.2 Knowledge and Individual Beliefs

Hayek's subjectivist methodological choice leads him to investigate the features of a 'cognitive' individual rationality, to use the distinction between cognitive and instrumental rationalities used by Boudon in this volume. The cognitive capacities that individual agents must mobilize refer to their own 'mental map'. What Hayek calls the 'map' is 'the semi-permanent apparatus of classification', which 'provides the different generic elements from which the models of particular situations are built' (Hayek 1952b, p. 89).

In fact, the idea of a mental map conveys the cognitive limits of the mental considerations of individuals. Rather than 'a sort of schematic picture of the environment' it supplies 'a sort of inventory of the kinds of things of which the world is built up, a theory of how the world works' (ibid.). For Hayek, this approach does not conflict with some of the tools commonly used in microeconomics, what he calls the formal 'logic of the choice'. However, he thinks they require adaptation. So, during the debate on 'socialist calculation', Hayek underlines the fundamentally subjective representation according to which agents interpret the 'data' or 'fundamentals' of the general economic equilibrium scheme, such as the qualities of consumer goods or the description and implementation of the available techniques of production (Hayek 1935).

Therefore, the economic behaviour of each individual agent is embedded in the framework of his own theory of how the world works. It means that each individual makes decisions according to his own set of 'structural' individual beliefs, to use Walliser's terminology in this volume. These structural beliefs shape what we could call 'circumstantial' beliefs, namely, beliefs which govern specific decisions related to particular circumstances and to particular expected economic results at a given point of time.

These decisions give rise to actions which, in their turn, produce results which the agent compares with his own expectations. The divergence perceived by the individual between his expectations and the actual outcomes of his actions leads him to revise his circumstantial and sometimes, albeit less frequently, his structural beliefs. This revision process is stronger when the observation of actual results convinces the agent of the 'errors' in his 'attempt' and provides him with the opportunity to eliminate certain beliefs. If, on the other hand, the 'attempt' is successful, a true selection of beliefs takes place. Indeed, in the long run, as pointed out by Garrouste (1999, p. 891), structural beliefs become stronger and are gradually transformed into individual abstract rules, comparable to genuine routines. In fact, the agent becomes aware that his structural beliefs help him obtain results that are superior to the other possible beliefs.

However, despite the fact that individual beliefs are subjective, they are not independent from those of the other agents.

3.3.3 Individual Beliefs and Social Rules

If economic agents were only to follow their beliefs and individual routines, it would be difficult to understand how even a minimal social order could result from a multitude of unco-ordinated economic actions. Hayek is clearly aware of this problem which, he believes, arises out of the need to distinguish 'social phenomena' or group actions from 'individual actions' (Hayek 1948, p. 48). This problem turns out to be particularly complex for two main reasons.

First of all, co-ordination of individual behaviours is contextual. This observation is not surprising in a Hayekian context: here 'fundamentals' are allowed to vary continuously and, moreover, it is impossible to grasp them objectively, even at a *given* point in time (Arena 1999, p. 851). Referring to the context thus implies that the same set of individual rules of conduct can lead to very different social orders, if the context is associated with different 'circumstances of time and place'.

Secondly, there is some divergence between the strictly individual motives of agents and the criteria allowing the ranking of preferences in favour of one social order instead of another: Hayek actually notes 'that there is no other way toward an understanding of social phenomena but through our understanding of individual actions directed toward the people and guided by their expected behavior' (Hayek 1948, p. 6). Moreover, 'the reason for this is simply that [...] wholes or social structures are never given to us as natural units, are not definite objects given to observation, that we never deal with the whole of reality but always only with a selection made with the help of our models' (ibid., p. 74).

In this context, it seems that there is a significant gap between the rules that govern the pursuit of individual self-interest and those allowing the emergence of a social order: 'knowledge of society' cannot be reduced to the sum of individual beliefs. As shown by Vanberg (1986), this is a serious problem in Hayek because he is unable to provide a convincing framework ensuring the compatibility between his subjectivist approach to the spontaneous order and his later theory of 'cultural evolution'. However, a first answer can be sketched out based on his writings.

In considering Hayek's cognitive approach, Birner (1999, pp. 67–8) underlines the analogy, developed by Hayek himself, between the organization of the human brain and that of society. This marks the limits of Hayekian subjectivism, because 'knowledge and beliefs of different people' are not completely diverse but 'possess a common structure which makes communication possible' (Hayek 1952b, p. 49). In this perspective:

> individuals which compose society are *guided* in their actions by a classification of things or events according to a system of sense qualities and of concepts which has a common structure and which we know because we, too, are men. [...] Not only men's action toward external objects but also all the relations between men and all the social institutions can be understood only by what men think about them. Society as we know it is, as it were, built up from the concepts and ideas held by the people, and social phenomena can be recognized by us and have meaning to us only as they are reflected in the minds of men. (Hayek 1952a, pp. 57–8, our emphasis)

This therefore implies that the rules of conduct which guide the behaviour of agents are clearly dependent on the mental 'common structure' of men. Thus it is easy to understand why Hayek admits that individuals belonging to the same historic and/or socio-cultural environment tend to share common individual beliefs. This viewpoint is obviously reinforced by the importance Hayek attributes to the relation between innovative and imitative individual decisions in the process of emergence of behavioural regularities.

Vanberg (1986) notes that this approach is still unsatisfactory: if the self-organization of the agents is the emanation of individual choices, it does not however lead inevitably to a socially optimal state. Hayek postulates the social superiority of the market order without demonstrating it in a convincing way, when he refers to the notion of 'empirical tendency toward equilibrium', or to a notion close to Pareto's optimum or even to the idea that there exists a dominant social group (cf. Arena 2003). If one wants to abandon this type of *petitio principii*, one should go back to the notion of social order and its foundations in a Hayekian perspective. However, before we examine them, it is necessary, first, to pay attention to the concept of social rule in Hayek.

3.3.4 Social Rules and Collective Beliefs

Up until this point, we have used the word 'beliefs' in the sense of 'individual beliefs'. We saw at first how these beliefs could give rise to a self-reinforcement process and thus lead to the emergence of real individual rules of conduct. We then underlined how agents could converge towards shared individual beliefs, through social communication and imitation. One could thus infer from these two observations that, in Hayek, the social rules of conduct that explain the regularity and co-ordination of individual behaviour may, in turn, be defined as shared individual rules. In fact, the situation is more complex.

As some commentators have noted (Ioannides 1999, pp. 874–6; Garrouste 1999, pp. 887–91), the features of social rules of conduct that in Hayek underline the formation of a spontaneous social order similar to the one found in market societies are threefold. First, they must be *tacit*, that is, 'supra-conscious', to use Hayek's expression. To put it another way, individuals follow rules of conduct, without knowing explicitly that they are doing so. Secondly, these rules must be *abstract*. Thirdly, tacit and abstract rules must necessarily be *general*. This means that they must be *valid* for all individuals and apply to an infinite number of particular cases. To put it another way, the content of these rules is independent from the particular individuals who adopt them or from the particular types of actions in which they are put into practice. This does not mean that their ultimate origin is not linked to the individual beliefs of agents. Simply, these rules are the result of a process of adaptation which tends to gradually erase its origin (Hayek 1960, p. 27).

With the passing of time and the repeated use of individual rules of conduct, their tendency to become more and more abstract and general creates the conditions of their growing autonomy vis-à-vis the individuals who have implemented and/or adopted them. In the long run, these forms of conduct 'consist of what we call "traditions" and "institutions", which we use because they are available to us as a product of cumulative growth without either having been designed by any one mind' (ibid., p. 27).

This interpretation is confirmed by Hayek's analysis of the 'properties' that social rules are supposed to possess in order to produce a global order that appears to be independent from individual actions. These 'properties' explain how *individual* rules (even shared rules) can be transformed into *social* rules, i.e. 'normative' rules which 'tell' individuals what they can or cannot do. As already noted, the social process of standardization of rules first results from similarities between individual mental processes. Its origin can also be found in the existence of a 'common cultural tradition'. Finally, it can be enforced by, say, the State or the law, and imply sanctions in case of violation. The above remarks confirm that social facts or norms have gradually acquired such a large autonomy with respect to individuals, that they appear to them as strictly exogenous (customs, convention, culture, law, etc.). This is why they appear to be the real causes of the process of social standardization of individual rules. Therefore, if shared individual beliefs often imply true social beliefs, it is mainly because individuals usually choose their individual rules of conduct within the repertoire of the available social rules.

It then remains to understand how the mechanism of selection between rules and available social beliefs works. This mechanism is essential since it allows us to understand the emergence of rules or *optimal* social beliefs. The answer Hayek puts forward corresponds to his theory of cultural evolution:

> All that we can know is that the ultimate decision about what is good or bad will be made not by individual human wisdom but by the decline of the groups that have adhered to the 'wrong' beliefs. (Hayek 1960, p. 36)

However, one can still wonder how the process of selection of social rules leads to a situation of relative autonomy with respect to individual knowledge beliefs, even if Hayek strongly advocates subjectivist individualism. This autonomy is taken into account by Hayek through his reference to the 'knowledge of society' (ibid., p. 25).

Individuals have no direct access to this kind of knowledge (ibid. p. 25). On the other hand, for Hayek, the simultaneous recourse, by individuals, to their own particular knowledge leads each of them to benefit from what one could call positive externalities stemming from social interaction. All that remains then is to understand how individuals can benefit *indirectly* from this knowledge.

Hayek's answer is obvious: tradition provides agents with a set of rules that are superior or 'wiser' than human reason (Hayek 1988, p. 73). Fleetwood elaborates on this answer, noting that 'by drawing upon these rules as surrogates, then, agents avail themselves of the collective wisdom of an evolving society, and are thereby enabled to initiate socioeconomic activity, although they can never know or articulate this collective wisdom' (Fleetwood 1997, p. 170).

To sum up, Hayek actually allows for the existence of a 'knowledge of society', or 'of the impersonal process of society', which differs from the mere juxtaposition of individual kinds of knowledge (Hayek 1960, p. 65). This means that, for Hayek, we must distinguish between two analytical levels (see, for instance, ibid., p. 28). The first is entirely governed by the methodology of subjectivist individualism and, therefore, only refers to individual beliefs, be they shared or not. The second corresponds to a kind of knowledge that individuals cannot access directly. It is the outcome of the interactive effects of their actions. In order for this impersonal knowledge to be as efficient as possible, it is first necessary that a social process of selection generate rules allowing men to live together in an open society, in other words, in a type of social order that permits individuals to make free but compatible decisions. It is also necessary that these selected rules produce the largest and best 'knowledge of society'.

It is on this last point that Hayek's failure is self-evident: the author fails to provide a satisfactory explanation of the social effects of individual beliefs on the working of market economies. Like von Mises, Hayek takes the tendency of the market to move towards equilibrium for granted without proving it rigorously. His solution is, however, more elaborate – essentially because of its ability to take into account the tacit as well as the unconscious aspects of individual knowledge. Moreover, through the introduction of the analytical device of the 'knowledge of society', it entails an evolutionary dimension which did not exist in von Mises. This level of knowledge turns out to be essential for Hayek's intellectual construct, but its relative autonomy does not question the individualistic and subjectivist methodology of the author since no individual is capable of appropriating it *directly*. Finally, if one is willing to place Hayek's treatment of knowledge into a framework based on self-organization and if one gives up the postulate of a determinist and systematic tendency of the economy towards a unique and stable equilibrium, Hayek's solution seems more promising than the one put forward by von Mises.

3.4   JOSEPH SCHUMPETER: THE SOCIAL FOUNDATIONS OF INDIVIDUAL BELIEFS

At first sight, it might seem surprising that we chose to include Schumpeter's contribution in this chapter. Although Schumpeter was born within the Austro-Hungarian Empire, he is not usually considered as a member of the so-called Austrian School. However, this hesitation does not stand up to scrutiny. Schumpeter was strongly influenced by the first generation of the School, in particular by von Wieser (Arena and Gloria-Palermo 2001). Moreover, he dedicated a great number of contributions to the study of rationality and individual beliefs (see above all Schumpeter [1940] 1991), a point that is often neglected in the literature. This is why we believe that his contribution deserves particular attention.

3.4.1   The Schumpeterian Analysis of the Foundations of Beliefs and Individual Motives

According to Donzelli (1983, p. 639), Schumpeter was the first to introduce the expression 'methodological individualism'. In fact, an entire chapter of his 1908 work entitled *Das Wesen und der Hauptinhalt der theoretischen Nationalökonomie* is dedicated to providing a precise definition and to a detailed discussion of methodological individualism and its main alternative: methodological holism. The approach favoured by Schumpeter does not consist in establishing the superiority of one of these two methods over the other but in specifying their respective domains of relevance.

One of the fundamental purposes of the author in this context is to estimate the impact of the existence of social classes or groups on the functioning of society. In his 1927 essay on the social classes ('Social classes in an ethically homogenous environment'), Schumpeter writes the following in referring to the Marxian analysis of investment:

> Manifestly, the captures surplus value *does not invest itself* but must *be invested.* This means on the one hand that it must not be consumed by the capitalist, and on the other hand that the important point is *how* it is invested. Both factors lead away from the idea of objective automatism to the field of behavior and motive – in other words, from the *social* 'force' to the individual – physical or family; from the *objective* to the *subjective.* [...] But the crucial factor is that the social logic or objective situation does not unequivocally determine *how much* profit shall be invested, and *how* it shall be invested, *unless individual disposition is taken into account.* Yet when that is done, the logic is no longer inherent solely in the system as distinct from the individuality of the industrialist himself. (Schumpeter [1927] 1951, p. 155)

For Schumpeter, the task of the social scientist is, therefore, to study individual specificities as well as their context embedded in the reality of social structures.

Schumpeter's reference to these structures, and, in particular, to the division of society into social classes does not impair the methodological individualism of the author. For Schumpeter:

> The ultimate foundation on which the class phenomenon rests consists of individual differences in aptitude. What is meant is not differences in an absolute sense, but differences in aptitude with respect to those functions which the environment makes 'socially necessary' – in our sense – at any given time. (ibid., p. 210)

Thus, for Schumpeter, the degree of self-interest and class interest for agents varies according to the social context. If one considers, for example, 'traditional' societies, interest for the group and holism prevail. If, on the other hand, one is interested in market economies, which is the case for part of the field of pure economics, the individualistic approach becomes essential.

These developments are radically different from the approaches of both von Mises and Hayek, whose explicit purpose was to explain the functioning of markets in an individualistic and subjectivist way. For his part, Schumpeter combines, in an eclectic way, the methods of individualism and holism, and examines the problems of rules and agent beliefs within this framework. This is also the key to reading Schumpeter's remark which states that 'it is society that shapes the particular desires we observe [... and] the field of individual choice is always, though in very different ways and to very different degrees, fenced in by social habits or conventions and the like' (Schumpeter 1934, p. 91).

This position is obviously unusual within the Austrian tradition, which is not favourably disposed towards methodological holism *a priori*. Indeed, in complete contradiction with Hayek and von Mises, Schumpeter does not hesitate to underline that social classes are not 'our making' or a 'creation of the researcher' but 'social entities that we observe', or 'social organisms, living, acting and suffering as such' (Schumpeter [1927] 1951, p. 137).

3.4.2 From Motives to Routines

Following Hayek, and unlike von Mises, Schumpeter accepts the possibility of beliefs or unconscious motives for agents. These can be of two types.

First, agents who are present in market economies have substantial but unconscious traces of collective beliefs inherited from the past and accepted within certain social groups. Modern economic rationality is not, for Schumpeter, a natural given fact but a slow and progressive construction.

So, the behaviour of agents is the result of motives, beliefs and composite determinants which well illustrate the mixture of holism and individualism advanced by Schumpeter. Agent behaviour indeed results from the combination of a rational motive based on the pursuit of self-interest and from collective beliefs unconsciously inherited from the past. From this angle, economic rationality itself is not a natural characteristic of agents but rather a kind of collective belief in the need to apply three principles to a growing segment 'of the sector of social life' (Schumpeter 1942, p. 122):

> First, by trying to make the best of a given situation more or less – never wholly – according to their own lights; second, by doing so according to those rules of consistency which we call logic; and third, by doing so on assumptions which satisfy two conditions: that their number be a minimum and that everyone of them be amenable to expression in terms of potential experience; the utility of the economic calculation based on optimization; the acceptance of the 'rules' of usual logic; the use of simple hypotheses based on experience. (Ibid.)

There are also other unconscious motives in Schumpeterian agents. They concern the weight of the past and the experiences to which it has given rise. These experiences are linked to the personal trajectory of an agent and they influence him unconsciously by limiting the scope of the possible behaviours he is able to conceive of. So, if the agent does not see any reason to change his activity, he will adopt a behaviour based on a mere extrapolation from circumstances that have occurred in the past. This explains the existence of real routines that contribute to create what the individual considers to be 'normality' (Schumpeter 1939, p. 4). Reference to this normality allows the agent to formulate a structural belief, what Schumpeter calls a 'full idea of that logic which is inherent in economic things and which it is the task of scientific economics to formulate somewhat more rigorously' (ibid., p. 5). The kind of experience described above also affects the idea an agent forms about the situation of the environment through observation. We are hinting at 'the rules by which [the agent] form[s] his judgment about existing business situations' (ibid.).

It is this 'situation' that implies that 'all knowledge and habit once acquired becomes as firmly rooted in ourselves as a railway embankment in the earth' (Schumpeter 1934, p. 84). Schumpeter here evokes the existence of real rules of conduct inherited from an agent's personal trajectory as well as from autonomous social factors, which sink into the 'strata of [his] subconsciousness' (ibid.).

3.4.3 The Weight of the Diffusion of Beliefs

In compliance with his Wieserian conception of economic sociology, and in line with an Austrian characteristic already identified in von Mises and Hayek, Schumpeter considers that, whatever the social environment that is considered, people always divide into two groups: leaders and imitators. Schumpeter does not consider the former as superior beings or 'great men' (Schumpeter [1927] 1951, p. 216). They do not possess specific intellectual qualities which would lead them to play a pre-eminent role of a particular kind. However, they do have to exercise the both individual and social function of leadership, which is 'to command, to prevail, to advance' (ibid., p. 217).

The motives of the leaders are linked to their 'instinctive urge to domination' (Schumpeter [1919] 1951, p. 15), or to their 'excess of energy' (ibid., p. 34). These 'urges' – or *Trieb* (ibid., p. 83) – express the fact that the motives of the leaders are more connected to their 'instinct', a fact that explains their creativity and entails permanent changes in the sphere to which they belong. The imitators are characterized essentially by a behaviour based on the pursuit of habits as described in the previous section. They generally adopt a passive role and contribute by diffusing the beliefs, rules or innovations of the leaders. They can help reinforce these beliefs or rules and improve their dissemination in society as a whole, by adopting imitative behaviour or by demonstrating their confidence in the decisions of the leaders. They can also resist them, by postponing the processes of diffusion or sometimes by preventing their mechanisms from working altogether.

The phenomenon of 'leadership' is not independent from the social context within which it appears. Thus, when referring to warlike civilizations, Schumpeter insists on the fact that leadership results from the excess energy of individuals but also contributes to the social reproduction of the group to which they belong.

The social phenomenon of leadership also contributes to the explanation of institutional change. Indeed, unlike the imitators, the leaders do not agree, partly unconsciously, to conform to the dominant rules and to minimize their efforts in order to reach a given objective. On the contrary, they adopt a conscious behaviour of innovation and, from individual beliefs of a new type, they invent new rules intended to attain new objectives. This invention – or more exactly, this innovation – requires the production of an effort. Leaders can make this effort because they have an excess of energy that is obviously useless when individual behaviour relies on routines and appears in a purely 'hedonistic' form.

The success of an economic or social innovation does not, however, depend on its intrinsic characteristics but on its acceptance by the community of the imitators. Imitators can show resistance to change an inclination towards routine behaviour. Schumpeter analyses the reasons for this. One of these is particularly interesting in this context because it concerns the existence of a conflict between two forms of beliefs: those based on routine lead us to view changes as destabilizing factors, affecting established interests and increasing potential uncertainty; the others, on the contrary, lead us to see innovation as a factor of economic or social progress (Schumpeter 1939, p. 100).

One thus recognizes, in Schumpeter, a process of diffusion and sharing of beliefs similar to those found in von Mises and Hayek in many respects. One notes, however, that Schumpeter attaches specific importance to history and economic sociology in the analysis of this process.

3.4.4   The Weight of Class Interest

When considering social classes as 'social entities', Schumpeter is quite naturally led to analyse the concept of class interest, which seems holist *a priori*. Schumpeter defines social classes as 'social entities which we observe but which are not our making' (Schumpeter [1927] 1951, p. 137). In this way, social classes can be considered as distinctive 'living, acting, and suffering' entities that must be 'understood as such' (ibid.). More exactly, for our author, a social class is a group of individuals who are capable, within a specific social context, of exercising a given social function.

This is why Schumpeter does not think that it is possible to define social classes on either a purely holistic or a purely individualistic basis:

> We cannot help those who are unable to see that the individual is a *social* fact, the psychological an *objective* fact, who cannot give up toying with the empty contrasts of the individual *vs.* the social, the subjective *vs.* the objective. (ibid., p. 211)

This characteristic of social classes explains why class interest may exist as such and why belonging to a social class influences an individual; his behaviour, in fact, does not only depend on his own will but also on what Wieser called the 'forces of compulsion' (Wieser 1927, p. 155). It would be inaccurate to attribute to Schumpeter a definition that would make the social class the outcome of shared beliefs among its members. Schumpeter is extremely clear on this point:

> Class is something more than an aggregation of class members. It is something else, and this something cannot be recognized in the behavior of the individual class member. A class is aware of its identity as a whole, sublimates itself as

such, has its own peculiar life and characteristic 'spirit'. (Schumpeter [1927] 1951, p. 140)

Therefore, according to Schumpeter, a social class is an autonomous entity which gives rise to collective beliefs (and not the other way around). That is why Schumpeter does not hesitate to refer to 'class interest' and to suggest a convergence of the vision of the world among members of a social class (ibid., p. 140). The class interest ever-present in all members of this class thus constitutes an autonomous social determinant 'originally quite independent of [their] will' (ibid., p. 143).

To summarize, the conception of beliefs developed by Schumpeter differs sharply from the ones of von Mises and Hayek. On the one hand, Schumpeter puts forward the idea that any economic action entails individual motives as well as autonomous social determinants. This clearly makes him stand apart from the subjectivist individualism of Hayek and von Mises. On the other hand, Schumpeter admits the existence of collective beliefs peculiar to each social class; this constitutes a further divergence from Hayek and von Mises since neither of them, while sticking to the notion of shared individual beliefs, ever admitted this notion.

Conversely, one finds in Schumpeter the Austrian idea of the diffusion of beliefs by innovation/imitation, but, unlike in Hayek for example, its introduction is not intended to justify the existence of a natural tendency of the economy to converge towards a unique equilibrium. One recognizes here the complexity of the short-term as well as long-term Schumpeterian dynamics and the importance attached to the role of economic sociology (cf., for instance, contributions dedicated to this dynamics in Arena and Dangel-Hagnauer 2002).

We have now reached the limits of Schumpeter's approach. If his eclecticism allows him to provide us with a more relevant conception of economic evolution from the viewpoint of its empirical scope, it also entails a certain number of inadequacies. The one that we most want to emphasize here is the absence of a true economic explanation of the formation of collective beliefs. In Schumpeter's mind, this explanation falls essentially within the province of economic sociology, though economic sociology would be unable to provide a satisfactory answer to the economists in this context. This absence of a solution is partly the result of an unsatisfactory economic analysis in Schumpeter of the ways in which social interaction works.

3.5 CONCLUDING REMARKS

Our analysis has shown the great variety of approaches to the problem of beliefs in the economy within the Austrian tradition. Although this fact is not completely surprising for a reader familiar with the history of economic thought, its examination has the virtue of highlighting three types of solution to the problem. The approach put forward by von Mises consists in refusing any form of social or collective belief and in interpreting the processes of co-ordination through the sharing of individual beliefs. Hayek admits to the existence of a social kind of knowledge, which is both superior to and different from the sum of individual types of knowledge, but denies individuals or groups of individuals the possibility of appropriating it; the 'knowledge of society' is, therefore, only a necessary analytical device. Finally, Schumpeter's analysis admits the possibility of collective beliefs and also develops the thesis according to which these beliefs affect the actions of both individuals and groups of individuals.

The Austrian tradition thus provides a considerable – though not exhaustive – overview of possible angles from which this problem could be tackled, thereby also illustrating its importance. In this sense, it is striking to notice how many questions which appear new to many contemporary economists seemed natural to economists who, in their time, refused to allow their discipline to become divorced from the other social sciences.

REFERENCES

Arena, R. (1999), 'Hayek et l'équilibre économique: une autre interprétation', *Revue d'Economie Politique*, **109** (6).

Arena, R. (2003), 'Beliefs, knowledge and equilibrium: a different perspective on Hayek', in S. Rizzello (ed.), *Cognitive Developments in Economics*, London: Routledge.

Arena, R. and Dangel-Hagnauer, C. (eds) (2002), *The Contribution of Joseph Schumpeter to Economics: Economic Development and Institutional Change*, London: Routledge.

Arena, R. and Gloria-Palermo, S. (2001), 'Evolutionary themes in the Austrian tradition: Menger, Wieser and Schumpeter on institutions and rationality', in Pierre Garrouste and Stavros Ioannides (eds), *Evolution and Path Dependence in Economic Ideas: Past, Present*, Aldershot: Edward Elgar.

Birner, J. (1999), 'The surprising places of cognitive psychology in the work of F.A. Hayek', *History of Economic Ideas*, **7** (1–2), 43–84.

Böhm-Bawerk, E. von (1914), 'Macht oder ökonomisches Gesetz', in *Zeitschrift für Volkswirtschaft, Socialpolitik und Verwaltung*, **23**.

Donzelli, F. (1983), 'Schumpeter e the teoria economica neoclassica', *Ricercche Economiche*, **XXXVII** (4), 634–90.

Fleetwood, S. (1997), 'Hayek III: the necessity of social rules of conduct', in Stephen Frowen (ed.), *Hayek: the Economist and Social Philosopher – A Critical Retrospect*, London: Macmillan.

Garrouste, P. (1999), 'La firme "hayekienne" entre institution et organisation', *Revue d'Economie Politique*, **109** (6), 885–902.

Hayek, F.A. (1935), *Collectivist Economic Planning: Critical Studies on the Possibilities of Socialism*, London: G. Routledge & Sons.

Hayek, F.A. (1945), 'The use of knowledge in society', *American Economic Review*, **XXXV** (5), 519–30. Reprinted in Hayek (1948).

Hayek, F.A. (1948), *Individualism and Economic Order*, Chicago: University of Chicago Press.

Hayek, F.A. (1952a), *The Counter-Revolution of Science: Studies on the Abuse of Reason*, Glencoe, Illinois: The Free Press.

Hayek, F.A. (1952b), *The Sensory Order: An Inquiry into the Foundations of Theoretical Psychology*, Chicago: University of Chicago Press.

Hayek, F.A. (1960), *The Constitution of Liberty*, Chicago: University of Chicago Press.

Hayek, F.A. (1978), 'The primacy of the abstract', in *New Studies in Philosophy, Politics, Economics, and the History of Ideas*, London: Routledge and Kegan Paul.

Hayek, F.A. (1988), *The Fatal Conceit*, London: Routledge.

Ioannides, S. (1999), 'The market, the firm, and entrepreneurial leadership: some Hayekian insights', *Revue d'Economie Politique*, **109** (6).

Mises, L. von ([1924] 1981), *The Theory of Money and Credit*, 2nd edn, Indianapolis: Liberty Classics.

Mises, L. von ([1949] 1996), *Human Action: A Treatise of Economics*, 4th revised version, San Francisco: Fox & Wilker.

Mises, L. von ([1962] 1979), *The Ultimate Foundations of Economic Science*, 2nd edn, Kansas City: Sheed Andrews and McMeel.

Schumpeter, J.A. ([1919] 1951), 'Zur Soziologie der Imperialismen', *Archiv für Sozialwissenschaft und Sozialpolitik*, **46**, 1–39. Translated into English as 'The sociology of imperialisms', in J.A. Schumpeter (1951).

Schumpeter, J.A. ([1927] 1951), 'Die sozialen Klassen im ethnisch homogen Milieu', *Archiv für Sozialwissenschaft und Sozialpolitik*, **57**, 1–67. Translated into English as 'Social classes in an ethnically homogenous environment', in J.A. Schumpeter (1951).

Schumpeter, J.A. (1934), *Theory of Economic Development*, Cambridge, MA: Harvard University Press.

Schumpeter, J.A. (1939), *Business Cycles*, 2 volumes, New York: McGraw-Hill.

Schumpeter, J.A. ([1940] 1991), 'The meaning of rationality in the social sciences', reprinted in R. Swedberg (ed.), *Joseph Alois Schumpeter, The Economics and Sociology of Capitalism*, Princeton University Press.

Schumpeter, J.A. (1942), *Capitalism, Socialism and Democracy*, New York: Harper & Bros.

Schumpeter, J.A. (1951), *Imperialism and Social Classes*, edited by P. Sweezy, New York: Augustus M. Kelley.

Vanberg, V. (1986), 'Spontaneous market order and social rules: a critical examination of F.A. Hayek's Theory of Cultural Evolution', *Economics and Philosophy*, **2**, 75–100.

Wieser, F. von (1927), *Social Economics*, New York: Adelphi Company. Reprinted by
    M. Kelley Publishers in 1967. English translation of *Theorie der Gesellschaftlichen
    Wirtschaft*, 1914.

4. General equilibrium, co-ordination and multiplicity on spot markets

Roger Guesnerie

4.1 INTRODUCTION

Before embarking on our main argument, we should point out that any economic or social theory based on the assumption that individuals enjoy a degree of autonomy must explain both their motivation and their cognitive representations of the world. Economic theory often postulates the rationality of motives, to which it associates preferences described through utility functions. Representations or beliefs in this context take the form of expectations, a functional reduction that comes naturally into general equilibrium theory, the subject to which this contribution is mainly devoted.

The world of static general equilibrium may be imaginary but it is a world whose understanding has proved surprisingly instructive in deciphering the complexity of interactions between real markets. In this world, the only information affecting agents' decisions, apart from any private information they may have, is embodied in equilibrium prices, supposing that the mechanisms leading to their realization are in place. In a sequential context, the relevant beliefs concern future prices. Such beliefs on future prices are captured in formal models by estimates in the form of probabilistic expectations. In this context, a reflection on beliefs is therefore tantamount to a reflection on price expectations.

The objective of this chapter is not to present an exhaustive retrospective of the history of research on expectations in Walrasian general equilibrium models. While attempting to sketch out a general overview, what follows touches upon certain aspects of this history, focusing on finite horizon general equilibrium models and stressing the difficulties associated with the multiplicity that can affect spot market equilibria. These aspects of the work on expectations in general equilibrium models are not among the best known in economics but, I believe, are of unquestionable relevance to both economic theory and economic history.

Section 4.2 of this chapter presents the inter-temporal version, à la Radner, of the Arrow–Debreu general equilibrium model; it discusses the role that the related concepts of completeness and of 'rationality of expectations' have for allocative efficiency. In this context, section 4.3 introduces the (at times) contradictory but often complementary positions taken by research on expectations (section 4.3.1), then goes on to evoke the problem of inter-temporal equilibrium multiplicity in infinite horizon models (section 4.3.2), particularly in models that place the analysis of expectations centre stage (overlapping generation models). Section 4.4 describes the problem of expectation co-ordination that follows from the possibility of multiple 'spot' equilibria over time, as discussed in section 4.4.1. Attention is then turned to the analysis of stochastic equilibria by focusing on the effects of *ex ante* and *ex post* insurance (section 4.4.2) and the possible roles of redundant assets (section 4.4.3). Section 4.5 returns to the theme of uniqueness versus spot multiplicity (section 4.5.1) and introduces incompleteness into the analysis. In section 4.6, in order to get a quick glimpse of the rest of the panorama, the focus moves from multiplicity to learning and particularly to eductive learning, which emphasizes the 'cognitive' stability of expectations, setting aside the problem of multiplicity.

4.2   FROM THE ARROW–DEBREU EQUILIBRIUM TO THE EQUILIBRIUM OF PLANS, PRICES AND PRICE EXPECTATIONS

Let us start from a retrospective on the emergence of the theme of expectations and more specifically of rational expectations in general equilibrium theory after the 1970s.

4.2.1   The Arrow–Debreu Model

The mathematical economics of the 1950s and 1960s transformed the Walrasian general equilibrium model into the Arrow–Debreu model. There is little point in emphasizing the merits of this work in this context. The rigour and the greater generality of the argument in particular allow an at times considerable extension of the interpretations. By distinguishing goods by date or even by the state of nature in which they become available, this formally static theory takes both time and uncertainty into account.

An Arrow–Debreu intertemporal equilibrium specifies prices for dated goods: these are discounted prices and the evolution of the prices of a physical good over time gives rise to interest rates that are specific to this good. In this model, the prices are announced and the decisions to exchange and consume are taken at the beginning of the time, even if transactions only take place at the moment in which the goods become available.

In order to illustrate the model, in what follows I shall examine an exchange economy with two goods in each period and two types of agents (to simplify, I assume that each type is constituted by a continuum of identical infinitesimal agents whose total mass comes to ½, so that everything takes place as if there were two representative agents). I shall at times refer to this model as the 2×2×2 model.[1] The reader will note that this simple economy has the advantage that it can be graphically represented within an Edgeworth box.

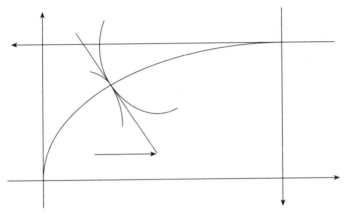

Figure 4.1   Spot equilibrium in the 2×2×2 model

The markets for dated future goods are forward markets and the Arrow–Debreu model therefore describes a system in which, in traditional language, spot markets for goods available today (in period 1 for the two-period model) coexist with forward markets for each of the goods available tomorrow.

4.2.2   The Sequential Model

We can substitute a purely sequential organization to the type of forward market organization just introduced. Now goods are only negotiated on spot markets, in other words, when they become available; the only forward markets – where a trade and the actual realization of the transaction occur at different dates – are financial markets. In the simple 2×2×2 model used to illustrate the argument, during the first period, the sequential organization means spot markets for available goods coexist with a financial market that operates as a medium of exchange between income (or the numeraire) in period one and income (or the numeraire) in period two. In period two, there exist only spot markets where the available goods are exchanged.

We can formalize the competitive equilibrium of the sequential organization in a variety of ways. In the logic of the old temporary equilibrium, expectations are treated, similarly to preferences, as exogenous. Preferences can be made endogenous by using rational expectations: in the 2×2×2 model this would consist in making them perfect in the sense of assuming perfect foresight.

This is exactly what the concept of equilibrium of prices, plans and price expectations (EPPPE) proposed by Radner (1972) does in this context.[2]

The new formalization recognizes the sequential character of the exchanges, so that in this sense it appears to be more 'realistic' than the Arrow–Debreu story.

The idea of the superiority of realism would, however, be more convincing if it were supported by a theory explaining the formation of markets. Outlining such a theory goes beyond the scope of this chapter, even though, as we shall see later, a complete answer to the issues that will be raised would require a more satisfactory analysis of the conditions for, and obstacles to, the creation of markets.

4.2.3   Efficiency and the Sequential Organization of Exchange

In the framework just outlined, the allocations of the forward market model are identical to those of the spot market, as long as the system of financial markets is sufficiently 'deep'. In the 2×2×2 model, the proof of the identity of the Arrow–Debreu and Radner equilibrium allocations is particularly simple. However, the property is more general. As long as markets are essentially complete in the Hahn (1973) sense, as Arrow (1953) had suggested and as Guesnerie and Jaffray (1974) proved quite generally in a context combining both time and uncertainty, the equilibrium allocations of the two finite horizon models coincide.[3]

The sequential organization of exchange actually allows the emergence of an Arrow–Debreu (Pareto-optimal) equilibrium: Muth's rational expectations hypothesis, the fact that agents do not make systematic errors in predicting the future state of the economy, which in this context leads to a Radner-type EPPPE, is in some ways the missing link between the static competition model and the dynamic competition model. Once again, we find rational expectations going hand in hand with an optimistic vision of the functioning of markets, as was already the case when the rational expectations hypothesis was introduced into monetary macroeconomics.

We should, of course, emphasize the conditions under which the above report is true. Intuitively, the rationality of expectations, which guarantees the absence of forecast errors in the sense adopted by the EPPPE, should be a necessary condition for efficient allocation. It is a sufficient condition only when combined with the assumption that markets are essentially complete.

The required 'depth' of the financial markets is easy to analyse in the context of the 2×2×2 model: a securities market in period one is sufficient. This can be a lot more difficult to assess in other contexts: such an assessment inevitably raises the issue of 'incompleteness', the subject of a new chapter in general equilibrium research in the 1980s.

Moreover, the co-ordination of expectations inherent in an EPPPE, which is 'perfect', because the expectations are identical and accurate, raises issues relating to the realization of equilibrium that are a lot more delicate than may at first appear. It is to these that we shall now turn.

4.3 THE CO-ORDINATION OF EXPECTATIONS IN EPPPE

4.3.1 Foreword

The first difficulty reflects the most obvious form of the multiplicity problem. Let us imagine that there are many intertemporal Arrow–Debreu equilibria, and therefore many sequential PPPE equilibria. The assumption of perfect foresight and rational expectations does not lead to a unique prediction. Neither the external observer nor the model's agents can get a univocal idea of the evolution of the economy by simply calculating the equilibrium.

The second difficulty is still related to multiplicity but in a less direct way. Let us suppose that only one intertemporal Arrow–Debreu equilibrium exists and, therefore, that there is only one sequential PPPE equilibrium. This sequential equilibrium defines a vector of equilibrium prices in each set of spot markets. However, this vector of equilibrium prices is not necessarily, and generally has no reason to be, the only vector of spot equilibrium prices! There may well be 'spot' multiplicity along the intertemporal path of the (unique) equilibrium. Figure 4.2 illustrates the phenomenon in the case of a 2×2×2 model. The arrow shows the change in initial endowments associated with the exchange of numeraire-denominated securities during the first period. The unique intertemporal equilibrium consists in two price vectors, p_1, p^a_2. However, if we take the security transactions (equilibrium transactions) into account, there are three spot equilibrium vectors $p^a{}_2$, $p^b{}_2$, $p^c{}_2$.

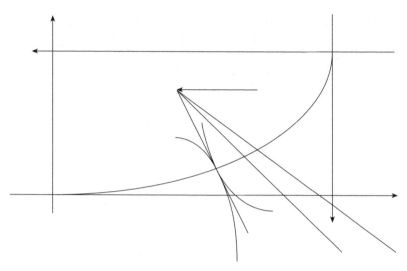

Note: The equilibrium price vectors are $p^a{}_2$, $p^b{}_2$, $p^c{}_2$ (budget lines from the left to the right).

Figure 4.2   Spot multiplicity, second period

The third difficulty is not related to multiplicity: how can we ensure that agents will co-ordinate along the spot equilibrium price vector, even when this happens to be unique?

Let us try to make a certain number of polar conditions on co-ordination more explicit in order to place the problems that we have just informally mentioned into a better-defined perspective.

Hypothesis 1: the intertemporal 'Scarf agency'

Assume the information on preferences and allocations is public. If so, a control agency endowed with adequate computational capabilities can calculate the Arrow–Debreu equilibrium, deduce the PPPE equilibria, choose one (if there is more than one) and announce the prices to the markets in each period. These announcements, whether they refer to effective prices or to price forecasts, will be self-fulfilling. In other words, they will become true if they are believed. According to this interpretation, all the co-ordination difficulties will be resolved due to the activity of a central agency – which is informed and endowed with adequate and credible computational capabilities – and not thanks to the cognitive activity of the agents. We refer to an intertemporal Scarf agency rather than to an intertemporal Walrasian auctioneer in order to emphasize the fact that the agency is endowed with computational and information-gathering capabilities that exceed those that Walras attributed to his auctioneer.[4]

Hypothesis 2: 'common knowledge' equilibrium co-ordination

Let us imagine that this central co-ordination agency no longer exists, but that all the information on endowments and preferences is public and therefore accessible to each agent, who, moreover, is endowed with infinite computational capabilities. Let us also imagine that every agent knows that each co-ordinates on a specific equilibrium, or that co-ordination on a particular equilibrium is common knowledge. This strong cognitive hypothesis ensures, in the case in which the intertemporal equilibrium is unique, that the agents will compute it and co-ordinate around it. However, in the case of multiple equilibria, a further intervention is necessary, in other words, there needs to be at least a public signal highlighting one of the equilibria.

Hypothesis 3: potential common knowledge of the equilibrium co-ordination with independent 'Scarf agencies'

Although the agents are potentially capable of computing the equilibria, the calculations and announcements are made by independent agencies acting sequentially. Thus, in the 2×2×2 model, the second period equilibrium prices will be announced by an agency whose rules of operation are known, but which is not necessarily synchronized with the agency operating in period one. The prices announced in the second period will, of course, take into account the transactions carried out in the first period. In line with the previous example, the agency in the second period will have three possible *a priori* choices, p^a_2, p^b_2, p^c_2. Without being too precise at this stage as to the underlying formal model, let us say that the independence of the second period agency means the first period agency is unable to make unique predictions on the prices of the second period. Despite this fact, the agents are assumed to anticipate prices correctly.

Hypothesis 4: common knowledge of rationality

In this hypothesis, the equilibrium in the first period depends on the activity of an agency whose operation does not interfere with the process of agents' expectations formation. The agents' forecast is the result of a collective, though private, cognitive activity which rests on two hypotheses: a sufficient knowledge (in the sense of common knowledge) of rationality, preferences and endowments of the other agents and the expectation that the operations carried out in financial markets, the second period spot equilibrium,[5] will be competitive.

This list of possibilities, which has been cursorily reviewed and whose description remains deliberately informal, does not exhaust all the possibilities. However, it has the advantage of setting out the limits of this exposition (essentially the research based on Hypothesis 3 and set out in sections 4.4 and 4.5), while also briefly presenting the difficulties associated with Hypotheses 1 and 2, the subject of what follows, and those relating to Hypothesis 4, discussed in section 4.6.

4.3.2   A Parenthesis: Co-ordination Problems due to Intertemporal Equilibrium Multiplicity

A standard finite horizon general equilibrium model with complete markets can have many PPPE intertemporal equilibria. This multiplicity raises a co-ordination problem that an intertemporal Scarf agency as outlined in Hypothesis 1 could resolve, but which destroys the predictive ability associated with the common knowledge of equilibrium co-ordination associated with Hypothesis 2. A move to infinite horizon models would exacerbate the co-ordination difficulties due to intertemporal multiplicity. Without delving too much into the details of the literature that has focused on this problem, let us review some of the most pertinent results for our purposes in order to place this text into a wider perspective.

Difficulties do not mainly originate from the infinite horizon hypothesis (though we should point out that the difficulties examined in the following paragraphs increase with the length of the horizon and, in a way, do so more than proportionally), but from the passage from a finite to an infinite number of agents.[6] This move calls into question both the *efficiency* of the PPPE intertemporal competitive equilibrium and its 'determinacy', in other words the fact that the equilibria are generally finite and topologically 'isolated'. These two phenomena can be easily observed in the simple overlapping generation models put forward by both Allais and Samuelson (Allais 1947, Samuelson 1958). In the model without money, where agents have (too) poor endowments when they are 'old', autarchy becomes an inefficient equilibrium. In the model with money, which can be viewed either as a bubble or a kind of co-ordinated sequence of lump-sum transfers, we know that the stationary monetary equilibrium can be indeterminate: in that case there is a continuum of perfect forecast equilibria, which converge towards this stationary equilibrium as time tends to infinity. Each of these phenomena (indeterminacy, inefficiency) is robust, as is clearly shown in a context of intermediate generality (*n* goods, one step forward-looking, memory 1) by the work of Kehoe and Levine (1985).

Indeterminacy poses a problem of co-ordination of expectations that is a lot more complicated than that posed by finite horizon intertemporal multiplicity. This is not the only problem: in the neighbourhood of a given equilibrium (which is stationary and deterministic in the overlapping generations model referred to earlier) there can be infinite neighbouring equilibria (which are not stationary but are deterministic in the same example). Also, sunspot equilibria in the sense of Cass and Shell (1983), which are regular in the sense of being stationary, can arise founded on extrinsic uncertainty. For example, in an overlapping generations model with money, stationary sunspot equilibria (Azariadis 1981, Azariadis and Guesnerie 1982) exist once the deterministic stationary equilibrium is 'indeterminate'. All these equilibria are, of course, rational expectations equilibria or equilibria that are based on perfectly indexed forecasts on the sunspots (note the semantic ambiguity). *De facto*, these equilibria are stochastic quasi-cycles and coexist with solutions of another class, the deterministic cycles *à la* Grandmont (1985).[7] Although the structure of the set of rational expectations equilibria (in particular the so-called sunspot equilibria) in finite horizon models is not fully elucidated except in the one-dimensional, one-step forward-looking overlapping generations model (see Grandmont 1989, Chiappori and Guesnerie 1991, Guesnerie and Woodford 1992, and Guesnerie 2001a), the potential generality of the phenomena outlined here is not questionable and is largely illustrated by existing research.

4.4 SPOT MULTIPLICITY AND CO-ORDINATION

Let us revert to our more limited finite horizon outlook and go back to Figure 4.2, which provides a graphic representation of a case of spot market equilibrium multiplicity.

Again, the unique intertemporal equilibrium consists in two price vectors, p_1, p^a_2. However, taking into account the securities trades (equilibrium trades) there are three spot equilibrium vectors, p^a_1, p^b_2, p^c_2.

How should we translate the idea that co-ordination does not result from a perfectly centralized mechanism and that the selection of the spot equilibrium is carried out by an independent agency?

4.4.1 On the Operation of the Independent Agency

To start with, we can imagine that the agency makes use of a deterministic choice mechanism, a mechanism that the logic of independent agencies suggests should depend on nothing else but the characteristics of the second period 'problem', for example the vector of initial endowments modified by the realization of trades associated with the securities market (the starting point of the budget lines on Figure 4.1 and Figure 4.2).

However, a greater difficulty appears here: it is well known that the rule that has just been referred to, i.e. that the spot market equilibrium price is a function of the endowments (modified by previous financial commitments), cannot be continuous if there are multiple equilibria in the domain of initial endowments under consideration.[8] This remark suggests that the independent functioning of tomorrow's market agency (in the 2×2×2 model) might be incompatible (for certain configurations of the intertemporal economy) with the existence of an equilibrium. This conjecture is not as mysterious as it might appear at first sight. If the 2×2×2 model illustrated here has only a single intertemporal equilibrium and if the rule of the independent co-ordination agency specifies that $p_2 = p^B_2$ for the configuration of initial endowments W', then there is no (perfect foresight) equilibrium that is compatible with the choice of the agency.

Another way we could try to compensate for the difficulty that arises due to the independence of the second period Scarf agency would consist in allowing for complete insurance against the uncertainty of the announcement of a further equilibrium. For example, it is tempting to see the choice of the second period co-ordinator in our 2×2×2 model as the operation of a sunspot that takes the three values r, g and v and to make the assumption that the signal is not only observable but also verifiable and contractible. An insurance market would then allow income exchanges, arising from previous trades on contingent securities, that would precede the choice of equilibrium. However, if all contingent securities exist, the market is complete and the Pareto-optimal equilibrium vis-à-vis the set of random (and not only deterministic) allocations coincides, in a convex economy, with the initial equilibrium. This is the Cass and Shell (1983) 'ineffectivity' theorem. For example, in our 2×2×2 model, the new equilibrium allocations with the new securities coincide with the initial equilibrium allocations. Still, have we solved our problem? No, the new securities are not exchanged at equilibrium and, paradoxically in view of our objective, the number of spot equilibria remains unchanged. We have not advanced by an iota towards the solution of the multiplicity problem. The ineffectivity s theorem, contrary to what a superficial reading might suggest, does not imply that the problem of multiplicity can be resolved by an insurance that proceeds *ex ante* to the choice of the spot equilibrium.

What lessons can we learn from this first analysis? That in a 'complex' sequential market the *deus ex machina* of co-ordination on the unique intertemporal equilibrium operates with less force. Short of co-ordinating the co-ordinators (the independent agencies in this case) the emergence of a fully co-ordinated and efficient equilibrium is problematic.

It would appear inevitable, under the independence hypothesis we envisage, to make the choice of the agency random in the case of spot multiplicity. It would then be described by probability distributions over the equilibrium prices that would vary continuously with the vector of modified initial endowments. This assumption would allow enough flexibility in the choice of probabilities to make the distribution continuous, and it should also succeed in restoring the existence of an intertemporal rational expectations equilibrium (with a random, but rationally expected, choice of tomorrow's spot equilibrium prices). Despite the fact that the construction put forward by Mas-Colell (1991) and generalized by Gottardi and Kajii (1999) cannot be directly transposed[9] to the 2×2×2 model, it suggests that, in the case of Figure 4.2, we can find a stochastic equilibrium of the type I have just described.[10] We note that an equilibrium of this kind is a rational expectations equilibrium (co-ordination is maintained) though it ceases to be efficient!

4.4.2   Should we Insure against Spot Multiplicity?

Let us admit that, in the case of spot multiplicity, the independent Scarf agency chooses randomly. Let us call stochastic equilibrium or sunspot equilibrium the equilibrium that corresponds to such a choice. The noise introduced, which destroys the first best efficiency, justifies the introduction of insurance. How does it perform?

Let us call *ex ante* insurance a system of income transfers that, conditional on the equilibrium choice, would occur at the same time as the equilibrium choice. This *ex ante* insurance,[11] which, as we have already seen, is not in a position to solve the multiplicity problem, would in principle attenuate the effects of a random choice of prices. It is, however, more reasonable to think that in this case, *ex post* insurance would be a better theoretical choice. The introduction of such an insurance mechanism would require us to complete our 2×2×2 model by introducing a third period. In this third period, after having undone all the previous trades that were contingent on the equilibrium prices, the spot markets would be reopened. We note that the securities that we have just introduced are reminiscent of options. As the analyses of Chichilnisky et al. (1992) have shown, the *ex post* options considered here play the role of imperfect insurance *vis-à-vis* the choice of a co-ordinator *à la* Scarf.

4.4.3   Multiplicity and Redundant Assets

There is perhaps another solution to the problem of insuring against the hazards of the choice of equilibrium in the case of spot multiplicity.

Returning to the 2×2×2 model, we observe that the initial allocations that determine the problem of the computation of the equilibrium in the second period are not independent, for a given intertemporal equilibrium, of the securities actually present on the financial market. For example, Figure 4.3 shows security trades when the security assigns rights on good 2 in the subsequent period.

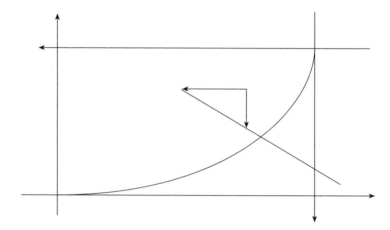

Figure 4.3   Visualization of the exchange of securities, depending on whether they are labelled in good 1 (horizontal arrow) or in good 2 (vertical arrow)

As the figure shows, although the spot equilibrium remains the same, the excess demand functions change. This remark suggests that the choice of financial assets affects our problem and that redundant assets, in other words the assets in excess of those required to make the market essentially complete, could play a favourable role in the co-ordination of expectations. Indeed, Mas-Colell (1991) has shown that the introduction of a redundant asset makes the stochastic equilibria disappear in a framework that is not too distant from the model we are considering here. His argument applies here and more generally to the *n* goods version of the two-period model considered here. It shows that if the number of independent assets allowing for the forward exchange of independent baskets of goods is equal to the number of goods, then a stochastic equilibrium does not exist. Since the hypothesis on the assets thus introduced goes back to assuming that the market is complete in an Arrow–Debreu sense and not only essentially complete, the intuition of the result is, in a certain sense, immediate: the addition of Radner-type assets does not have any effect on the intertemporal Arrow–Debreu allocation. Despite this, the careful Mas-Colell (1991) reader will note that, setting aside the lack of realism of the assumption on the number of assets, the result does not fully satisfactorily resolve the co-ordination problem arising from spot multiplicity (when this is present). At the equilibrium he describes, the agents are indifferent between trading securities in the first period and engaging in further trades of goods, and co-ordination, which assumes equilibrium of security trades today, must, in one way or another, have some centralized aspect.

4.5 UNIQUENESS, MULTIPLICITY, INCOMPLETENESS

The stochastic equilibrium that we have just described, and whose existence we have briefly discussed, has the following characteristics: after the trades have taken place there are three spot equilibria and one of these is chosen randomly. We can see this, using the commonly accepted terminology, as a sunspot equilibrium. In this particular case though, the sunspot equilibrium is tied to spot multiplicity. Is this necessary?

4.5.1 Sunspots and Spot Uniqueness

Let us imagine, for example in the 2×2×2 model, that there exists only one spot equilibrium in quite a large domain of initial allocations. Is the uniqueness of the spot equilibrium compatible with the existence of a stochastic sunspot equilibrium correlated to an extrinsic random variable $s \in S$? The answer is clearly no in the two extreme cases:

- No assets exist allowing insurance against sunspots. For example, with the single security on the numeraire postulated at the beginning of this chapter for the 2×2×2 model, the uniqueness of the spot equilibrium makes any stochastic allocation impossible in the second period, and therefore any intertemporal stochastic equilibrium impossible as well.
- Enough assets ($> S$) exist to be fully insured against sunspots. In this case the allocation is Pareto-optimal and therefore, if the economy is convex, deterministic. It should, moreover, be noted that one consequence of the redundancy argument mentioned earlier, despite the limitations we highlighted, is that it is not necessary to have an infinite number of insurance markets in order to be fully insured against sunspots, even if the potential number of sunspots is infinite. Along similar lines, the argument put forward by Kajii (1997) shows that the addition of a sufficiently large number of 'call' options to a financial security can eliminate extrinsic uncertainty, whatever the number of sunspots considered.

The answer to the question posed (stochastic equilibrium despite spot uniqueness) cannot therefore be positive unless the number of assets is intermediate, for example, if our 2×2×2 model has $S = 3$ and two negotiable assets in the first period. The example provided by Hens (2000a) is set against this kind of framework. Although the example entails an error (Barnett and Fisher 2002), it can be modified in such a way as to save the conclusion (Hens 2000b): when insurance markets against sunspots are incomplete, despite spot uniqueness, a stochastic intertemporal equilibrium can exist.

4.5.2   Multiplicity, Incomplete Markets and Sunspots

Our argument is set out in the context of the 2×2×2 model in which the financial market renders the economy essentially complete at least vis-à-vis intrinsic uncertainty. What happens when this is no longer the case? Without attempting to answer the question at a very general level, we can tackle the issue within the maintained framework of the 2×2×2 model by supposing that there is intrinsic uncertainty in the second period (applying to either preferences or endowments) and that it is associated to two signals. If the signals are not verifiable, then no contingent asset is viable and, for example, only the initial financial market is open. Figure 4.4 shows the equilibrium allocation with such an incomplete market.

In this case, the PPPE equilibria are no longer efficient in terms of first best Pareto efficiency. However, in the case of second period spot multiplicity, a further hurdle is added to the difficulty of co-ordinating equilibrium choices – the subject of the preceding paragraph. Paradoxically, this difficulty appears when extrinsic uncertainty (the one tied to sunspots etc.) is, as in the paragraph that follows, contractible and can therefore act as a support to a security of the following type: a numeraire unit if the sunspot is in that state. If the securities are traded in the first period and are realized before the second period spot equilibrium has been reached, then if the number of spot equilibria in the model without extrinsic uncertainty is p, the number of equilibria in the model with extrinsic uncertainty, and insurance against it, is $2p - 1$: in other words, there exist necessarily $p - 1$ stochastic equilibria. This is the result obtained by Guesnerie and Laffont (1988) in a context of n goods, which holds for the 2×2×2 model with intrinsic uncertainty referred to here. It implies there that, in the absence of endowments in the first period, so that the non-contingent security is not tradable in the absence of non-contingent securities, if there were initially 3 spot equilibria in each non-insurable intrinsic state (hence 9 Radner equilibria), the number of stochastic equilibria when all sunspot contingent securities are available is, in the case suggested by Figure 4.4, 8!

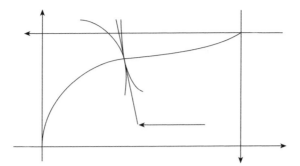

*Figure 4.4   Spot equilibrium (second period), intrinsic (and unverifiable)
state of nature 1*

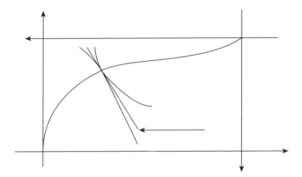

*Figure 4.5   Spot equilibrium (second period), intrinsic (and unverifiable)
state of nature 2*

One must also understand that the just suggested increased intertemporal equilibrium multiplicity will not, at least in general, reduce the multiplicity of the spot equilibria contingent on the states of an extrinsic nature. In this case the co-ordination difficulties are exacerbated: in our example, the number of intertemporal equilibria goes to $p - 1$, but in each case it is plausible that the number of spot equilibria is equal to 3. Paradoxically, the new markets created to take the sunspots into account are responsible for this exacerbation of the difficulty. Their creation increases price volatility and is an additional source of inefficiency.

The analysis put forward by Bowman and Faust (1997) is even more intriguing in a certain sense. In their analysis, in a (three-period) model where we cannot insure against intrinsic uncertainty (a shock on preferences) but where there is spot uniqueness, the introduction of a 'call option' leads to the emergence of a Pareto-optimal equilibrium, a point that is in line with the results of traditional analysis (Ross 1976). However, the introduction also gives rise to new sunspot equilibria that can be 'less good' than the equilibrium without the option. What is more, although the market is initially essentially complete, the addition of a redundant option, and hence one that can be priced using Black–Scholes-type techniques, can introduce, in addition to the efficient equilibrium that remains attainable, sunspot equilibria.

The conclusion of these exploratory thoughts is not crystal clear. Let us say that if the phenomenon of a sunspot stochastic equilibrium in finite horizon general equilibrium models is not the necessary consequence of spot multiplicity, this makes it more formidable. The multiplication and/or redundancy of assets has ambiguous effects on co-ordination.[12] The subject deserves to be examined in greater depth, so that the results of Hens (2000b), Guesnerie and Laffont (1988) and Bowman and Faust (1997) can be placed into a unified and improved framework.

4.6   COGNITIVE CO-ORDINATION PROCESSES

We have seen how the problem of multiplicity in finite horizon general equilibrium models that could initially appear minor takes a more complex turn once we allow for spot equilibrium multiplicity, even when the intertemporal equilibrium is unique. By concentrating on this difficulty and associating it to the problem of co-ordination between agencies charged with computing the equilibrium in each period, we implicitly admitted that the only difficulty in the forecast of the second period price depended on the hazards of the choice of the Scarf agency and not on the uncertainty of the conditions in which it operated. In other words, in the 2×2×2 model, we assumed that the vector of modified initial endowments, which was the starting point of the analysis, was perfectly predictable. We now abandon this hypothesis and assume that, in line with the logic of what we called Hypothesis 4, individual agents have to forecast all the data of the second period. This problem is clearly independent from the multiplicity problem, be it intertemporal or spot.[13] The analysis will therefore be carried out in relation to models with both intertemporal and spot uniqueness and which include learning.

4.6.1   Learning the Equilibrium: Evolutionary and Eductive Points of View

Standard evolutionary procedures (those of evolutionary learning) are based on the application of mechanical rules that start from a limited understanding of the functioning of the system or from a limited rationality, and lead to a correction of expectations when these are found to be inaccurate. For example, in this case the agents would revise the second period price expectations that turned out to be wrong and the process would continue until convergence, for each repetition of the two period economy considered. The revision mechanisms studied are generally simple (e.g. adaptive rules) and such that their repeated application can allow agents to learn the equilibrium, in the sense that the only resting state of the system that is compatible with the revision rule is the equilibrium state itself. There is a considerable number of works on evolutionary learning.[14]

Work on eductive learning starts from a different idea, the iterated elimination of the strategies that are not best responses, a process that leads to the set of rationalizable solutions.[15] Alternatively, this procedure can be seen as stemming from the model's assumptions of common knowledge and individual rationality.[16] I have suggested associating the success of a local eductive procedure, which, in my words, establishes the strong rationality of expectations, to the convergence of the elimination process triggered by an assumed common knowledge of a local restriction on the state of the system. Research of this kind affects both models where decisions taken independently today affect the state of the system tomorrow and infinite horizon models where the eductive expectation stability criterion is confronted with alternative criteria.[17] A detailed review of this work is presented in Guesnerie (2002).

4.6.2 Eductive Learning in Standard General Equilibrium Models: A Brief Introduction

I would like to refer to some of the studies on the eductive stability of expectations in the general equilibrium model (a two-period exchange economy) a little less briefly. In this model, the agents in the first-period must 'educe' the second period equilibrium price before providing the necessary information to the agency charged with computing the first period equilibrium. However, assuming the second-period equilibrium prices are unique for the sake of simplicity, these depend in a way on the ability of agents to calculate the wealth transfers (through saving between the first and second periods) that are decided simultaneously by the agents. The collective eductive process affects both the savings forecast and the equilibrium price simultaneously. This occurs because in the 2×2×2 model, with spot uniqueness on the point expectation of initial endowments modified by the financial market's transactions (in Figure 4.1), the plausibility of the rational expectations hypothesis (in the sense of the aforementioned eductive stability criterion) increases with the insensitivity of tomorrow's equilibrium price to the distribution of purchasing power or the insensitivity of savings to the goods' interest rates. Both these properties depend on the agents' preferences in their intertemporal and static aspects (see Ghosal 2000, Guesnerie and Hens 1999).

The last two models I would like to refer to are situated within a macroeconomic framework where firms today make hiring decisions (Guesnerie 2000b). These decisions determine the volume of product brought to market, a volume that will be sold at the competitive price, given the total revenue distributed during production. It can be shown that the eductive stability of the Keynesian equilibrium (fixed salary) is favoured by a weak price elasticity of supply of the producers (which makes errors in the cross forecast of each agent's price expectations less significant), a strong demand elasticity (which makes tomorrow's price less uncertain) and a high value for the elementary Keynesian multiplier (the inverse of the marginal propensity to consume), which gives a positive role to the strategic complementarities associated with the increased revenue and new job opportunities by reducing the strategic substitutabilities. Curiously enough, the same factors favour the eductive stability of the flexible wage Walrasian equilibrium. Despite this, in this last case, the generalization of the argument to an *n* good model shows that the stabilizing force of the Keynesian multiplier is reduced (Guesnerie 2000c).

4.7   CONCLUSION

This brief review of contemporary thinking on expectations is both subjective and incomplete. It is subjective because it assigns a privileged place to the works I know best and therefore, among others, my own contributions and in particular those in sections 4.3.2 and 4.5, which only incompletely touch on important subjects and considerable areas.

It is incomplete because I have only summarily treated one of the least known chapters of theoretical developments, the one relating to spot equilibrium multiplicity in finite horizon models, in this case in two period models. This choice, even if we have often gone beyond the strict problems of spot equilibrium multiplicity, is clearly debatable, given that the degree of pertinence of the phenomenon of spot equilibrium multiplicity for the understanding of economic phenomena is an open question: which stylized facts are, or could be, explained by spot equilibrium multiplicity? Even if Hildebrand's work (1994) on the plausibility of the law of demand is an important exception, too few works allow us to approach this question with the seriousness it deserves in relation to the analyses referred to in this chapter.

NOTES

1. In the 2×2×2 model, an Arrow–Debreu equilibrium consists in p_1, p_2, two price vectors of R^n (good 1 of the first period being the numeraire whose price equals 1), an intertemporal consumption plan for each of the agents, $\left(\overline{x_1^i}, \overline{x_2^i}\right)$, $i = 1, 2$, such that:

   1. $\left(\overline{x_1^i}, \overline{x_2^i}\right)$ is the solution of the following programme:

   $Max\ u\left(x_1^i, x_2^i\right)$

   $p_1 x_1^i + p_2 x_2^i \leq p_1 \omega_1^i + p_2 \omega_2^i$

   1. $\sum \overline{x_1^i} \leq \sum \omega_1^i, \sum \overline{x_2^i} \leq \sum \omega_2^i$

2. In the 2×2×2 model, an EPPPE consists in two given price vectors, p_1, p_2, of R^n (good 1 being in each period the numeraire whose price equals 1), an interest rate i, an intertemporal consumption plan for each of the agents, $\left(\overline{x_1^i}, \overline{x_2^i}\right)$, $i = 1,2$, and positions $\left(\overline{y^i}\right)$, $i = 1,2$, on the financial market such that:

   1. $\left(\overline{x_1^i}, \overline{x_2^i}\right)$ is the solution of the following programme:

   $Max\ u\left(x_1^i, x_2^i\right)$

   $p_1 x_1^i + y^i \leq p_1 \omega_1^i$

   $p_2 x_2^i \leq p_2 \omega_2^i + \left(1+i\right) y^i$

   1. $\sum \overline{x_1^i} \leq \sum \omega_1^i, \sum \overline{x_2^i} \leq \sum \omega_2^i$

3. In an infinite horizon model with a finite number of participants (a fact that implies a certain number of them have an infinite lifespan) and under the hypothesis that they remain small, the identity of allocations also obtains (see Kehoe and Levine 1985).
4. We could indeed see behind it the ideal 'Commissariat du Plan' as set out by Massé (1971)
5. Which we could, in the first instance, consider to be unique.
6. Which in a certain sense affects the power of the transversality conditions.
7. In the simple overlapping generations model, these two classes of solution are intimately related to each other, as shown by Azariadis and Guesnerie (1986): (binary) sunspot equilibria exist if, and only if, cycles of order 2 exist.
8. See for example Balasko (1981).
9. Mas-Collel's argument requires three goods and therefore is valid in the 2×3×2 version of our model.
10. However, it is not fully enlightening on the conditions under which variations of the probability distributions would make the existence of an equilibrium with a stochastic agency probable.
11. Whose formal definition if not realization, the reader will verify, is not trivial.
12. A different argument, in a different model, is put forward by Guesnerie and Rochet (1992): in this case redundancy contributes to the destabilization of expectations.
13. We re-examine the problem in a different way, that is more modest and more ambitious at the same time. It is more modest, because, considering the recurrent character of multiplicity, we look amongst all equilibria for those that are the most credible candidates from the point of view of expectation co-ordination. It is more ambitious because the criteria that we adopt can lead to the rejection of a model's unique equilibrium.

14. The majority of studies on learning do not take place within a general equilibrium context, with the exception of those that fall within the framework of overlapping generations models. In this context, many studies have been made on evolutionary learning of the stationary state (de Canio 1979; Marcet and Sargent 1989a, 1989b), of cycles (Grandmont and Laroque 1986; Guesnerie and Woodford 1992), or of sunspot equilibria (Woodford 1990; Desgranges and Negroni 2003). The interested reader can usefully consult the review and recent work of (Evans and Honkaphoja 1997, 2000).
15. In the framework of a strategic complementarity case, this set has a simple structure and, if the equilibrium is unique, it is reduced to it (see Cooper and John 1989; Milgrom and Roberts 1990).
16. See Bernheim (1984), Pearce (1984), Guesnerie (1992).
17. See for example Evans and Guesnerie (2003) and Gauthier (2003) on the restrictions, the support but also the reasons that the eductive viewpoint provides for the choice of saddle point solutions.

REFERENCES

Allais, M. (1947), *Economie et intérêt*, Paris: Imprimerie Nationale.
Arrow, K. (1953), 'Le rôle des valeurs boursières pour la répartition la meilleure des risques', *Cahiers du séminaire d'économétrie*, **40**, 41–8.
Azariadis, C. (1981), 'Self-fulfilling prophecies', *Journal of Economic Theory*, **25**, 380–96.
Azariadis, C. (1993), *Intertemporal Macroeconomics*, Cambridge, MA and Oxford: Blackwell.
Azariadis, C. and Guesnerie, R. (1982) 'Prophéties Créatices et Persistance des Théories', *Revue Economique*, **33**, 787–806.
Azariadis, C. and Guesnerie, R. (1986), 'Sunspots and cycles', *Review of Economic Studies*, **53**, 725–36.
Balasko, Y. and Shell, K. (1981), 'The overlapping-generations model, I, II', *Journal of Economic Theory*, **24**.
Barnett, R.C. and Fisher, E. (2002), 'Do sunspots matter when equilibria are unique?', *Econometrica*, **70** (1), 393–6.
Bernheim, B.D. (1984), 'Rationalizable strategic behavior', *Econometrica*, **52**, 1007–28.
Bowman, D. and Faust, J. (1997), 'Options, sunspots and the creation of uncertainty', *Journal of Political Economy*, **105**, 5, 957–75.
Cass, D. and Shell, K. (1983), 'Do sunspots matter?', *Journal of Political Economy*, **91**, 409–26.
Chiappori, P.A. and Guesnerie, R. (1991), 'Sunspot equilibria in sequential markets model', in W. Hildenbrand and H. Sonnenschein (eds), *Handbook of Mathematical Economics*, Amsterdam: North Holland, pp. 1682–762.
Chichilnisky, G., Dutta, J. and Heal, G. (1992), 'Endogenous uncertainty, derivative securities and incomplete markets', Working Paper, Graduate School of Business.
Cooper, R. and John, A. (1989), *Coordinating Coordination Failures in Keynesian Macroeconomics*, 242–64.
De Canio, S.J. (1979), 'Rational expectations and learning from experience', *Quarterly Journal of Economics*, **93**, 47–58.
Desgranges, G. and Negroni, G. (2003), 'Expectations coordination on a sunspot equilibrium: an eductive approach', *Macroeconomic Dynamics*, **7** (1), 7–41.

Evans, G. and Guesnerie, R. (2003), 'Coordination on saddle path solutions: 1-Linear univariate models', *Macroeconomic Dynamics*, 7, 42–62.

Evans, G. and Honkhapojha, S. (1997), 'Learning dynamics', in J.B. Taylor and M. Woodford (eds), *Handbook in Macroeconomics*, Amsterdam: North Holland.

Gauthier, S. (2003), 'On the dynamic equivalence principle in linear rational expectations models', *Macroeconomic Dynamics*, 7 (1), 63–88.

Ghosal, S. (2000), 'Eductive stability in an exchange general equilibrium setting', mimeo, University of Warwick.

Gottardi, P. and Kajii, A. (1999), 'Generic existence of sunspot equilibria: the real asset case', *Review of Economic Studies*, 66, 713–32.

Grandmont, J.M. (1985), 'On endogenous competitive business cycles', *Econometrica*, 33, 995–1045.

Grandmont, J.M. (1989), 'Local bifurcations and stationary sunspots', in W. Barnett, J. Geweke and K. Shell (eds), *Economic Complexity: Chaos, Sunspots, Bubbles and Non-Linearities*, Cambridge: Cambridge University Press.

Grandmont, J.M. and Laroque, G. (1986), 'Stability of cycles and expectations', *Journal of Economic Theory*, 40, 138–51.

Grandmont, J.M. and Laroque, G. (1991), 'Economic dynamics with learning: some instability examples', in W.A. Barnett et al. (eds), *Equilibrium Theory and Applications: Proceedings of the Sixth International Symposium in Economic Theory and Econometrics*, Cambridge, UK: Cambridge University Press.

Guesnerie, R. (1992), 'An exploration of the eductive justifications of the Rational Expectations Hypothesis', *American Economic Review*, 82, 1254–78.

Guesnerie, R. (2001a), *Assessing Rational Expectations: 1-sunspot Multiplicity and Economic Fluctuations*, Cambridge, MA: MIT Press.

Guesnerie, R. (2001b), 'Short run expectational coordination: fixed versus flexible wages', *Quarterly Journal of Economics*, 116 (3), 1115–47.

Guesnerie, R. (2001c), 'On the robustness of the analysis of expectational coordination: from 3 to n+2 goods', in G. Debreu, W. Neuefeind and W. Trockel (eds), *Economic Essays, a Festschrift for Werner Hildenbrand*, Springer, pp. 141–158.

Guesnerie, R. (2002), 'Anchoring economic predictions in common knowledge', *Econometrica*, 70, 439–80.

Guesnerie, R. (2005), *Assessing Rational Expectations: 2-eductive Stability in Economics*, Cambridge, MA: MIT Press.

Guesnerie, R. and Hens, T. (1999), 'Expectational stability in a two-period exchange economy', mimeo.

Guesnerie, R. and Jaffray, J.Y. (1974) 'Optimality of equilibria of plans, prices and price expectations', in J. Dreze (ed.), *Uncertainty, Equilibrium, Optimality*, London: Macmillan, pp. 71–86.

Guesnerie, R. and Laffont, J.J. (1988), 'Notes on sunspot equilibria in finite economies', in *Volume en l'honneur d'Edmond Malinvaud: Economica*, EHESS, pp. 118–43.

Guesnerie, R. and Rochet, J.C. (1992), '(De)stabilizing speculation: an alternative viewpoint', *European Economic Review*, 37, 1043–63.

Guesnerie, R. and Woodford, M. (1991), 'Stability of cycles with adaptive learning rules', in *Equilibrium Theory and Applications: Proceedings of the Sixth International Symposium in Economic Theory and Econometrics*, Cambridge, UK: Cambridge University Press, pp. 110–33.

Guesnerie, R. and Woodford, M. (1992), 'Endogenous fluctuations', in *Advances in Economic Theory*, Econometric Society Monograph, Cambridge: Cambridge University Press, 289–412.

Hahn, F. (1973), 'On transaction costs, inessential sequence economies and money', *Review of Economic Studies*, **40**, 449–62.

Hahn, F. (1982), *Money and Inflation*, Oxford: Blackwell.

Hens, T. (2000a), 'Do sunspots matter when spot equilibria are unique?', *Econometrica*, **68** (2), 435–41.

Hens, T. (2000b), 'Corrections to "Do sunspots matter when spot equilibria are unique?"', Universitat Zurich, mimeo.

Hildenbrand, W. (1994), *Market Demand*, Princeton: Princeton University Press.

Kajii, A. (1997), 'On the role of options in sunspot equilibria', *Econometrica*, **65** (4), 977–86.

Kehoe, T.J. and Levine, D.K. (1985), 'Comparative statistics and perfect foresight in infinite horizon economies', *Econometrica*, **53**, 433–54.

Marcet, A. and Sargent, J. (1989a), 'Convergence of least squares learning mechanisms in self referential linear stochastic models', *Journal of Economic Theory*, **48**, 337–68.

Marcet, A. and Sargent, J. (1989b), 'Convergence of least squares learning in environments with hidden state variables and private information', *Journal of Political Economy*, **97**, 1306–22.

Mas-Colell, A. (1991), 'Three observations on sunspot and asset redundancy', in P. Daguspta, D. Gale, O. Hart and E. Maskin, *Economic Analysis of Markets and Games*, Cambridge, MA: MIT Press, pp. 464–73.

Massé, P. (1971), *Le plan ou l'anti-hasard*, Paris: Dunod.

Milgrom, P. and Roberts, J. (1990), 'Rationalizability, learning and equilibrium in games with strategic complementarities', *Econometrica*, **47**, 1337–51.

Pearce, D. (1984), 'Rationalizable strategic behavior and the problem of perfection', *Econometrica*, **52**, 1029–50.

Radner, R. (1972), 'Equilibrium of plans, prices and price expectations', *Econometrica*, **40**, 289–303.

Ross, S. (1976), 'Options and efficiency', *Quarterly Journal of Economics*, **90**, 75–89.

Samuelson, P.A. (1958), 'An exact consumption-loan model of interest with or without the social contrivance of money', *Journal of Political Economy*, **66**, 467–82.

Woodford, M. (1990), 'Learning to believe in sunspots', *Econometrica*, **58**, 277–307.

PART II

Knowledge and Beliefs in Game Theory

5. Justifications of game theoretic equilibrium notions

Bernard Walliser

5.1 INTRODUCTION

In line with the spirit of Walrasian equilibrium, game theory is based on various equilibrium notions that convey the manner in which rational players co-ordinate their actions to give rise to some relatively stable state. Any equilibrium notion is, however, defined from the modeller's viewpoint, an equilibrium state being only subject to the necessary condition that, if the actors are involved in it, they find no interest in deviating unilaterally from it. Hence, no concrete process of reaching an equilibrium state, grounded solely on the actors' deliberations and actions without outside intervention, is described by the modeller. Similarly to the Walrasian auctioneer, who delivers the equilibrium prices to the economic agents, it is possible to introduce a fictitious entity, the Nashian regulator, who calculates the equilibrium actions and suggests them to the actors. However, the actors would have to effectively adopt them, which is the case only if they have a good reason to think that their opponents will also adopt them, the stability condition postulated for an equilibrium not being necessarily sufficient.

The aim of 'cognitive economics' is to study the beliefs and reasoning that economic actors use in order to adapt to dynamic situations of mutual interaction (Walliser 2000). One of its major themes is to explain the concrete processes by which the actors, invested with an instrumental as well as cognitive rationality, are susceptible of co-ordinating, on their own, on an equilibrium state. The exhibited processes must permit, in one movement, the justification of one or another equilibrium notion stated *a priori* and the selection of one or another associated equilibrium state in case of multiplicity. A first approach tries to give 'eductive justifications' to the equilibrium, that is, to base the equilibrium only on the reasoning of autonomous actors equipped with an extremely strong rationality. A second approach tries to give 'evolutionist justifications' to the equilibrium, that is, to make the equilibrium appear as an asymptotic state of some dynamic process followed by actors endowed with a very bounded rationality.

In what follows, the first section deals with eductive justifications of the usual static equilibrium notions (Nash equilibrium, rationalizable equilibrium, correlated equilibrium). The second section deals with eductive justifications of the dominant dynamic equilibrium notion (subgame perfect equilibrium) with reference to the 'backward induction paradox'. The third section deals with evolutionist justifications of the static as well as dynamic equilibrium notions, for various learning and evolution processes. Each section is subdivided into three parts: the first part is devoted to the necessary analytic tools, the second to their application to the games under consideration and the third to the expression of the main results.

5.2 EDUCTIVE JUSTIFICATIONS OF STATIC EQUILIBRIA

5.2.1 Logical Principles

Formalization of an actor's belief structure is carried out within the framework of epistemic logic (a type of modal logic), under the two usual syntactic and semantic forms that can be shown to be equivalent. In syntax, the actor's referential physical universe is described by 'propositions' and the actor's knowledge about it is expressed by a 'belief operator' that indicates whether or not he knows a proposition. In semantics, the physico-psychological states of the universe (combining material properties and the actors' beliefs) are described by 'possible worlds' and the actor's belief is expressed by an 'accessibility domain', indicating the worlds he is unable to distinguish in any particular world; moreover, one possible world is set out as the real world. The transfer from syntax to semantics is achieved simply by associating an event with each proposition, i.e. the set of worlds where it is true. In addition, an actor believes a proposition in some world if the associated event is true in all the worlds accessible from this world.

The syntactic representation allows the definition of a set of strong axioms, assumed to be satisfied by the actor's beliefs about his environment and about himself as well (self-hierarchical beliefs). These are the axioms of logical omniscience (the actor knows all the consequences of what he knows), veridicity (what the actor knows is true), positive introspection (the actor knows what he knows) and negative introspection (the actor knows what he does not know). The syntactic axioms have semantic counterparts in the form of properties imposed to the accessibility domains or to the associated accessibility relations (one world is linked to another if it belongs to its accessibility domain). In fact, logical omniscience is automatically satisfied in the retained semantics, whereas the three other axioms refer respectively to reflexivity, transitivity and Euclideanity of the accessibility relation. Concerning veridicity, the most controversial property, what an actor considers is usually qualified as 'knowledge' when it proves true (in the modeller's sense) and as 'belief' when it may be false.

The preceding beliefs were defined within a propositional (or set-theoretic) framework, where the knowledge is expressed as all or nothing, the actor either knowing or not knowing a given proposition. In semantics, when all properties are simultaneously satisfied, the actor is endowed with a partitional knowledge on the possible worlds, in the sense that the accessibility domains form a partition. Alternatively, the beliefs can be defined in a probabilistic framework within which knowledge is more finely shaded, the actor knowing a proposition with some probability. In semantics, having defined the generalized properties of knowledge, the actor considers a probability distribution in each world for all the worlds. In practice, a mixed semantic 'information structure' tends to obtain and is defined, on the one hand, by a prior probability distribution on the worlds, common to all actors and conveying objective public information, and, on the other hand, by a set-theoretic knowledge partition, specific to each actor and conveying his private information.

Furthermore, in an almost certain context (Monderer and Samet 1989; Brandenburger 1992), the passage from the set-theoretic framework to the probabilistic framework can be accomplished by taking a whole range of intermediate beliefs into account (Stalnaker 1996). On one side, the actor has a set-theoretic belief available that nobody can question (no contradictory message can arise). On the other side, the actor is provided with a 1-belief (belief with probability 1), which can prove false (a surprising message may arise). In a first intermediate situation, the actor has a 1-belief, in the real world, that what he believes is true (no surprise can arise in the real world). In the second intermediate situation, the actor has a 1-belief 'robust to truth', i.e. his belief is confirmed if he receives a true message in the world under consideration (a surprise becomes possible, even in the real world). In all probabilistic cases, when a belief revision becomes necessary regarding a non-contradictory message, the revision rule assumed to be used is the Bayes rule.

In a syntactic context involving many actors, these will adopt crossed beliefs (hetero-hierarchical beliefs) such as 'I believe that you believe that I believe'. The distribution of these beliefs between individuals goes, with increasing strength, from a shared belief ('each actor believes X') to a common belief (each actor believes X, believes that the other believes X and so forth to infinity). The latter notion was introduced by Lewis (1969). Each collective belief level is symbolized by an autonomous belief operator, obedient to remarkable axioms derived from the axioms of individual belief operators. In semantics, the distributed beliefs are expressed by accessibility relations obtained simply from individual accessibility relations. In particular, if the individual beliefs are partitional, the common belief is also interpreted as a partition, i.e. the finest partition in the set of partitions that are coarser than those of individual actors. When moving from a set-theoretic framework to a probabilistic framework, common belief once again proves to be more or less demanding, ranging from common knowledge to common 1-belief through a number of intermediate positions (Stalnaker 1996).

5.2.2 Assumptions

In a (static or dynamic) game context, a player can have different types of beliefs, affected by different degrees of uncertainty, regardless of whether these are expressed in a set-theoretic or a probabilistic form. 'Structural beliefs' relate to the structure of the game, in other words the 'choice characteristics' (opportunities, beliefs, preferences) of the other players and their rationality. In this context, a player is assumed to know his own characteristics. 'Factual beliefs' relate to past plays of the game, that is, the past actions of other players. Once again, a player is assumed to know his own past actions. 'Strategic beliefs' relate to the future plays of the game, namely to the expected actions of the other players, known as 'conjectures'. A player knows his own intended actions in this context as well. Given that players are involved in strategic interactions (in the sense that the effects of a player's action depend on the actions of others), they are naturally engaged in a system of crossed beliefs about their respective future actions, actions which are themselves grounded in a system of crossed beliefs about their respective characteristics.

In a static game, a player's opportunities are defined by the set of actions (or pure strategies) he can mobilize, whereas his preferences are derived from a utility function that depends both on his own actions and on those of the other players. As far as a player's beliefs are concerned, they depend on the other player's characteristics, especially his beliefs. An available combination of the other's characteristics defines the other's type, chosen from a set of possible types. In addition, a player is endowed with Bayesian rationality (which means that his decision rule consists in maximizing expected utility), subject to his beliefs about the others' types. Actors make their choices under various forms of uncertainty without any external mediation, because all external influences are considered more or less integrated into their beliefs. The outcome of a game, defined by the players' joint actions (or rather by their joint intentions) effectively comes down to a 'belief equilibrium' state, in the sense that in this state no player is willing to modify his beliefs.

The semantic framework starts from a universal uncertainty space in which the possible worlds include both the player types and their intentions. Players know their own types in this context as well. Given that each player has mixed information about the possible worlds (whose prior probability may or may not be the same for all), it follows that uncertainty can be expressed in probabilistic form (and is even partially shared). Each player chooses a strategy defining the actions he would take in each of the possible worlds. Since a player is assumed to know his own intended actions in a particular world, it follows that the same action applies to two non-distinguished worlds. The player's (*ex post*) rationality is defined by the choice of the strategy that maximizes his expected utility based on his conjectures. Since a player's conjecture is a probability distribution over the others' actions, any mixed strategy can be interpreted as a probabilistic belief of the others about a player's action.

5.2.3   Results

The first result, as is to be expected, asserts that under the assumptions of common knowledge of the game structure and of the players' Bayesian rationality, all iteratively strongly dominated strategies are eliminated (Tan and Werlang 1988). An actor's strategy is said to be (strongly) dominated if there is another strategy, such that the last yields (strictly) more utility than the first one, for every possible combination of strategies of the opponents. A strategy is said to be iteratively dominated if it is eliminated in the following process: in the initial game, the dominated strategies for each player are eliminated; then, in the residual game, the strategies that have become dominated are eliminated, and so on. The iterative elimination of the dominated strategies can be eductively explained by the fact that each player will eliminate his dominated strategies, knows that the others will do likewise, and so on. The iterative elimination of dominated strategies generally produces a number of outcomes, so that a mutual choice cannot generally be made without the help of additional conditions.

A second result asserts that if common knowledge of the players' independence is postulated (over and above common knowledge of the game structure and the players' rationality), one obtains a 'rationalizable equilibrium' (Bernheim 1984, 1986; Pearce 1984). Rationalizable equilibrium is defined by considering that each player determines his best response to the expected strategy of the others, this being expected to be the best response to the adverse expected strategies, and so forth, until reasoning loops at some level. In fact, it is obtained through the iterated elimination of the players' inferior strategies, an inferior strategy being a strategy that is never a best response. Such equilibria are eductively explained by the fact that knowledge of the players' independence (which means that their intentions are not correlated) allows each player to break down the conjectures on all strategies into conjectures relating to each strategy. Any rationalizable strategy is iteratively undominated, though the reverse is not always true. Yet this is the case in two-player games, where the condition of independence between players is automatically satisfied.

A third result asserts that if, in addition to common knowledge of the game structure and of the players' rationality, one assumes that the players' beliefs about their respective strategies result from a common prior probability distribution, one obtains a 'correlated equilibrium' (Aumann 1987). A correlated equilibrium is characterized by a probability distribution defined on all the (pure) outcomes of the game; an external entity (the 'correlator') draws by chance some outcome of the game, in conformity with his probability distribution, and suggests the corresponding strategy to each player. At equilibrium, each player should follow the correlator's recommendation if the others do the same. From an eductive point of view, the players are now pre-coordinated by their prior common beliefs on the worlds, reflecting exogenous states of nature which condition the possible outcomes. Once again, a correlated equilibrium strategy is iteratively undominated, although the reverse is not the case; on the other hand, it is not directly comparable to a rationalizable strategy.

A fourth group of results revolves around Nash equilibrium, the most prominent equilibrium notion and one that obtains when each player strategy is a best response to the equilibrium strategies of the others. For games with two players, a first result (Tan and Werlang 1988; Brandenburger and Dekel 1989), soon weakened (Aumann and Brandenburger 1995), asserts that, under the assumptions of shared knowledge of the game structure, of the players' rationality and of the players' conjectures, these conjectures constitute a Nash equilibrium (in mixed strategies). For games with more players, a more demanding result (Aumann and Brandenburger 1995) states that, under the assumption of shared knowledge of the game structure and of the players' rationality, and under the assumptions that the players' beliefs result from a common prior probability distribution and that their conjectures are common knowledge, the conjectures of all players on a same player match and again define a Nash equilibrium.

Nash equilibrium appears as a weakening of both the rationalizable equilibrium (the beliefs about the other's actions are looping from the second level onwards) and of the correlated equilibrium (the probabilities assigned to the outcomes break up into probabilities on the strategies of each player). However, the results obtained are very restrictive since they assume that the players are aware of the others' conjectures, which are not immutable structural characteristics of these players, but fluctuating beliefs the origin of which is not described. In the case of more than two players, additional and even more drastic conditions are necessary to ensure that the conjectures of two players about a same third player are identical. The difficulty of eductive co-ordination between players comes from the fact that a Nash equilibrium is basically based on an interaction loop between these players. The latter appears, in fact, as a self-fulfilling equilibrium, i.e. the players' expectations on their (Nash) strategies bring about their realizations.

If the preceding results deal with the problem of the definition of a notion of equilibrium, the problem of the selection of an equilibrium state in case of multiplicity remains. In the case of rationalizable equilibrium, given that each player chooses a rationalizable strategy independently, one cannot conceive of any co-ordination on a particular outcome. In the case of correlated equilibrium, the fictitious correlator selects a particular outcome according to the relevant probability distribution. In Nash equilibrium, knowing (without specifying how this occurs) the other's conjecture again leads to selecting a certain outcome. However, in specific games – such as co-ordination games (where all equilibrium states are utility-equivalent) – the selection can take place thanks to 'conventions' that are common knowledge among the players.[1] These conventions act directly on 'focal states' of the game (Schelling 1960), the salience of which reflects cultural phenomena outside the model of the game, or they affect the choice criteria between states, such as symmetry or Pareto-optimality. Finally, if the game is repeated, it is its very history that is likely to bring out prominent characteristics (Crawford and Haller 1990).

5.3   EDUCTIVE JUSTIFICATIONS FOR DYNAMIC EQUILIBRIA

5.3.1   Logical Principles

When considering a dynamic framework, an additional problem arises, the genesis and evolution of the actor's beliefs. In fact, epistemic logic does not deal with the problem of belief formation directly, but confines itself to the problem of the change of prior beliefs (the origin of which is not clarified). Traditionally, one distinguishes between two main contexts of change, characterized by the type of message that transforms an initial belief into a final belief about some universe. When *revising*, the message can either reinforce or invalidate an initial belief about a stable universe. When *updating*, the message indicates the way in which the universe, considered as evolving, is changing. A third context is concerned with *focusing*: in this case the message relates to some object, drawn randomly within a universe made up of a population of objects. However, focusing can be reduced to a revising principle associated with a projection principle (transforming a belief about the population into a belief about an object).

In syntax, axiom systems for belief revision were developed originally for propositional beliefs (Alchourron et al. 1985; Katsuno and Mendelzon 1992). A family of axioms is common to the two main contexts. For instance, the *success* axiom asserts that the final belief must validate the message, a postulate that gives priority to the message (supposedly true) against the initial belief (possibly false). Similarly, the *inclusion* axiom states that the part of the initial belief that is compatible with the message is retained in the final belief. This postulate effectively embodies a weak 'conservation principle' (one keeps what can be kept). Other axioms are context dependent. When revising, the *preservation* axiom states that, if the message is compatible with the initial belief, the final belief is limited to the part that is common to both, a postulate that embodies a strong 'conservation principle' (what has to be changed is changed as little as possible). When updating, the *monotony* axiom states that, for a given message, if the initial belief is weakened, the final belief will also be weakened. Once again, this is a postulate that embodies a minimal change principle.

In semantics, the revision rules are inferred from the axiom system by representation theorems. When revising, everything happens as if there were a set of concentric coronas around the initial belief, reflecting worlds that move further and further away from this initial belief. The final belief is then simply the intersection between the message and the first corona intersecting the message. Reinterpreted in syntactical terms, this revision rule gives each proposition a degree of 'epistemic entrenchment', adds the message to the initial belief and removes from the system thus established the less entrenched propositions until reaching again logical coherence. When updating, everything takes place as though there were a group of concentric coronas surrounding each world, depicting worlds that are further and further away from this world. The final belief here is the result of a union, for all the worlds of the initial belief, of the intersections of the message with the first corona intersecting the message.

This process can be extended from a set-theoretic framework to a probabilistic framework, by conceiving of a (set-theoretic) message that allows the transformation of a prior probability distribution into a posterior probability distribution (Walliser and Zwirn 2002). In syntax, the above axioms can be weakly transcribed (in terms of support of the probability distributions) or strongly transcribed (in terms of numerical values attributed to the probabilities). In semantics, the revision rules for probability distributions are derived from transcribed axioms through representation theorems. When revising, with a weak transcription of the axioms, the satisfactory rule is the generalized *conditioning* rule. The rule most commonly used by game theorists, the Bayes conditioning rule, is singled out only due to a very strong transcription of the axioms; it receives an epistemic justification (in opposition to a decisional justification through bets carried out by a decision-maker) in a very restrictive context. When updating, with a weak transcription of the axioms, the satisfactory rule is the generalized *imaging* rule proposed by Lewis.

Belief revision can be considered as a fundamental form of reasoning insofar as various other forms of reasoning can be reduced to it (Walliser et al. 2002). This is the case for 'non-monotonic reasoning' of the type 'from facts A, one normally infers facts B', which weakens the usual deduction by considering exceptions, and which can be reinterpreted as belief change in a revising context. It is the same for 'abductive reasoning' of the type 'from facts A, one abduces hypothesis B', which is a form of inverse explanation and which can also be reinterpreted in two different ways in a revising context. This is particularly true for 'conditional reasoning' of the type 'if the antecedent A were the case, then the consequent B would be true', which is a reinforcement of material implication and which can be reinterpreted in an updating context. A conditional has a truth-value that is based on a physical transformation of the universe in order to render the antecedent true, even if this transformation remains virtual.

In syntax, the conditional reasoning distinguishes a pro-factual proposition when the antecedent is true from a counterfactual proposition when the antecedent is false. A conditional proposition A>B is distinguished from a material implication A→B insofar as the latter is (deceptively) true as soon as its antecedent is false. The conditional reasoning is subjected to an axiom system of which we can give some examples. The *reflexivity* axiom attests that a conditional whose consequence is identical to its antecedent is always valid. The *infra-classicality* axiom asserts that a conditional whose antecedent is true coincides with the intersection of the antecedent and the consequent. The *cautious monotony* axiom affirms that if two conditionals with the same antecedent are valid, so is the conditional built by taking, as antecedent, the conjunction of the common antecedent and one consequent and, as consequent, the other consequent. Additional axioms have a more 'topological' role (right *and*, left *or*).

In semantics, conditional reasoning is expressed by a 'selection function' which, in each world w, associates to each hypothetical event H a selected event K, eventually reduced to a unique world (Stalnaker 1968). Considering only the topological axioms, the selection function can again be derived from a set of concentric coronas bringing worlds which are further and further apart from the world under consideration (Lewis 1973). Linking syntax and semantics, a conditional is then valid if, in the worlds which are closest to the world under consideration and where the antecedent is true, the consequent is equally true. More substantial axioms correspond to properties assigned to the selection function (or equivalently to the set of coronas). The *satisfaction* property imposes that the event selected from a world and a hypothetical event be part of the last. The *preservation* property requires that, if a world is situated in the hypothetical event, it remains situated in the event selected from it and this hypothetical event.

A variant (Samet 1996) creates a more direct connection between classical reasoning and conditional reasoning. In syntax, one associates to the usual belief operator a hypothetical belief operator (parametrized by a hypothetical proposition); the latter reduces to the former when the hypothetical proposition is just the tautology. Both operators are subjected to a list of axioms that generalize the axioms of the first (logical omniscience, positive and negative introspection) and combine them. In semantics, with the support of the partition associated to usual belief, one defines once again a 'hypothesis transformation function', which associates a selected event with any world and any hypothetical event. The hypothesis transformation function then satisfies both preceding properties of satisfaction and preservation. It can be shown (Halpern 1999) that classical conditional reasoning is restored by understanding the hypothetical belief operator as 'if the antecedent is accepted, then the consequent is known' (a proposition is said to be accepted if it is not known to be false).

5.3.2 Assumptions

Conditionals were first integrated in decision theory in a configuration where the actions are likely to influence the states of nature. The two decision rules which were proposed have in common the preservation of the expected utility maximization principle, but differ regarding the probability affected to the states (Gibbard and Harper 1978). The 'evidential decision theory' retains the probability of the state conditional to the action, expressing a simple probabilistic correlation without causal dependence between action and state (due for instance to a common factor which influences both parties). The 'causal decision theory' retains the probability of the conditional 'if such action, then such state', expressing this time a direct causality between action and state. Both rules have been used in the analysis of the traditional 'Newcomb problem' in order to show that the first rule (usual expected utility maximizing action) leads the actor to take one box whereas the second rule (choice of the dominant action) leads him to take two boxes.

Conditionals were brought up early, otherwise actually used, to deal with extensive form games, expressed in the form of a game tree (which describes the possible sequential moves and the utilities resulting from any game play). Selten and Leopold (1982) emphasize that it is what takes place outside the equilibrium path which justifies the choice of the equilibrium path itself, and discuss the relevance of various theories of conditionals. Harsanyi and Selten (1988) observe that a strategy must be expressed by a conditional rather than a material implication. These reflections have been more recently followed up by attempting to describe various aspects of a game by using conditionals. This work is restricted to the category of generic games (games without ties between the outcomes for a same player or such that, when there is a tie for one player, there is a tie for the others too) with perfect information (each player knows at any moment where he is in the game tree). In addition, the game structure is considered as common knowledge.

First of all, conditional reasoning can be applied to the game structure itself, that is, to the game tree. It indicates that in an intermediate node, the player must retain one action (and only one), and in a terminal node, the player receives some utility. It indicates, conversely, that any node can only be reached if a specific move has been previously played. In fact, conditional reasoning does not differ here from material implication and only conveys the physical constraints and the utilitarian rules relative to the game. Furthermore, conditional reasoning is naturally applied to the definition of the strategy of a player, that is to the virtual action that this player would play in any intermediate node of the game tree (if he is arbitrarily landed there). It refers to a pro-factual conditional if the node is actually on the followed path, or to a counterfactual conditional if the node is outside this path. Limiting oneself to a material implication here is insufficient because it would allow any action outside the equilibrium path.

By combining the two preceding uses, conditional reasoning serves to express in a non-ambiguous way the player's rationality, always analysed from a strictly individual point of view. This rationality is caught both in each intermediary node of the game tree and in each possible world. Since the possible worlds again convey the players' types (essentially their beliefs), the strategies retained by the players are naturally conditional to these worlds. The rationality of a player is more precisely defined by considering the other players' strategies as fixed (by the player's conjecture in the given world) and by seeing if he should deviate from his own strategy, in relation to what is happening downstream from the node under consideration (consequential principle). However, it nevertheless receives numerous and more or less persuasive alternatives, in relation to the individual choice rule considered, to the type of node where it is actually evaluated and to the beliefs attributed to the player in this node.

First of all, expressed in set-theoretic terms, rationality can be content with stating that the player does not know that he can do better with another action, or else insists that the player has full knowledge that he cannot do better. In probabilistic terms, it can be expressed by the fact that the player knows, almost certainly, that he cannot improve his expected utility. This last assumption is intermediary between the two previous assumptions. Next, rationality is said to be 'substantial' (Aumann 1995) if it is defined in any node, conditionally to the fact of reaching this node, that is to say, through a conditional. It is termed 'material' if it is defined only in the nodes reached by the equilibrium path, that is to say, through a material implication. Material rationality is naturally weaker than substantive rationality. Finally, rationality is defined *ex ante* when evaluated with the beliefs available at the start of the game or *ex post* when evaluated with the beliefs available at the time of playing. The second is, in all evidence, stronger than the first.

In semantics, conditional reasoning is expressed by a selection function defined in each world, taking for a hypothetical event the attainment of a certain node. The general conditions previously required for this function now receive a more concrete interpretation in relation to the strategies followed by the players in this world (Halpern 2001). The satisfaction property indicates that the strategies adopted, in the nearest worlds from the considered one, lead to a path which goes through the node under discussion. The preservation property indicates that if the node under discussion is attained by the strategies related to the world being considered, the nearest worlds confine to this world. Moreover, an additional 'uniqueness property' requires that, on the subtree beginning at the node under discussion, the strategies relative to the world considered and to the nearest world coincide; it guarantees that the strategies dictate exactly what the players are going to do if the node under discussion is actually reached.

5.3.3 Results

For a game in extensive form and with perfect information, the basic equilibrium notion is the 'subgame perfect equilibrium'. This notion is stronger than Nash equilibrium, which remains, however, applicable since the game in extensive form can be translated in normal form thanks to the strategy concept. Subgame perfect equilibrium has the advantage of existing and of being unique for any generic finite game, because it is obtained by a constructive procedure, the 'backward induction procedure'. In a terminal node, the player who has to move chooses his best action; in a preceding node, the player who has to move chooses his best action, considering the next one as already given; the procedure continues from node to node until the initial node. If the (subgame) perfect equilibrium notion at first seemed somewhat paradoxical, the paradox progressively disappeared when it was justified or invalidated by a variety of analytical results, based on epistemic assumptions which differ only in a very subtle way.

Binmore (1987) considers the possibility of justifying the perfect equilibrium notion by postulating common belief of the players' rationality, and puts in evidence what he calls the 'backward induction paradox'. This paradox lies in the fact that the player's reasoning must work in both directions of the time arrow: in the reverse sense to define the strategies in relation to the beliefs (instrumental rationality), in the direct sense to revise the beliefs in relation to the information collected (cognitive rationality). It states that since the actor's rationality is based on his action in nodes outside the equilibrium path, it is necessary to consider concretely the possibility of a deviation from that path and to examine the actor's revised belief at deviating nodes. However, the player's beliefs in a node outside the equilibrium path are no longer compatible with common knowledge of rationality, which precisely served to define the equilibrium, at least if the other structural assumptions are assumed to be kept (Reny 1992).

A first result (Aumann 1995) shows however that, if the players have common knowledge of their respective rationality, the intended strategies determine a subgame perfect equilibrium. It relies on the assumption that player's rationality is set-theoretical, weak, substantial and *ex ante*; no belief revision and no conditional is considered. The result is *a fortiori* valid with a stronger form of rationality, especially Bayesian rationality or *ex post* rationality. However, rationality is assumed to be common knowledge in a strong sense (it is never questioned in virtue of the veridicity axiom) and this assumption cannot be weakened. The result indicates, in fact, that under the assumption of common knowledge of rationality in any node, no player would deviate from his perfect equilibrium path under pain of breaking it. This is reminiscent of the virtual works theorem in mechanics, which indicates the very path a material system will take in a set of virtual paths, even if these last are never achieved.

This result set off a debate between Aumann (1996) and Binmore (1996), the former considering that one can maintain the assumption of common knowledge of rationality against all odds, the latter insisting that one cannot free oneself from considering and interpreting what goes on outside the equilibrium path. If he finds himself in an out-of-equilibrium node, a player must indeed choose, among all assumptions justifying the equilibrium, which one must be questioned (Walliser 1996). This assumption can come about from the degree of epistemic entrenchment that the player attributes to each, a degree which may depend on the game under consideration (in chess, even if the perfect equilibrium strategies are unknown, observed deviations will be attributed to the shortcomings of the opponent's cognitive rationality rather than to a lack of knowledge of the game structure). The degrees of epistemic entrenchment and, more generally, the belief revision rules then become part of the characteristics of the players and can themselves become the object of common knowledge. According to the assumption questioned in the revision, it turns out that it is precisely the perfect equilibrium or other equilibrium notions which prove to be eductively justified.

The first assumption which may be considered is the 'resolution' of the players, an assumption which states that the retained actions of a player are indeed those which he further implements. It is easy to see that perfect equilibrium will remain if this assumption is questioned in the form of a 'trembling hand', i.e. every player is affected by successive random and independent trembles when he carries out his intentions of action (Selten 1975). Indeed, any deviation of another player will then be interpreted by a player as purely accidental and revealing nothing regarding the future behaviour of this player. A second assumption concerns common knowledge of the game structure. Kreps et al. (1982) showed (in a framework differing slightly from epistemic logics) that other solutions than the perfect equilibrium can be obtained when a player is uncertain about the type of the other players. Any deviation of another player is then interpreted by a player by the fact that he is playing a different game from the true game or even that he believes that a third party is playing a different game.

The most sensitive assumption is, however, that of common knowledge of the players' rationality, because it allows no surprise. On one hand, if considering no more than common 1-belief that what the agents believe is true, the perfect equilibrium remains because a surprise is no longer conceivable (Stalnaker 1996). On the other hand, if weakening in common 1-belief robust to truth, the perfect equilibrium is generally no longer guaranteed (Stalnaker 1996). If there is simply common 1-belief, the perfect equilibrium is *a fortiori* not guaranteed because a surprise is explicitly considered. For example, Ben Porath (1992) shows that if there is a common 1-belief of players' rationality at the start of the game, the relevant equilibrium is obtained by a first-stage elimination of weakly dominated strategies, followed by sequential elimination of strongly dominated strategies. Stalnaker (1998) obtains a similar equilibrium notion when assuming common knowledge that the players are rational and apply a 'rationalisation principle'. Moreover, in a game of length m, perfect equilibrium remains justified with m-common knowledge of players' rationality (Bicchieri 1988), but it is no longer guaranteed by common 1-belief.

One may finally turn to the rationality assumption itself, in spite of its strong degree of epistemic entrenchment. The basic result justifying the perfect equilibrium does not continue to hold if substantive rationality is replaced by material rationality, except for some particular classes of games (Aumann 1998). More precisely, if rationality is evaluated not in each world under consideration, but in the nearest world in the sense of a selection function, the result is invalidated (Stalnaker 1998). The selection function, supposedly identical for all the players and satisfying the three conditions mentioned beforehand, contributes to belief revision when a node outside equilibrium is reached. Even if, in the considered world and in the nearest world, the downstream strategies coincide, the beliefs are going to differ (Halpern 2001). A similar result (Samet 1996) shows that, if introducing a conditional reasoning with the help of a hypothetical belief operator, the perfect equilibrium is no longer guaranteed. It is restored only under very strong additional conditions (sequential hypothetical beliefs).

Related to the players' rationality assumption is the assumption of independence between the players' choices, considered by Stalnaker under two aspects. The assumption of 'causal independence', inherent to the idea of a non-cooperative game, just considers that the players play independently. The assumption of 'epistemic independence' is more demanding and states that what a player learns about another, particularly what this player thinks about a third player, does not affect what he himself thinks of a third player. Causal independence does not entail epistemic independence, since the former does not prevent the beliefs from being eventually correlated. Seen from this angle, Aumann (1995) justifies perfect equilibrium by the assumption of causal independence associated with a strengthened assumption of epistemic independence, that is, the independence between successive moves of a same player (insensitive to the received messages). Stalnaker (1998) shows however that, if the players' beliefs satisfy an assumption of epistemic independence between players, but differ at each node, the adequate equilibrium concept well remains that of perfect equilibrium.

In fact, the condition of epistemic independence plays the same role as a fourth property (added to those of satisfaction, preservation and uniqueness) attributed to the selection function (Halpern 2001). This last states that if a first world is accessible from a world chosen by the selection function, there exists a second world which is accessible from the considered world such that the strategies in both worlds are identical on the subtree starting with the node under discussion. This very demanding property can be understood by the fact that, in an intermediate node, the player keeps the same beliefs about the others in the world under consideration and in the nearest worlds. As a result, the strategies that a player considers in the worlds chosen by the selection function are a subset of those considered in the world under consideration. If, as it has been stated, the three first properties of the selection function are not sufficient to guarantee the perfect equilibrium, the fourth permits assuring it again.

5.4 EVOLUTIONIST JUSTIFICATIONS OF EQUILIBRIA

5.4.1 General Principles

Evolutionist game theory considers a base game sequentially played over a generally infinite set of periods. It is grounded on five major modelization principles. Only the *satisfaction principle* is in common with classical game theory and makes explicit the (unchanging) characteristics of the players. It details the structure of the base game, i.e. the set of actions for each player and the utility for each player resulting from the combination of their joint actions. Whether the base game is static or dynamic, these characteristics will be represented in the form of a game matrix or of a game tree. It also states the manner in which the players aggregate the utilities obtained during successive instances of the game (generally by discounting the successive utilities). The other four principles concern the usually random dynamic process according to which the base game is repeated, and describe the physical interactions between the players as well as the psychical reasoning which moves them.

The *confrontation principle* clarifies the nature of the interactions between the players, notably the way in which they meet. The base game can be played by specific players as well as populations of players. When the game is asymmetric, one introduces as many populations as basic game players (multi-population game). When the game is symmetric, one can do the same (multi-population game) or consider that the players form only one and the same population (mono-population game). Each player can potentially meet up with any other individual (global interactions) or only those located in his 'interaction neighbourhood' (local interactions). As a result, the individuals are often located on different figures (line, circle, plane, torus) and situated on a network drawn on this figure, thus defining geometrically the interaction neighbours. In each period, a player may meet all the players situated in his neighbourhood or meet only a sample of them (eventually reduced to one player).

The *information principle* describes the information that each player gathers as much about the game structure as about its past plays. The structural information is often very reduced, the player knowing his possibilities for action, but not necessarily his preferences and, *a fortiori*, the others' characteristics. The factual information is richer and is presented in two aspects. On the one hand, he may observe the past actions played by the other players (he knows his own past actions). On the other hand, he may observe the utilities which he obtains from his implemented actions (and more exceptionally the utilities obtained by the others). All information is collected in his 'information neighbourhood', a set of players generally included in his interaction neighbourhood. There again, he observes the global information available or receives it only from a random sample of players. Finally, as will be seen later, he obtains information either as a spontaneous sub-product of the game play (passive experimentation) or willingly by displacing his 'normal' action (active experimentation).

The *evaluation principle* concerns the interpretation and processing of the information in order to obtain condensed information in view of the action. On the one hand, the player can concentrate his attention on the statistical distribution of his opponents' past actions in order to take out some invariants. Moreover, he is going to use these retrospective indicators to form (usually probabilistic) expectations about the others' future actions. On the other hand, the player can calculate indexes relating to past performances of his own strategies (or all strategies). Moreover, he is going to suppose that these indicators remain valid in the future and may compare them with normative aspiration levels, evolving also (increasing or decreasing according to whether they were, or were not, reached in the past). More exceptionally, he will try to reveal, from utilities he himself experienced, his own preferences, and even (from observation of the others' actions) some others' structural characteristics, especially their preferences.

The *decision principle* clarifies the choice rules adopted by each player, based on the previously combined information. Taking into consideration the strategic dimension of the information he is likely to acquire, two types of behaviour are usually distinguished. The *exploitation* behaviour consists in using the already existing information to his best interests. The *exploration* behaviour consists in moving from the preceding action, more or less randomly, to test the opponent and acquire new information used in the future. The player faces, in fact, a trade-off between 'exploration' and 'exploitation', i.e. weighs up between a loss of utility in the short term compensated by a gain of utility in the long term (informational investment). This arbitration (usually not optimal) is often implicitly or explicitly included in the choice rule, which combines the two behaviours. In particular, exploration should appear as more important at the beginning of the process and exploitation as more important at the end.

5.4.2 Taxonomy

Three families of evolutionist models, which correspond to rather contrasted illustrations of the previously mentioned principles, are usually considered

(Walliser 1998). They attribute to the player less and less information, weaker and weaker cognitive rationality (adequacy between available information and adopted beliefs) as well as instrumental rationality (adequacy between available means and pursued objectives). *Epistemic learning* is based on a belief revision process of the player about the others' strategies. *Behavioural learning* is based on the strengthening by a player of his own most outstanding strategies. *Evolutionary process* is based on a Lamarckian mechanism of natural selection among players gathered into populations. These three types of models can be combined in hybrid models, which associate various principles. In addition, since the second and third families present a formal isomorphism, it is possible to restrain to the first two families, which are the most realistic.

Epistemic learning assumes that the actors know their utility function and are even able to observe their respective actions. Relying on these observations, they revise their beliefs about the others' future strategies. Relying on their utility function, they choose their best response to these beliefs, hence applying an exploitation behaviour. This best response can, however, be disturbed by random actions, in accordance with an exploration behaviour. The simplest model which fits this scheme is the FP (*fictitious play*) model. Each player first calculates, after observation, the frequency of each action used by the other; he then transforms this past frequency into a future probability of implementation of the other's action and finally chooses his best response regarding the expected utility for each of his actions. The model of *stochastic fictitious play* is a variant, which supposes that the player no longer maximizes, but plays an action with a probability increasing with its expected utility.

Behavioural learning assumes that the actors observe only the results (in terms of utility) of their own past actions. They calculate an aggregated performance index of each action, eventually compared with an aspiration level. They adopt a probabilistic choice, the probability of playing an action increasing with its index. This choice simultaneously presents an exploration component (by the fact that any action always has a non-negligible probability of being used) and an exploitation component (by the fact that the most performing actions are the most frequently played). They may also imitate the behaviour of the best performing players if they can observe their results. The simplest model fitting this scheme is the CPR (*cumulative proportional reinforcement*) model. Each player observes first the utility resulting from the action he put in operation; he next calculates the cumulated utility obtained by this action since the start of the game; finally, he takes a probabilistic decision by choosing each action with a probability proportional to its index.

The evolutionary process assumes that the actors no longer observe anything (except the others' actions if their strategies depend on them) and no longer have beliefs. They have a fixed strategy, but form populations of individuals who are in the same position as far as the game structure is concerned. They undergo a 'selection process' which favours the reproduction of those who obtain the best utility (utility is assimilated to biologists' *fitness*); selection expresses the exploitation behaviour. They eventually experience a 'mutation process' randomly modifying their strategy or adding new strategies; mutation expresses an exploration behaviour. The simplest model fitting this scheme is the '*replicator* model'. In a multi-population or mono-population framework, individuals of opposite populations meet randomly; they reproduce proportionally to the utility they obtain from their interactions. A variant (the *stochastic replicator*) considers, moreover, mutant individuals randomly introduced into the population at each period.

5.4.3 Results

Looking at asymptotic states of the preceding processes, the last can as easily converge towards stationary states (punctual attractors) as not converge (cyclical or chaotic attractors). The problem of selection of an equilibrium state, crucial from an eductive point of view, is no longer relevant in an evolutionist one because the system's path is always directed (at least in probability) toward a specific outcome. The obtained results are valid only for particular categories of dynamic processes and specific classes of games. They are also relative to the type of stability imposed on the asymptotic path as well as on the time scale considered (long term in the absence of stochastic disturbances, very long term with such disturbances). These results prove not to be very robust against slight modifications of the model specifications and are particularly sensitive to the various stochastic elements introduced by the different principles (modes of interaction, sampling of information, formation of expectations, rules of decision).

The convergence results, first of all, concern the dynamic processes relying on static base games. In fact, the only really general result concerns the elimination of the strongly dominated strategies as well as of the iteratively strongly dominated strategies. This result has been proved for rather extended evolutionary processes, including the standard replicator (Weibull 1995), as well as for various learning processes. However, it is not maintained for the (iteratively) weakly dominated strategies. Samuelson and Zhang (1992) indeed showed that in the case of an evolutionary process, more precisely with the replicator dynamics in the presence of noise, the weakly dominated strategies can be preserved. This result applies as well to dynamic base games, since they can be translated into static games thanks to the notion of strategy. They ensure that the subgame perfect equilibrium state, which is never strongly dominated, but often weakly dominated, is not systematically eliminated.

If one looks at Nash equilibria for static games, they appear as resting points for most of the dynamic processes (if a player is initially in such a state, he stays here). More ambitiously, the strict Nash equilibria in pure strategies can be obtained as limit states in some processes because any deviation leads to a strict utility loss. Thus, with the CPR rule (Laslier et al. 2001), the learning path converges with a positive probability towards any strict Nash equilibrium in pure strategies, if some exist. In the same way, with the standard replicator dynamics in a multi-population framework, a state is asymptotically stable if, and only if, it is a strict Nash equilibrium. However, the Nash equilibria in mixed strategies are much more difficult to obtain. Always with the CPR model, the convergence of the game path with positive probability towards such an equilibrium state is achieved only for particular classes of games, for example those with only one equilibrium. For the *stochastic fictitious play* model, such a convergence with global stability is, however, ensured (Hofbauer and Sandholm 2001) for various classes of games (zero sum, potential, supermodular).

Refinements of the Nash equilibrium can sometimes be obtained, always for static base games. Thus, Young (1993) considers a stochastic fictitious play model where each player is provided with a bounded memory, observes only a sampling of the others' actions and chooses his action either as the best response to his observations (with some probability) or in a random fashion (with complementary probability). He shows that, for co-ordination 2×2 games, the stochastically stable equilibrium corresponds to a selection of the Nash equilibria in pure strategies, that is, the 'risk-dominant' equilibrium. This selection is due to random disturbances, which lead the system path to the most extended attraction basins. A related result is obtained by Kandori et al. (1993), who study a special stochastic fictitious play process (each player defines his best response to the distribution of the others' actions in the previous period, with the possibility of a random deviation of the action).

More recent results concern static games in which the players are situated on a network and have only local interactions. More precisely, they are dispersed on a circle and interact or gather information only from their immediate neighbours. Ellison (1993) takes up the model of Kandori et al. (1993) without disturbances and shows that the game path can only finish at a limit cycle or converge towards a Nash equilibrium. By adding a (spatial) stochastic sampling procedure for the information in Young's style, Durieu and Solal (2000) show that it is possible to eliminate the limit cycles and keep only the Nash equilibria; the risk-dominant equilibrium may even be obtained when the players are able to proceed to some experimentation. In more general cases, especially for a grid pattern, one can obtain asymptotically diverse spatial structures, for instance a segmentation of the field with such and such an equilibrium in some zones and such and such in other zones.

Some results have finally been obtained for dynamic base games (generic and with perfect information), that is a convergence toward the (unique) subgame perfect equilibrium. In relying on a particular epistemic learning process allowing random mutations, Nöldeke and Samuelson (1993) showed that any 'locally stable' issue is clearly a perfect equilibrium, although a perfect equilibrium can be situated in a locally stable component with other equilibria. As for a behavioural learning process, it applies differently to that of static base games: it operates on the actions stemming for each node of the game tree and no more on the global strategy; the utility obtained for a taken path being assigned to each of its composing actions (Pak 2001). For instance, with the CPR model, the convergence of the process toward the perfect equilibrium is guaranteed by the fact that each action is played an infinite number of times (Laslier and Walliser 2005). Similar results are obtained with evolutionary processes.

5.5   CONCLUSION

The results obtained in an eductive and an evolutionist perspective present, with regard to the dispersion of the considered contexts, both strong similarities and strong differences. The (iteratively) strongly dominated strategies are unanimously eliminated. More specifically, in an evolutionist framework, the pure strict Nash equilibria are often justified, and even mixed Nash equilibria for epistemic learning as well. Conversely, in an eductive framework, the Nash equilibria can be obtained, whether they be pure or mixed, only under very drastic conditions. Weaker equilibrium notions are however justified in an eductive framework, like the rationalizable equilibrium or the correlated equilibrium, which have no clear counterpart (for the moment) in an evolutionist framework. Finally, the subgame perfect equilibrium is obtained in both perspectives, possibly with other equilibria, in a less robust manner in an eductive framework, and in a more robust manner in an evolutionist framework.

The results obtained prove to be very sensitive to the details of modelization and require a very sharp formalization to specify the conditions of validity of each equilibrium notion. Those carried out in an eductive perspective brought particularly into evidence the existence of implicit rationality assumptions, which play a fundamental role in the conclusions. Moreover, past work led to the development of traditional analytical tools and enlisted new tools, and this quest is still being pursued today. The eductive perspective can be enriched with new logical tools such as temporal logics, whereas the evolutionist perspective relies on original theorems concerning stochastic processes applied to networks. Finally, the efforts already undertaken throw light on some more concrete problems, if these can be expressed in terms of game equilibrium. It is so for the problem of the genesis of institutions, whether they result from the actors' conscious design or from a partially unconscious learning process.

NOTE

1. See Chapter 9 by André Orléan in this volume.

REFERENCES

Alchourron, C.E., Gärdenfors, P. and Makinson, D. (1985), 'On the logic of theory change: partial meet contraction and revision functions', *Journal of Symbolic Logic*, **50**, 510–30.
Aumann, R.J. (1987), 'Correlated equilibrium as an expression of Bayesian rationality', *Econometrica*, **55**, 1–18.
Aumann, R.J. (1995), 'Backward induction and common knowledge of rationality', *Games and Economic Behavior*, **8**, 6–19.
Aumann, R.J. (1996), 'Reply to Binmore', *Games and Economic Behavior*, **17**, 138–46.
Aumann, R.J. (1998), 'A note on the centipede game', *Games and Economic Behavior*, **23**, 97–105.
Aumann, R.J. and Brandenburger, A. (1995), 'Epistemic conditions for Nash equilibrium', *Econometrica*, **63**, 1161–80.
Basu, K. (1990), 'On the non-existence of a rationality definition for extensive games', *International Journal of Game Theory*, **19**, 33–44.
Ben Porath, E. (1992), 'Rationality, Nash equilibrium and backward induction in perfect information games', working paper, University of Tel Aviv.
Bernheim, D. (1984), 'Rationalizable strategic behavior', *Econometrica*, **52**, 1007–28.
Bernheim, D. (1986), 'Axiomatic characterization of rational choice in strategic environments', *Scandinavian Journal of Economics*, **88**, 473–88.
Bicchieri, C. (1988), 'Strategic behavior and counterfactuals', *Synthese*, **76**, 135–69.
Bicchieri, C. (1989), 'Self-refuting theories of strategic interaction: a paradox of common knowledge', *Erkenntnis*, **30**, 69–85.
Binmore, K. (1987), 'Modeling rational players', *Economics and Philosophy*, **3**, 9–55; **4**, 179–214.

Binmore, K. (1996), 'A note on backward induction', *Games and Economic Behavior*, **17**, 135–37.

Binmore, K. (1997), 'Rationality and backward induction', *Journal of Economic Methodology*, **4**, 23–41.

Binmore, K. and Brandenburger, A. (1990), 'Common knowledge and game theory', in *Essays in the Foundations of Game Theory*, Blackwell, pp. 105–50.

Binmore, K. and Samuelson, L. (1996), 'Rationalizing backward induction', in K.J. Arrow et al., *The Rational Foundations of Economic Behaviour*, Macmillan.

Bonnano, G. (1991), 'The logic of rational play in games of perfect information', *Economics and Philosophy*, **7**, 37–65.

Brandenburger, A. (1992), 'Knowledge and equilibrium in games', *Journal of Economic Perspectives*, **6**, 83–101.

Brandenburger, A. and Dekel, E. (1987), 'Rationalizability and correlated equilibria', *Econometrica*, **55**, 1391–402.

Brandenburger, A. and Dekel, E. (1989), 'The role of common knowledge assumptions in game theory', in F. Hahn (ed.), *The Economics of Missing Markets, Information and Games*, Oxford University Press.

Crawford, J. and Haller, M. (1990), 'Learning how to co-operate: optimal play in repeated co-ordination games', *Econometrica*, **58** (3), 571–96.

Damme, E. van (1987), *Stability and Perfection of Nash Equilibria*, Springer Verlag.

Dekel, E. and Gul, F. (1997), 'Rationality and common knowledge in game theory', in D. Kreps and M. Wallis (eds), *Advances in Economics and Econometrics*, vol. 1, Cambridge University Press, pp. 87–172.

Durieu, J. and Solal, P. (2000), 'Adaptive play with spatial sampling', *Games and Economic Behavior*, **43** (2), 189–95.

Ellison, G. (1993), 'Learning, local interaction and co-ordination', *Econometrica*, **61**, 1047–71.

Fudenberg, D. and Levine, D. (1998), *The Theory of Learning in Games*, MIT Press.

Gibbard, A. and Harper, W. (1978), 'Counterfactuals and two kinds of expected utility', in C.A. Hooker, J. Leach, and E.F. MacClennen (eds), *Foundations and Applications of Decision Theory*, Reidel.

Halpern, J.Y. (1999), 'Hypothetical knowledge and counterfactual reasoning', *International Journal of Game Theory*, **28**, 315–30.

Halpern, J.Y. (2001), 'Substantive rationality and backward induction', *Games and Economic Behavior*, **37**, 425–35.

Harsanyi, J.C. and Selten, R. (1988), *A General Theory of Equilibrium Selection in Games*, MIT Press.

Hofbauer, J. and Sandholm, W.H. (2001), 'Evolution and learning in games with randomly disturbed payoffs', mimeo.

Kandori, M., Mailath, G. and Rob, R. (1993), 'Learning, mutation and long run equilibria in games', *Econometrica*, **61**, 29–56.

Katzuno, A. and Mendelzon, A. (1992), 'Propositional knowledge base revision and nonmonotonicity', in P. Gärdenfors (ed.), *Belief Revision*, Cambridge University Press.

Kreps, D., Milgrom, P., Roberts, J. and Wilson, R. (1982), 'Rational co-operation in the finitely repeated prisoner's dilemma', *Journal of Economic Theory*, **27**, 245–52.

Laslier, J.F. and Walliser, B. (2005), 'A reinforcement learning process in extensive form games', *International Journal of Game Theory*, **33**, 219–27.

Laslier, J.F., Topol, R. and Walliser, B. (2001), 'A behavioral learning process in games', *Games and Economic Behavior*, **37**, 340–66.

Lewis, D. (1969), *Conventions: A Philosophical Study*, Harvard University Press.

Lewis, D. (1973), *Counterfactuals*, Harvard University Press.

Monderer, D. and Samet, D. (1989), 'Approximating common knowledge with common beliefs', *Games and Economic Behavior*, 170–90.

Nöldeke, G. and Samuelson, L. (1993), 'An evolutionary analysis of backward and forward induction', *Games and Economic Behavior*, **5**, 425–54.

Pak, M. (2001), 'Reinforcement learning in perfect information games', mimeo.

Pearce, D. (1984), 'Rationalizable strategic behavior and the problem of perfection', *Econometrica*, **52**, 1008–50.

Pettit, P. and Sugden, R. (1989), 'The backward induction paradox', *Journal of Philosophy*, **86**, 169–82.

Rabinowicz, W. (1998), 'Grappling with the centipede: defence of backward induction for bi-terminating games', *Economics and Philosophy*, **14**, 98–126.

Reny, P. (1992), 'Rationality in extensive form games', *Journal of Economic Perspectives*, **6**, 103–18.

Samet, D. (1996), 'Hypothetical knowledge in games with perfect information', *Games and Economic Behavior*, **17**, 230–51.

Samuelson, L. (1997), *Evolutionary Games and Equilibrium Selection*, MIT Press.

Samuelson, L. and Zhang, J. (1992), 'Evolutionary stability in asymmetric games', *Journal of Economic Theory*, **4**, 364–91.

Schelling, T. (1960), *The Strategy of Conflict*, Harvard University Press.

Selten, R. (1975), 'Re-examination of the perfectness concept for equilibrium points in extensive games', *International Journal of Game Theory*, **4**, 25–55.

Selten, R. and Leopold, U. (1982), 'Subjunctive conditionals in decision theory and game theory', in W. Stegmuller, W. Balzer, and W. Spohn (eds), *Studies in Economics, Philosophy of Economics*, Springer Verlag.

Stalnaker, R.C. (1968), 'A theory of conditionals', in N. Rescher (ed.), *Studies in Logical Theory*, Blackwell.

Stalnaker, R.C. (1996), 'Knowledge, belief and counterfactual reasoning in games', *Economics and Philosophy*, **12**, 133–63.

Stalnaker, R.C. (1998), 'Belief revision in games: forward and backward induction', *Mathematical Social Sciences*, **36**, 31–56.

Tan, T. and Werlang, S. (1988), 'The Bayesian foundations of solution concepts in games', *Journal of Economic Theory*, **45**, 370–91.

Walliser, B. (1996), 'Comment to Binmore and Samuelson', in K.J. Arrow et al., *The Rational Foundations of Economic Behaviour*, Macmillan.

Walliser, B. (1998), 'A spectrum of equilibration processes in game theory', *Journal of Evolutionary Economics*, **8**, 67–87.

Walliser, B. (2000), *L'économie cognitive*, Odile Jacob

Walliser, B. and Zwirn, D. (2002), 'Can Bayes rule be justified by cognitive rationality principles?', *Theory and Decision*, 95–135.

Walliser, B., Zwirn, D. and Zwirn, H. (2002), 'Abductive logics in a belief revision framework', *Journal of Logic, Language and Information*, **14**, 87–117.

Weibull, J. (1995), *Evolutionary Game Theory*, MIT Press.

Young, H.P. (1993), 'The evolution of conventions', *Econometrica*, **61**, 57–84.

Young, H.P. (1998), *Individual Strategy and Social Structure, An Evolutionary Theory of Institutions*, Princeton University Press.

6. Game theory and players' beliefs on the play

Christian Schmidt

6.1 INTRODUCTION

For over a decade, several game theorists, assisted by logicians and computer scientists, have been working to uncover the epistemic foundations of interactive situations between many agents. Their objective is to produce a general framework for investigating players' knowledge assumptions. However, due to information conditions, players' knowledge is not necessarily true. Therefore the term 'knowledge' has been replaced by 'belief'. The result has been the construction of belief systems, derived from modal logics, which are associated with the available data of the game.[1]

The simplest way to capture the main features of a belief system is to start with individual situations of decision-making *à la* Savage. The beliefs of the individual decision-makers are pictured by a set of finite states of the world, defined as a system of subjective partitions. In such a situation, the decision-maker's beliefs are independent of his chosen action. This is no longer the case in a game situation, where the states depend on the other players' actions and on the player's own actions. The consequence is an intricate system of degrees (beliefs, beliefs of beliefs, etc.) to formulate the system of players' beliefs as a hierarchical order encoded in a consistent format.

Supplementing a game by a system of players' beliefs changes the traditional perspective of game theory or, at least, its way of modelling a game situation. Roughly speaking, in the classical approach developed by game theory, a game situation raises a problem to be solved by the game theorists thanks to a solution concept. Such a well-known approach is summarized as 'problem-solution' by Aumann. In the belief perspective, the question to be investigated is different. The game theorists have to find which players' knowledge is required for reaching the solution. The status of the model is also different, because players' choices are now an inclusive part of the states of the world.

The quest for a logical structure of beliefs, consistent with a game situation, is obviously fruitful, but limited. The main limitation has been implicitly pointed out by Aumann himself in a joint paper with Brandenburger, as follows:

> As indicated above, belief systems are primarily a convenient framework to enable us – the analysts – to discuss the things we want to discuss: actions, pay-offs, beliefs, rationality, equilibrium and so on ... As for the players themselves, it is not clear that they need concern themselves with the structure of the model. But if they, too, want to talk about things we want to talk about, that's OK, it's just a convenient framework for them as it is for us. In this connexion we note that the belief system itself may always be considered common knowledge among the players. (Aumann and Brandenburger 1995, p. 1174)

One can wonder under which conditions the players of a game could use the logical system of beliefs developed by Aumann and others to reach the solution. They must first refer to the same categories as the analysts, so 'actions', 'pay-offs', 'rationality' and 'equilibrium' are supposed to be meaningful, identical from one player to another and provide all the necessary and sufficient information to all the players. Secondly, knowing the model of knowledge implies knowing all its logical implications. Therefore, the players are supposed to be logically omniscient. Thirdly, as mentioned by Aumann and Brandenburger, the model of knowledge becomes relevant for the players involved in a game situation if it is itself a common knowledge between them.

On one hand, the analysis of a game in the logical perspective of a belief system enlarges the understanding of a game situation by taking into account the players' knowledge. On the other hand, the assumptions about players' knowledge, which are necessary for using the belief system, reinforce the cognitive constraints of the players in an unrealistic direction. The cognitive approach of individual decision-making has shown that decision-makers frame the perception of their situation through heuristic models, which reveal cognitive bias by contrast to pure logical models.[2] As for the game situation, it looks sound to suppose that players also organize their information on the game ('actions', 'pay-offs' etc.) according to a framing procedure which does not necessarily coincide with the logical belief system.

This chapter puts forward this alternative approach to the players' beliefs. Instead of searching for the best way to formalize players' theoretical knowledge, which is logically required for solving the game situation, we would start with what players actually believe about the rules and the structures of the game in which they are playing. At variance with classical game theory, we conjecture that a same game situation can give rise to different descriptions for different players. In other words, the game is no longer considered as a given for the players, but rather as the result of a cognitive construction from various available information. Such an alternative approach to players' beliefs suggests a revision of the solution concepts as the issue of an adjustment process leading to a belief co-ordination.

6.2   WHAT DO PLAYERS REALLY KNOW ABOUT THE GAME THEY ARE PLAYING?

For game theorists, a 'game' designates every situation of interactions between several agents, when the final outcome is the common result of their individual choices. Starting from such a general and unspecified definition, game theorists use different models to describe the various situations which refer to a typology accepted by the scientific community (cooperative games, non-cooperative games, differential games, evolutionary games etc.). The information on the game, which is incorporated by those models, varies from one type of model to another as the chosen form to describe the game (normal form, extensive form, characteristic form). Nevertheless, beyond the specificities of each type of model, all the information necessary for modelling any game situation can be grouped into three main accepted categories: the structures of the game (players, actions, outcomes, evaluations), the rules of the game (moves, sequences order, time-schedule) and the issue of the game (solutions). The first two sets of information have an empirical content, whereas the third is just derived from a conceptual construction. The complete description of a game situation in the language of game theory requires the three kinds of information. If these categories are self-evident for the game theorists, one can wonder whether they are also meaningful for the players.

One can first question how players discriminate between a cooperative and a non-cooperative situation. Apart from institutional specific rules, the players do not really know in concrete situations whether the agreements are binding or not. On one hand, the rules and the structures of a game seem so closely linked from the players' perspective that their distinction appears meaningless for them. Indeed, a move makes sense for a player when it is related to definite pay-offs. On the other hand, players' knowledge on the knowledge of other players is problematic. Other players' knowledge on the game cannot be confused with the content of information concerning other players which can be provided by the game theory model. Indeed, this knowledge crucially depends on the other players' representation of the game. Thus, the knowledge of other players' knowledge raises a difficult question when the description of the game is not assured to be derived from a common 'framing'. Finally, for the player, the solution of a game situation cannot be directly derived from the rules and the structures of the game, thanks to a conceptual construction. Players reach a solution in playing the game. Additional information, which does not belong to the rules and the structures of the game, is therefore necessary, as to the moves really chosen by the other players during the play and the players' conjecture about the 'common belief' of a solution. Once again, rational assumptions, whatever their level, are not sufficient and, perhaps, not even relevant for solving such difficulties.

This quick check shows that to question what the players really believe about the game they are playing requires investigating how the game is framed by the individual players. In order to clarify the point, let us come back to an old distinction between a 'game' and its 'plays'.

6.2.1   The Game and its Plays

Parlour games offer a powerful metaphor to give an intuitive idea of the gap between the objective description of a game and the representation of its play by the players. In a parlour game, the rules are supposed to provide the players with all the necessary and sufficient information on the game to play it. In the case of a chess game, for instance, the rules incorporate the complete description of the chess board, the moves allowed and forbidden in all possible situations, the time limitation and the precise definition of 'winning', 'losing' and 'tying'. Thus, knowing the rules of chess is tantamount to knowing the chess game. Chess players are supposed to have a complete knowledge of the chess rules and to know that the other players also know the chess rules. The assumption that the chess rules are common knowledge among chess players is quite obvious and does not raise any problem. It is easy to verify that if this assumption is relaxed, players can no longer play chess. Indeed the rules of the game can be encoded differently by different players so that the possible cognitive biases at this level are not determinant for the understanding of the game.

The course of a determined chess play cannot be induced only from the information provided to the players by the structures of the chess play. Even if we suppose that the chess players know all the logical inferences of the chess rules, i.e. that they are logically omniscient about the game, such knowledge does not uncover the chess play. The discrepancy between the information derived from games like the chess game and the understanding of their play has been underlined by von Neumann and Morgenstern from the very beginning of game theory:

One must distinguish between the abstract concept of a *game* and the individual *plays* of that game. The *game* is simply the totality of the rules which describe it. Every particular instance at which the game is played in a particular way – from the beginning to the end – is a *play*. (von Neumann and Morgenstern 1944, p. 49)

As a consequence of this distinction, von Neumann and Morgenstern proposed to call 'moves' all the trajectories which are consistent with the rules of the game and 'choices' actual consequences of players' decisions during the play. To sum up, the game consists for von Neumann and Morgenstern of sequences of moves and the play of a sequence of choices.

Let us draw on the distinction between a game and its play from the view-point of agents' knowledge. The set of information of a game belongs to only one category, its abstract rules. Other kinds of information are necessary to describe a play, all along its process. These kinds of information refer to individual players. Some of them are factual, such as the past moves of other players, while others are speculative, like the expected moves of other players. Therefore, a formal description of a play must capture – in addition to the abstract implications of possible moves – the material implications of real moves which can be known by the players. The following example illustrates the logical gap between the description of a game and the description of its corresponding play which can lead to contradictions.

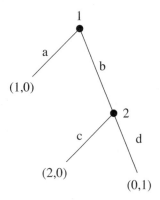

Figure 6.1

This is a non-cooperative game, where players' moves are sequential. Each player has to choose individually one move from alternative possible moves. According to the rules of the game, player 1 must choose between a and b, player 2 between c and d. Such information, however, does not capture an essential feature to model the play. Indeed, if player 1 chooses to play a, the alternative between c and d really disappears for player 2. Therefore, player 2 has nothing to choose. In other words, the outcome of the game does not depend on player 2's choice. Translated into formal logic, a $\rightarrow \neg$ b (material implication), then a $\rightarrow \neg$ c V d. Therefore, c $\wedge$ d becomes possible and the formula a $\wedge \neg$ b $\wedge$ c is perfectly consistent in the language of the play, but in contradiction with the rules of the game as previously recalled.[3]

The description of the play does not only depend on players' positions during the play, but also, more fundamentally, on their own representation of the play. In extending the meaning of a game to the logical riddles, several well-known paradoxes, such as Newcomb's problem, provide good examples. Newcomb's game can be described as follows:

There are two boxes. One box is transparent and contains €100. The other box is opaque. In the opaque box a highly reliable predictor has already placed €1 million if he predicted that you will choose to take the opaque box alone, and, otherwise, nothing. You have two options: (a) to take the contents of the opaque box, (b) to take the contents of the two boxes.

Such rules are quite consistent with two different plays, according to the personal belief of the players, derived from the game information. On one hand, due to the time order, the choice between a and b cannot have any consequences on the playing decision of the predictor. On the other hand, as the predictor is supposed to be almost infallible, choosing between a and b is tantamount to ratifying the previous decision of the predictor.[4] There are plenty of arguments in favour of the first evidence and some arguments in favour of the second, which have been discussed at length by the logicians.[5] It proves that both plays can be considered as logically possible. However, the player who chooses a does not have the same mental representation of the play as the player who chooses b. One can wonder now how the first category of player could convince the second category of player that the play he has in mind is the actual play (and vice versa). Such a kind of difficulty is rather similar to Wittgenstein's paradox of private language.[6]

Newcomb's problem is traditionally discussed as a matter of rationality. However, behind the justifications, it questions the plurality of framing a decision-making situation and opens the way to the study of its consequences when the different framing of the play belongs to the same game.

6.2.2 From Parlour Games to Social Games

When we leave parlour games and riddles for social situations, the distinction previously proposed between the game and its plays becomes less clear. Intuitively, there is a temptation to couple this distinction with the different forms that are used by game theorists to model the situation. For instance, the normal form of a non-cooperative game could describe the game and its extensive forms, the corresponding plays. Indeed, the same normal form of a game is most often consistent with several extensive forms which capture additional details of the plays (sequences, players' set of information, indirect strategies, etc.).

Let us consider the following normal form:

	c	d
a	3,2	1,1
b	2,3	2,3

Figure 6.2

This pay-off matrix is obviously compatible with several different extensive formulations, such as the following extensive forms – which correspond to different assumptions on the sequence moves.

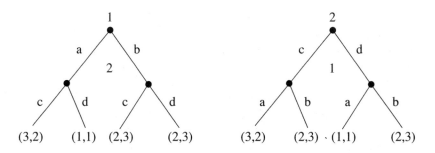

Figure 6.3   *Figure 6.4*

Figure 6.5 brings together these two possible games. Due to the difference in sequence moves, Figures 6.3, 6.4 and 6.5 picture different games – if these differences are understood as the consequences of different rules to be followed by the players. On the other hand, the extensive forms (Figure 6.3, Figure 6.4 and Figure 6.5) refer to the same normal form (Figure 6.2), which is also supposed to describe the game. Therefore, one can argue that Figure

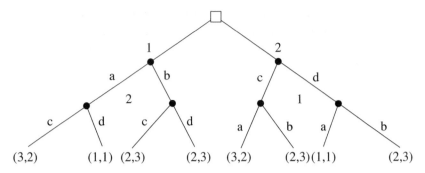

Figure 6.5

6.3, Figure 6.4 and Figure 6.5 are no more than different representations of the same game expressed by the normal form corresponding to Figure 6.2. As the sequences of the moves are related to the sequences of the players' choices, the different extensive forms associated with this game look like different ways to play it.

In spite of this consideration, such an analogy with the distinction between a game and its plays, previously discussed, is largely fallacious. Indeed, the normal form and the extensive form of a non-cooperative game can be considered as different ways to select and frame the information on a game. However, all of them concern the analysts and not the players. A previous example (Figure 6.1) has underlined the difference between the representation of a game in its extensive form and the players' representation of its play. Whereas the extensive form describes what the analysts know about the possible trajectories of the game's moves, the model of the play pictures what the players know (or believe) about its play during its actual process.

This comparison with the different standard descriptions of a game in the traditional 'problem-solution' approach is not uninteresting, because it clarifies the basic differences between the parlour games and the social games situations. In a parlour game, the observers (as well as the players) have a complete knowledge of the rules, and, then, of the game, but both categories do not know in advance the play. In the social game, the analysts know the rules of the game they are modelling, but the players have to discover the rules of the game they are playing. In addition, game theory provides analytical tools for modelling the plays, but the use of these tools by the players is bounded by very stringent cognitive conditions.

The cornerstone of this difference is to be found in the meaning of the solution concept in the two kinds of games. In parlour games, the solution concept is embedded in the description of the rules of the game, even if the logical existence of a definite solution is not insured by the rules.[7] This is not the case for social games, where the solution does not belong to the set of rules and where, most often, several solutions are consistent with the same structures, according to different concepts. These concepts are therefore closely dependant on the different descriptions of the games. Thus, the solution which is to be proposed by the analysts is connected to their chosen description of the game.

Therefore, some authors have considered the different solution concepts proposed for solving non-cooperative games as the consequences of something like a 'framing effect', due to the specific features of those descriptions. Such a perspective justifies the quest for invariance to be found at the level of the structures of the game captured by its normal form (Kohlberg and Mertens 1986). However, this does not concern the players, who do not frame the game as the analysts do and ignore, at least at the beginning of the play, its solution concept.

6.2.3 Solution Concepts and Players' Rationality

In order to reduce the gap between the representation of a game situation and its knowledge, game theorists have elaborated a new approach to the solution concept. A solution concept is now defined as a set of conditions (or restrictions) on the description of the game situation, such that rational players who would follow (or accept) these conditions would reach the solution. If so, the solution of the game becomes a direct implication of players' rationality. The problem raised by the players' knowledge of the game seems to be solved as a pure question of epistemic logic. However, it lets down several crucial assumptions about players' actual competence.

Let us focus on the simplest case: a two-person non-cooperative situation described by the normal form of a game with a unique Nash equilibrium solution, leaving out, for the moment, the additional difficulties generated by the plurality of a Nash equilibrium solution. The corresponding restrictions of its domain can be formulated in various ways. The most elaborated and convincing manner is to use the resources of epistemic logic. Nash's conditions are thus expressed in the formal language of a semantic model (Aumann and Brandenberger 1995; Stalnaker 1997). A more intuitive formulation is to consider the restrictions as a set of rules to be followed by the players for playing the game described by its normal form. One can use here, with a slight modification, Greenberg's verbal description of what he calls a 'Nash situation', which is characterized by some rules of deviation from a position in the studied game situation (Greenberg 1990). The following rules are self-sufficient for our purpose:

R1: Each individual player is allowed to deviate from any position whatever.

R2: The deviating player can choose any move at his disposal.

R3: The deviating move does not affect the moves chosen by the other player.

The game is described by its normal form: R1, R2 and R3 can be considered as the rules of a specific way to play this game and, thus, as an abstract description of the play. The distinction between the game and its play does not coincide here with the distinction previously discussed in the case of parlour games, due to the differences between parlour games and social games.

Anyway, for two players who know the information provided by the normal form of the game (pay-off matrix), and who know R1, R2 and R3, the Nash equilibrium is just the result of their rational choices. At first glance, the rational assumptions on players' behaviour seem to overlap all other considerations. The following example shows, however, that the role of players' rationality is over-weighted to the detriment of other assumptions concerning players' cognition, such as the knowledge of R1, R2 and R3.

	a	b	c
A	1,3	4,2	2,2
B	2,2	3,3	2,1
C	1,2	2,2	2,2

Figure 6.6

Rational players who know the pay-offs of the game (Figure 6.6) and the Nashian rules of its play (R1, R2, R3) will obviously choose C and c, which correspond to the unique Nash equilibrium in pure strategies, and, thus, to the expected solution.

Let us suppose now that the two players know the pay-off matrix, but ignore the Nashian rules. As C is dominated by A and B, and c by a and b, the dominance principle traditionally associated with rationality will stop them choosing C and c. However, this evidence does not preclude the open question of the relation between the rational behaviour of the players and the Nashian rules, which reappears at another level. Will the players find the Nashian rules and adopt them on the only ground of this pay-off knowledge and purely rational considerations?

The answer to this question is not convincing. First, it reverses the line of reasoning initially followed by the analysts. As previously mentioned, the Nash rules are supposed to formulate restrictions in order to bring together players' rational decisions and the solution of the game. Now, the rationality is claimed to justify those restrictions. So rationality seems to be used in a self-referential process of reasoning. Secondly, the rationality of the rules does not have the same meaning as the rationality of the individual acts. Such a distinction has been elaborated a long time ago by moral philosophers with regard to two kinds of utilitarianism, namely 'act utilitarianism' and 'rule utilitarianism'.[8]

There are different ways to approach this 'rule rationality'. One approach follows the theory of evolutionary games. What is called a solution in the evolutionary perspective means a trend toward a stable state through a more or less long process of trial and error. At first sight (C,c) is a *weak* stable state, in the sense that neither of the two players has an incentive to deviate from it. Unfortunately, this stability is purely static (or strategic). It is easy to demonstrate that choosing C and c does not lead, in a dynamic perspective, to an asymptotically stable set. Therefore, an evolutionary interpretation of the Nashian rules R1, R2 and R3 does not justify their rationality at a systemic level.

An alternative approach is to consider the Nashian rules to be the consequences of a preliminary choice of a set of rules, as a social contract between the players. Such a perspective has been successfully explored in a game theoretical mode by Binmore (1994, 1998). However, it requires additional assumptions concerning what Binmore calls the 'empathic preferences', which reinforce the cognitive constraints on the players. Must the empathic capacity of the players be considered as a component of a 'social rationality' in interactive situations? This assertion is to be discussed further below.

To sum up, the quest for purely rational reasons for discovering and accepting the Nashian rules by the players remains questionable (Schmidt 2001b). However, on the other hand, the belief of their common knowledge is quite necessary to accept them rationally. Indeed, the smallest uncertainty about the acceptance of those rules at any level of its knowledge by the players is sufficient to rule out the rationality of choosing C and c by reference to the dominance principle.

6.2.4   The Structures and the Rules

R1, R2 and R3 are closely related to the description of the structures of the game in its normal form. Thanks to the new definition of a solution concept, such a connection is almost tautological for game theorists. This explains the vagueness of game theory's terminology where the 'structures' and the 'rules' are so often associated that they seem interchangeable or at least interdependent. This floating terminology is derived from the implicit assumption that the structures of a game are captured by a unique description which remains the same whatever the level of its considered knowledge. As, for instance, the normal form of a game is not supposed to change when the analyst takes into account the first level of player 1's knowledge (player 1 believes ...), the second level (player 1 believes that player 2 believes ...) and so on. The set of rules which is defined in the normal form of the game can ambiguously be named 'structures'. Once again, what is self-evident for the analysts is much more questionable for the players. The universe of the players is not the game, but its plays. Different descriptions of a play during its process are consistent with what each player can know about the structure of the game. Furthermore, one cannot be sure in these conditions that what the different players know about the structures of the game is framed by a common reference model, the normal form of the game. The implicit assumption that the rules of the game are common knowledge for the players seems, for that reason, highly problematic.

Let us examine this point thoroughly. The matrix of pay-offs of the normal form, which organizes the available information about a two-person non-cooperative game, is to be understood as a code, or a small repertoire. The terms 'outcomes', 'pay-offs', 'moves', etc. belong to this repertoire. Thanks to this repertoire, such words are meaningful and their meaning unique. To know the structures of a game is tantamount to knowing this repertoire. The *raison d'être* of a repertoire is to support a common knowledge. Therefore, the structures of the game encoded in a normal form are without any discussion considered as common knowledge by the game theorists. However, such an obvious assumption implies, when it is applied to the players, that they use this repertoire to frame the information they select on the game in which they are playing. The following cases will show the limits of this condition.

Case 1

Let us come back to the game situation depicted by the graph of Figure 6.1. Player 2's strategic moves do not belong to the repertoire of the normal form of the game. As described in a normal form, the strategic moves of the players are rather the results of alternative choices (pure strategies) or are the consequence of chosen probability distribution on their set (mixed strategies). So, cVd → c, cVd → d, but CVd → cΛd is not a proposition consistent with the repertoire. This is the reason why player 2 cannot derive the framing of his play from his knowledge of the normal form of the game. For player 1, the question is much more intricate. Indeed, aVb → a, aVb → b according to the repertoire. Furthermore, he knows by material implication that a → ¬cVd and b → cVd, which are consistent in the repertoire. The traditional interpretation which is proposed to explain such a situation is to say that the structures of the game situation are not correctly captured by its normal form presentation. This is quite right. However, this inadequacy also concerns the extensive form and has a direct effect on the players' beliefs on the play. Player 2, who does not use exactly the same information as player 1 during the play, does not necessarily frame this information in the same way as player 1.

Case 2

Jane and Peter have to share the contents of a basket of fruit. Two kinds of fruit are available: a nice apple and a ghastly pear. At the beginning of the play, Jane declares to Peter: 'Please choose the fruit you prefer.' Peter obviously takes the nice apple, which leaves Jane disappointed. She regrets her initial proposal. While Peter thinks 'I do not understand Jane's disappointment. She has obtained what she expected to get', Jane, on her side, has in mind that if Peter was a gentleman, as she expected, he would certainly have taken the pear and left the nice apple for her. Contrary to Case 1, the game situation here is correctly described by its normal form. The strategic moves of both players belong without discussion to the repertoire of the normal form which is commonly know by them. The problem arises because the same proposition derived from this repertoire is integrated in different ways by each of them. Jane and Peter, who share a complete knowledge of the structures of the game and of the Nashian rules to be applied, have however different codes in mind when they implement those rules during the play. The codes are given from outside the game, but they can disturb its play. Such a dissonance is traditionally imputed to some rational failure. Peter's behaviour is certainly rational, but Jane's complaint seems more difficult to rationalize. According to Jane's reference code, however, her reaction is also quite rational. Does this mean that Jane's code is not rational? In this case, Peter may be able to convince her on the grounds of analytic argument to abandon her reference code. In the light of Wittgenstein's well-known paradox of private language, this is an almost hopeless task. The point is elsewhere. A common belief of the game does not necessarily entail a common belief of its play by the players.

Case 3

Paul and Jack have an appointment in a station, without any additional precision on the determined place. There are two meeting points in this station, the ticket office and the cafeteria. Each is distant from the other and located in an opposite direction. Paul and Jack have to choose one or the other direction. However, those characteristics of the station are well described in the normal form of the game, which is common knowledge between the players. At variance with Case 2, the repertoire of the game is self-sufficient and provides to both players a common interpretation of the play. In spite of all this, applying the Nashian rules does not lead the players to the solution, and thus does not help them to make their appointment.

There are many versions of this kind of story. Such a situation which is well-known since Schelling's seminal work (Schelling 1960) has been extensively discussed in game theory literature under the general label of 'pure co-ordination games'. Contrary to almost all examples previously described, players' knowledge exactly coincides here with the analysts' knowledge on the game. Therefore, the problem raised by this game situation is generally considered as a challenge for the theory in itself. Is it simply an extensive situation of selection among identical Nash equilibriums, or does it concern, more fundamentally, the failure of the restrictive conditions for implementing any equilibrium, whatever the solution concept?

We will propose a different interpretation of this situation. As in parlour games, players preferably know the structures and the rules of the game. However, this knowledge is not sufficient for the players to play the game. They must find 'outside' additional information. The quest for this information and its selection can be shared during the play in a game form which is more or less different from the initial game; for example, the rules of this new game are not predetermined, but must be discovered by the players thanks to the information they select during the play.

Case 1 shows that the transparence of the structures of the game is not self-evident for the players. Case 2 and Case 3 point out that the knowledge of the structures and the rules of the game cannot be self-sufficient to the players, who refer to additional information for understanding its play. Such information may interfere with the rules of the game (Case 2) or may supplement its solution (Case 3). Either way, the three cases prove that the assumption on players' knowledge about the game they are playing is neither trivial nor innocuous. All the examples concern non-cooperative games and Nash equilibrium solutions. However, these conclusions are also valid *a fortiori* for cooperative games with different solution concepts, where acceptance of the rules or justification of their acceptance is even more difficult for the players (Schmidt 2003).

6.3 HOW TO FRAME THE PLAYERS' FRAMING

The first section of this chapter stresses that the framework used by game theorists to describe a game situation does not necessarily coincide with players' framing of its corresponding play. Several examples have shown that this gap between the analysts and the players cannot be reduced to a quantum of information and to a divergence in the evaluation of this information. Its origin is rather to be found at the level of the basic system in which the information is decoded in both cases. The next step will be to pursue this analysis by identifying the limitations of the game theoretical framework, in order to suggest some alternative approaches to frame the players' framing.

We defend the idea that this failure is partially due to a common framework between Savage's approach to individual decision-making analysis and game theory modelling of decision-making in many players' interaction situations. Thanks to the tools of epistemic logics, Aumann and some researchers around him have contributed to re-establishing the semantic filiation between Savage's original treatment of individual decisions under uncertainty and the game theoretical treatment of many players' interactions. A critical survey of this common background illuminates the difficulties of using game theoretical categories to capture players' framing of the play. Moreover, it provides a starting point from which to classify the different directions to be explored for this purpose.

A first direction, which we propose to call 'conservative', tries to extend the Savagian framework for pushing further its limitations. The 'psychological games' (Geanakoplos et al. 1989) and their variants, such as the 'fairness reciprocal games', belong to this category (Rabin 1993). We will show why they cannot completely succeed in framing the players' framing.

Another direction, which we propose to call 'radical', rejects the Savagian framework and lays out new paths for alternative frameworks. The 'variable universe games' (Bacharach 1993) and some suggestions derived from Greenberg's *Theory of Social Situations* (Greenberg 1990) belong to the second category. We will suggest the reasons why this direction seems promising and is to be supplemented by experimental evidence.

6.3.1 Back to Savage's Framework

Savage's framework for analysing decision-making under uncertainty can be viewed, in retrospect, as a support for a belief system in the sense of the epistemic logic. Let us recall the well-known triplet <A, S, C> which is used by Savage as a general canvas. A designates the set of available acts, S, the set of possible states of the world, and C, the set of consequences generated by the acts in the different states of the world. These categories are related to an individual decision-maker noted i. So, the three dimensions of Savage's framework must be written A_i, S_i, C_i.

We focus for the moment on S_i, in order to elaborate a little more the belief system to which this framework refers. According to Savage, S_i expresses i's knowledge about the 'world', that is to say, all the information which concerns i's own interests for the purpose he has in mind to reach his chosen act (Savage 1954). In symbolic terms, s_1, s_2 .... $s_n \in S_i$, where s_1, s_2 .... s_n are finite partitions. Savage assumes that one of the possible states is the 'real' state of the world and that the decision-maker knows S_i. Therefore, S_i is not vacuous and the K_i (S_i) where K_i is i's knowledge operator. The first assumption is self-evident, the implication of the second assumption is more subtle. In verbal terms it means that i knows his knowledge on the world. Mixing together these two assumptions, i is necessarily supposed to know something about the 'world'. However, what precisely does this knowledge mean?

An oversimplified situation illustrates the question. A person is interested in the meteorological conditions for the purpose of an excursion. He selects a small 'world' of only two states: 'It's raining' (S_1); 'It is sunny' (S_2), knowing that neither S_1 nor S_2 provides any factual information about tomorrow's weather. Additional information is necessary about the event's occurrence. From a different perspective, however, a complete ignorance of meteorological partitions precludes any statement concerning tomorrow's weather. The knowledge of those partitions is to be used by the candidate for an excursion as a checklist, which allows him to make forecasts on meteorological events for tomorrow.

A clear-cut distinction emerges from Savage's framework between the referential knowledge (basic knowledge) and the 'beliefs' in the field of decision-making. Basic knowledge concerns the definition of the partitions of the states, while the occurrence of the states is the object of beliefs. In the previous meteorological example, the decision-maker knows $S_i = S_1 \, VS_2$, but he only believes that one of the two S's will be the true state tomorrow.

This schema can be extended in various ways; so the decision-maker can know that he knows (the states partitions) and so on, up to infinity. Such an extension by levels of a knowledge does not bring any additional information to the basic knowledge of the initial partition. He can also have beliefs on his beliefs, and so on. However, now the different levels of beliefs may be significant. Let us suppose, for instance, that his first level of belief comes from the expertise of another person; he may legitimately have his own beliefs on the expert's beliefs, on even a belief on these beliefs.

With relatively slight modifications, the Savagian categories can be revised to frame game situations. The normal form of a non-cooperative game refers to the triplet $<N, A, C>$ where N designates $1, 2 \dots n$ players; A, the set of their available acts and C, the set of consequences of their common action (Schmidt 2001a). The state of the world in the Savagian acceptance must be replaced here by the consequences, which can be interpreted as the 'states of the game'. Indeed, the states of the game are entirely endogenous *vis-à-vis* the players' actions. Thus the 'states' are not independent of the acts, as they are in the Savagian framework of individual decision. However, the meaning of the term 'consequence' in Savage's construction is not so clear and leaves the way open to various interpretations. Savage himself has proposed in the *Foundation of Statistics* to call 'personal states' the outcomes of the interactions between 'acts' and 'consequences' (Savage, 1954).[9] Jeffrey, from his perspective, defines these personal states as 'conditional consequences of the acts' (Jeffrey 1983).

Nevertheless, the transposition of Savage's categories to game situations is almost evident, as is shown by the following figures, which describe respectively a 2×2 individual decision situation *à la* Savage (Figure 6.7) and the normal form of a 2×2 game (Figure 6.8).

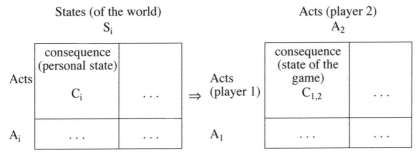

Figure 6.7   Figure 6.8

The reliability of Savage's categories to describe game situations in a game theoretical format suggests that a belief system that is derived from Savage's framework can also be extended, under additional assumptions, to many players interacting in a game situation. Unfortunately, such assumptions are not innocuous and still reinforce the gap between the analysts and the players about the representation of the game.

A comparison between Figure 6.7 and Figure 6.8 from the view-point of the decision-makers reveals several differences between an isolated individual and the players, both being framed *à la* Savage. The isolated individual (Figure 6.7) is supposed, by construction, to know A_i, S_i and C_i. The content of the information provided by those three categories is indeed purely subjective. Moreover, S_i is derived from i's partitions which describe his personal representation of the 'world'. If, for example, i is a well-informed meteorologist, the partitions will be much more numerous and finer than if i is a poor amateur. However, both of them are supposed to uses partitions for describing their own 'world' in the Savagian sense and such kinds of description do not raise any logical problem, whatever the decision-maker. It does not follow, however, that real decision-makers actually refer to those Savagian categories for framing their decisions. On the contrary, a very large sample of experiments tend to contradict this view and to question the relevance of Savage's categories for understanding the real process of decision-making.[10] However, this is another matter.

Let us turn now to Figure 6.8 from the view-point of player 1. He is supposed to know his acts, A1, as well as the isolated decision-maker in Figure 6.7. However, he must also know A2, i.e. the player 2's acts. Such an additional knowledge is absolutely necessary to identify the states of the game in the sense previously defined. Taking into account the distinction between the knowledge and the beliefs derived from the Savage schema, player 1 is also supposed to have beliefs on the act which will be chosen by player 2.

The normal form presentation of a 2×2 game reduces the states of the game to the intersection of players' acts, and more technically of players' pure strategies. However, the more general categories to define the states of the game are the players' partitions. So the players take into account their own partitions and what they may or may not know about all other players' partitions to describe the states of the game – and thus the game itself. In order to measure the immense distance between one player's partitions and another player's partitions in some extreme game situations, let us come back to the co-ordination game of the meeting point briefly surveyed above (p. 120). Player 1 is a blind man and player 2 a deaf person. However, each of them ignores the disability of the other. They obviously picture the two potential meeting points differently, according to acoustic signals for player 1 and visual signals for player 2. Indeed, acoustic and visual information give rise to partitions in both cases. However, the acoustic signals and the visual signals do not organize, in the same way, their respective information in the human brain. Therefore, player 1's and player 2's partitions not only differ quantitatively, as in the meteorological example, but, more seriously, refer to different categories which are hardly comparable. One must wonder in those conditions what player 1 can really know on player 2's partitions. After all, how can one be sure that the blind man and the deaf person are playing in the same game?

6.3.2 The States of the World, the States of the Game and the Mental States of the Players

In a single decision-making situation, the concept of individual partitions works out whatever its individual reference system. The decision-maker can be blind or deaf, this does not change anything in the definition of his 'world' in terms of states-partitioning. This is not the case in a many players situation, where the formal definition of players' partitions does not necessarily entail a common definition of the 'game' in terms of states partitions. Furthermore, the risk that the players fail to attempt a common description of the game in which they are playing increases with the number of players.

Aumann was perfectly aware of such a semantic obstacle, which he has often discussed since 1976 (Aumann 1976, 1987, 1992 and 1999). Thanks to the metaphor of a 'dictionary' by which players' partitions would only be different methods of classification in the *dictionary*, he finally recast the question in the following form:

> Can such a 'dictionary' be constructed? Isn't there some kind of self-reference implicit in the very idea of such a dictionary? If it can nevertheless be constructed, is the construction in some sense unique, 'canonical'? If not, which of the possible 'dictionaries' would the participants use? (Aumann 1999, p. 273)

And he rapidly concludes:

> The most convincing way to remove all these questions and doubts is to construct Ω and ... the K_i (players' partitions) in an explicit, canonical manner, so that it is clear from the construction itself that the knowledge operators are 'common knowledge' in the appropriate sense. (Aumann 1999, ibid.)

Starting from this intuitive idea of a referential dictionary from which players' partitions of the states of the world are necessarily derived, Aumann actually succeeds in constructing a canonical semantic system $<N, S, K_i, D>$, where N denotes a population of individuals (the players); S, the states (of the game); K_i, the knowledge operator associated with each individual i of the population, which allows the definition of players' partitions (players' knowledge of the states); and D, the dictionary from which the partitions are understandable for the players. Roughly speaking, with D and K_i, individuals can translate this information on the world in terms of propositions defined in a logical dictionary.

Let us observe first that such a construction is primarily relevant for a single individual. In this case, K and D are so closely connected in a 'private language' that knowing K_i implies, for i by construction, knowing D. Aumann's categories, however, are much more stringent for many individuals and his canonical system requires supplementary assumptions. When n=2, the model is still simplified, due to the semantic equivalence between 'It is common knowledge' and '1 and 2 know that it is common knowledge'. However, a two-person situation is a very specific case. Where n=3 or more individuals, Aumann's formulation becomes much more complex and necessitates additional distinctions. So, for instance, in a game with three players, 1, 2, 3, the statement that player 3 knows that some event x is common knowledge between player 1 and player 2 is obviously different from the statement that x is common knowledge between 1 and 2. Furthermore, and more subtly, this statement does not mean the same thing as that player 3 knows that x is not common knowledge between player 1 and player 2. Such an observation confirms that Aumann's canonical model for interactive situations is an extension of Savage's informal knowledge framework to individual decision-making situations.

A detailed discussion of Aumann's canonical model goes largely beyond our purpose here. However, the main lines of his argument are to be kept in mind for our investigation. The states partitions used by the players to describe what they know about the game imply that there is a kind of dictionary which gives them a code for understanding these partitions, such as the definition of the world in a dictionary, or the list of the letters in an alphabet. This evidence is valid for all the players, whoever. Therefore, if such a general dictionary exists, all the players know of it, and this knowledge can be considered as being common knowledge. Aumann's canonical construction proves that there exists at least one model (in the logical acceptance of the term) in which such a 'dictionary' is logically consistent.

This is all well and good, but players' partitions are considered as given, as well as their own preferences, their own expected utility and their own strategies. So Aumann's canonical model does not inform us how the players construct their partitions from the information they select and organize about the situation-game in which they are playing. In other words, Savage's belief system leads to describing the states of the game and does not concern the 'mental states' of the players about the play. The progress of Aumann's long intellectual road illuminates the enigmatic quotation recalled in the introduction of this chapter (p. 108), where Aumann specifies that belief systems are primarily a convenient framework for the analysts, and where he confesses that he does not really understand how they may also concern the players themselves. Nevertheless, such an incursion into Aumann's canonical model appears to be informative in our perspective for two reasons.

Thanks to a belief system, Aumann's players can take into account several levels of expectation in their personal framing but not necessarily up to infinity. Jane, for instance, in the game of Case 2 (pp. 119–20), expects (a) that Peter will be a gentleman (level 1), (b) that Peter himself will expect that she will expect that he is a gentleman (level 2). Indeed, Jane cannot be sure that (a) and (b) will really happen; thus (a) and (b) belong to Jane's beliefs about her interaction with Peter. So, framing the game situation means here for Jane to include these two levels of hierarchy in her understanding of the play with Peter.

Another feature of Aumann's construction helps us to approach a different dimension of players' framings, the reference to a dictionary as a foundation for the knowledge of a game situation. As we have seen, Aumann's dictionary is a purely logical device which does not mean anything for the real players. However, the quest for a common 'repertoire' may guide the players in their way to select information for framing the situation. So the main task for Paul and Jack in the co-ordination game (Case 3, p. 120) is to find, or at least to imagine, a 'repertoire' such that they can derive from it a common understanding for playing the game. Aumann's model assumes that such a preliminary difficulty has been solved on the grounds of a so-called knowledge of the structures of the game. This is precisely the limit of his epistemic approach for analysing the cognitive bases of players' framing.

6.3.3 'Editing' and 'Evaluation'

When Khaneman and Tversky introduced the notion of 'framing' in their new approach of individual decision-making under risk, they referred to a fruitful distinction between two different phases in the decision-making process, the 'editing phase' and the 'phase of evaluation'. This distinction illuminates the research programme they promoted around the core of the 'prospect theory' (Khaneman and Tversky 1979; Tversky and Khaneman 1992). During the editing phase the individuals select and organize the information in order to encode it in meaningful prospects. Then, they evaluate those prospects according to significant weighing procedures. The analytical distinction between the phase of editing and the phase of evaluation is still relevant for understanding players' framing in a game situation. Due to the specificity of the interactions, the concepts which have been elaborated by Khaneman and Tversky for modelling the prospect theory of individual decision-making (reference points, gains and losses asymetries) cannot be directly applied to game situations, where the expected outcomes of the players are generated by speculative mental processes of reciprocal beliefs.

Whereas the editing phase normally precedes the phase of evaluation, we will reverse this sequence with regard to the specific framework of game theory. Starting from the game theoretical description of a game situation, the first step for integrating players' framing is obviously to extend the definition of their pay-offs to other determinants than their expected utility in a narrow sense. Thanks to the model of hierarchical beliefs, players' different levels of reciprocal expectations can be taken into account in the evaluation of their outcomes. Investigating players' editing process requires going beyond the theoretical framework of a game situation. As we have previously pointed out, the problem in this second step is to identify the cognitive procedures which can be followed by the players to elaborate a more or less consistent system of common beliefs about the play they are playing.

Let us start with the evaluation. In the classical description of a game situation, players' pay-offs are supposed to measure their expected utility, at the termination of the play (normal form), or at each sequence of the game (extensive form). From this point of view, but only from this point of view, game theory models can be considered as extending the expected utility theory to many decisions-makers (cf. the Savagian framework above). The main idea is to enlarge the number of variables which enter into the utility function of each of the players and from which their pay-offs are derived. So, players' pay-offs depend not only on the material outcomes of the game, but also on their beliefs about other players, and on their beliefs about other players' beliefs on themselves, before and during the play. Different technical approaches have been followed, corresponding to different purposes. Gilboa and Schmeidler's 'information-dependant games' (Gilboa and Schmeidler, 1988) are a first step in that direction. The most interesting formulations for our quest of an editing procedure can be found in Geanakoplos, Pearce and Stachetti's 'psychological games' (Geanakoplos et al. 1989) and Rabin's 'fairness games' (Rabin 1993), because their models integrate explicitly in players' pay-offs several psychological patterns *vis-à-vis* their expectations. Both of them obviously lead to a revision of the solution concept derived from a Nash equilibrium.

Rabin has reinterpreted (in terms of this new kind of evaluation) several emblematic game stories – such as the battle of the sexes and the prisoner dilemma. Let us briefly look at the stag hunt game, as an illustration of this perspective.

	s	d
S	3,3; $X_1 X_2$	0,2; $X_1 X_2$
D	3,3; $X_1 X_2$	2,2; $X_1 X_2$

Figure 6.9

The numerical values of the pay-offs represent the physical outcomes, and X_1 X_2 denote player 1's and player 2's psychological evaluation derived from their beliefs. Only two levels of beliefs are taking into account.

Player 1 expects that player 2 would like to cooperate with him in the stag hunt (level 1), and that player 2 expects the same expectation for himself (level 2). Indeed, player 1 would be seriously disappointed if such optimistic expectations were contradicted by the behaviour of player 2 (who would prefer to trap a deer alone). If player 2 follows the same line of reasoning about player 1, the two players will reasonably leave the stag hunt. So the psychological expectations reinforce the attractiveness of the sub-optimal solution (D, d).

'Psychological games' open the path to several applications. Their most interesting contribution is probably to provide a convincing model of the deterrence mental processes. When a player announces, or simply suggests by a signal to another player, 'If you do ... so and so ..., then I shall do that ...' he speculates on the other player's beliefs evaluation. As I have explained elsewhere (Schmidt 1990, 2001a), the difference between the 'deterror' and the 'deterred' cannot be reduced to simple asymetric information; it must be connected to a more dramatic transformation of their belief perspective.

Modelling the editing phase is a much more difficult task because one cannot assume, as in the whole game theoretical literature, that the players even know their own strategies. The insights to be inferred from the large corpus of experimental games are relatively limited for this purpose. Their protocol is monitoring in such a way that the rules of the games are most often included in the instructions that are given to the subjects. The example of the well-known ultimatum game, in all its variants, shows the limits of the lessons which can be drawn from their results. This does not mean, however, that they do not provide useful information about the understanding of those rules by the players, in relation to their verbal presentation, and, especially, about the learning effect of playing the game.

Nevertheless, the main difficulty remains theoretical. As the rules and the structures of the game cannot be assumed to be common knowledge between the players, there is no justification for the 'real game' to be the same in all the players' possible worlds, at variance with the belief systems previously surveyed. Therefore, an alternative framework is necessary in order to capture the players' real understanding of the situation. The pure co-ordination games, where the common knowledge of the structures of the games does not help the players to find the solution, is a relevant case study for this investigation. It has suggested to Bacharach a stimulating model of 'variable universe games', where the belief states of the players do not refer to a fixed and unique world, but may vary from one player to another (Bacharach 1993, 1997).

A slightly modified example of the game of the meeting point (Case 3, p. 120) offers an informal illustration of Bacharach's heuristic approach to the players' problem in such a situation.

The two players have now six possible meeting points. Two of these meeting points have a green façade and four of them have a grey façade. One of those façades is slightly more illuminated and it is a grey one. Neither of the players knows exactly what the other knows of these different characteristics of the six possible meeting points. If we consider the colours, it is almost certain that if each player knew that the other player also knew the colours of the six meeting points, they would both deduce (on the basis of elementary statistical reasoning) to choose a green meeting point. With regard to the lighting of the façades, on the other hand, the same argument employed within a similar reasoning would make the two players prefer the point that is better illuminated.

The choice of the meeting point with the grey façade which is slightly better illuminated would definitely impose itself on both players, to the extent that it alone allows the singling out of the meeting point. The validity of this conclusion is, all the same, subject to one supplementary condition. Not only must each player know that the other player knows these two characteristics of the six meeting points, but he must also know that the other person estimates, as he does, that they provide both elements of pertinent information necessary to them to direct their choice. Such pertinence depends on the cultural repertoire of both players (colours, light etc.). If both players know that this repertoire is common, this second condition is fulfilled and the question is settled. If this is not the case, supplementary conditions concerning the translation of their respective cultural 'repertoires' have to be explored.[11] Indeed, Bacharach's heuristics is oversimplified in this example. It leaves aside the more particularly delicate question raised by the treatment of players' 'empathy'. However, it can be used as a starting point for further investigations concerning the players' mental processes.

6.4 CONCLUDING OBSERVATIONS

On the one hand, we have seen that game theory does not provide a well-adapted framework for studying how players frame the game in which they play. This can be strange at first sight, but not really surprising. Indeed, the very focus of game theory is the investigation into the properties of the games which have been already identified by their structures and their rules. Such primary information (the basic knowledge) becomes an obstacle when the focus of the research moves to the mental construction of the game's representations by the players during their play.

On the other hand, and for an opposite reason, the heuristics models of framing individual decisions are not more relevant. They lack the very specific dimension of players' interactions.

This exclusion from two disciplines or research programmes explains why players' framing in game situations has remained a domain of research rarely explored until now. To escape those difficulties we have proposed the consideration of players' framing as the issue of a sort of preliminary metagame, where the aim of the players is to find sufficient common categories, such as characteristic features and selective processes, for playing a game corresponding to their perceived situation. Such a tentative programme must now be tested in appropriate experimental protocols in order to prove its fruitfulness.

NOTES

1. Chellas (1980), *Modal Logic*, is the reference book for modal logic. For a survey of the applications to game theory, see Bacharach et al. (1997), *Epistemic Logic and the Theory of Games and Decisions*.
2. For a survey of this cognitive approach to decision-making, see Khaneman et al. (1982), *Judgement under Uncertainty: Heuristics and Biases*. An alternative heuristic framework has been elaborated by Gigerenzer, cf. Gigerenzer and Todd (1999), *Fast and Frugal Heuristics: the Adaptative Tool Box*. An evaluation of their contribution, from an economic point of view, can be found in Schmidt (2005).
3. This contradiction in the logical formulation of a game situation has been pointed out by Bonanno (1993) from a quite different perspective.
4. This statement is obviously reinforced when the predictor is supposed to be infallible.
5. Cf. Campbell and Sowden (1985), *Paradoxes of Rationality and Cooperation: Prisoner's Dilemma and Newcomb's Problem*.
6. Wittgenstein (1953), *Philosophical Investigations*. For an original treatment of Wittgenstein's paradox see Kripte (1982), *Wittgenstein on Rules and Private Language*.

7. As, for example, the logical existence of solutions for the chess game has to be proved mathematically.
8. For a critical survey of this literature see Sen and Williams (1982), *Utilitarism and Beyond*.
9. On that point, Aumann and Savage had an interesting exchange of letters during 1970; see Aumann (2000) *Collected Papers*, vol. 1, pp. 305–10.
10. The experimental failures of Savage's system of axioms derived from this framework have been the starting point for 'the bias and heuristic' approaches to individual decision-making under risk and uncertainty.
11. The problem raised by the indeterminancy of translation is classical in analytical philosophy. It has been seriously disccussed by Quine (1970).

REFERENCES

Aumann, R.J. (1976), 'Agreeing to disagree', *Annals of Statistics*, **4**, 1236–9.
Aumann, R.J. (1987), 'Correlated equilibrium as an expression of Bayesian rationality', *Econometrica*, **55**, 1–18.
Aumann, R.J. (1992), 'Knowledge and game theory', mimeo, *Summer Institute in Game Theory*, Stony Brook: New York State University.
Aumann, R.J. (1999), 'Interactive espistemology I, II', *International Journal of Game Theory*, **128**, 263–314.
Aumann, R.J. (2000), *Collected Papers*, vol. I, Cambridge: The MIT Press.
Aumann, R.J. and Brandenburger, A. (1995), 'Epistemic conditions for Nash equilibrium', *Econometrica*, **63**, 1161–80.
Bacharach, M.O.L. (1993), 'Variable universe games' in K. Binmore, A. Kirman and P. Tani (eds) *Frontiers of Game Theory*, Cambridge: Cambridge University Press.
Bacharach, M.O.L. (1997), 'The epistemic structure of a theory of games', in M.O.L. Bacharach, L.A. Gerard-Varet, P. Mongin and H.S. Shin (eds.), *Epistemic Logic on the Theory of Games and Decisions*, Dordrecht: Kluwer Academic Publishers.
Bacharach, M.O.L., Gerard-Varet, L.A., Mongin, P. and Shin, H.S. (eds) (1997), *Epistemic Logic on the Theory of Games and Decisions*, Dordrecht: Kluwer Academic Publishers.
Binmore, K. (1994), *Game Theory and the Social Contract, Playing Fair*, vol. I, Cambridge: The MIT Press.
Binmore, K. (1998), *Game Theory and Social Contract, Just Playing*, vol. II, Cambridge: The MIT Press.
Bonanno, G. (1993), 'The logical representation of extensive games', *International Journal of Game Theory*, **22**, 153–69.
Campbell, R. and Sowden, L. (1985), *Paradoxes of Rationality and Cooperation: Prisoner's Dilemma and Newcomb's Problem*, Vancouver: University of British Columbia Press.
Chellas, B.F. (1980), *Modal Logic*, Cambridge: Cambridge University Press.
Geanakoplos, J., Pearce, D. and Stachetti, E. (1989), 'Psychological games and sequential rationality', *Games and Economic Behavior*, **1**, 60–79.
Gigerenzer, G. and Todd, P.M. (eds) (1999), *Simple Heuristics That Make us Smart*, Oxford: Oxford University Press.
Gilboa, I. and Schmeidler, D. (1988), 'Information dependent games: can common sense be common knowledge?', *Economics Letters*, **27** (3), 215–21.

Greenberg, J. (1990), *The Theory of Social Situations*, Cambridge: Cambridge University Press.

Jeffrey, R.C. (1983), *The Logic of Decision*, Chicago: Chicago University Press.

Kahneman, D. and Tversky, A. (1979), 'Prospect theory: an analysis of decision under risk', *Econometrica*, **47**, 263–91.

Kahneman, D., Slovic, P., and Tversky, A. (eds) (1982), *Judgment Under Uncertainty: Heuristics and Biaises*, Cambridge: Cambridge University Press.

Kripte, S. (1982), *Wittgenstein on Rules and Private Language*, London: Basil Blackwell.

Kohlberg, E. and Mertens, J.F. (1986), 'On strategic stability of equilibria', *Econometrica*, **5**, 1003–37.

Quine, O. (1970), 'On the reasons for the indeterminacy of translation', *The Journal of Philosophy*, **67**, 178–83.

Rabin, M. (1993), 'Incorporating fairness into game theory and economics', *The American Review*, **83** (5), 1281–302.

Savage, L.J. (1954), *The Foundations of Statistics*, New York: John Wiley.

Schelling, T.C. (1960), *The Strategy of Conflict*, Cambridge: Harvard University Press.

Schmidt, C. (1990), 'Dissuasion, rationalité et magasins à succursales multiples', *Revue d'économie politique*, **2**, 297–304.

Schmidt, C. (2001a), *La Théorie des Jeux: Essai d'interprétation*, Paris: Presses Universitaires de France.

Schmidt, C. (2001b), 'Does Nash equilibrium imply the players' rationality in non-cooperative games?', Mimeo, LESOD, Paris, Université Paris-Dauphine.

Schmidt, C. (2003), 'The epistemic foundations of social organizations: a Game-Theoretic Approach', in S. Rizello (ed)., *Cognitive Developments in Economics*, London: Routledge, pp. 243–67.

Schmidt, C. (2005), 'Cognitive psychology and economic analysis of decision-making', mimeo, LESOD, Université Paris-Dauphine, 2–38.

Sen, A. and Williams, B. (eds) (1982), *Utilitarianism and Beyond*, Cambridge: Cambridge University Press.

Stalnaker, R. (1997), 'On the evaluation of solution concepts', in M.O.L. Bacharach, L.A. Gerard-Varet, P. Mongin and H.S. Shin (eds), *The Epistemic Logic and the Theory of Games and Decisions*, Dordrech: Kluwer Academic Press.

Tversky, A. and Kahneman, D. (1986), 'Rational choice and the framing of decisions', in M.R. Hogarth and M.W. Reder (eds), *Rational Choice*, Chicago: Chicago University Press.

Tversky, A. and Kahneman, D. (1992), 'Advances in prospect theory: cumulative representation of uncertainty', *Journal of Risk and Uncertainty*, **5**, 297–323.

Von Neumann, J. and Morgenstern, O. (1944), *Theory of Games and Economic Behavior*, Princeton: Princeton University Press.

Wittgenstein, L. (1953), *Philosophical Investigations*, London: Basil Blackwell.

PART III

Beliefs and Decision Theory

7. Beliefs and dynamic consistency

Jean-Marc Tallon and Jean-Christophe Vergnaud

7.1 INTRODUCTION

In this chapter, we apply the decision theoretic approach to the representation and updating of beliefs. The standard Bayesian approach developed by Savage (1954) sets out the conditions under which a decision maker whose preferences satisfy a certain number of 'rationality' axioms (among which is the famous 'Sure-thing principle') will have probabilistic beliefs. When these axioms are satisfied any decision maker is able (or acts as if he were able) to come up with a probability distribution over the possible states of nature (i.e. the sources of uncertainty) and also acts as if maximizing an expected utility with respect to this prior.

This construction underlies most of economic theory. However, as early as 1921, Keynes (1921) and Knight (1921) had already suggested that probabilistic beliefs failed to address an important issue, namely the confidence agents have in their own beliefs. Doubts about the fact that probabilistic beliefs could represent all types of uncertainty were also raised by Shackle (1952). These theoretical concerns were backed by experimental evidence showing that subjects often failed to deal with probabilistic information in the way predicted by the theory (Allais 1953). Moreover, the evidence showed that subjects found it difficult to come up with probabilistic priors when information was *a priori* too scarce (Ellsberg 1961).

In more recent years, more general axiomatic models of decision under uncertainty have emerged in which agents can have non-additive beliefs (Schmeidler 1989) or multiple-prior beliefs (Gilboa and Schmeidler 1989). These models are specifically meant to deal with the 'Ellsberg paradox', while retaining enough structure to have some normative appeal over and above their superior descriptive ability.

Given that the Ellsberg paradox has been central to the development of decision theory under uncertainty we shall briefly recall it here. Consider an urn containing 90 balls. The decision maker is told that there are 30 red balls and that the remaining 60 balls can be either black or yellow, though their proportion is unknown. The decision maker is then asked to choose among the following 'acts' (decisions):

	Red	Black	Yellow
f	100	0	0
g	0	100	0
f'	100	0	100
g'	0	100	100

Figure 7.1

Act f is the act of 'betting on drawing a red ball', g of 'betting on black', f' of 'betting on red or yellow' and g' of 'betting on black or yellow'. What the experiment shows is that a large majority of subjects prefer f to g, while also preferring g' to f'.

If one were to ascribe probabilistic beliefs to agents, the first preference would suggest that subjects think there are fewer than 30 black balls in the urn and hence think that there is a probability of less than $\frac{1}{3}$ of winning the bet f'. On the other hand, the second preference suggests that they think that there are more black and yellow balls than there are red and yellow balls, thus revealing (subtracting the number of yellow balls) that they think that there are more black balls than red balls (i.e. the probability of drawing a black ball is greater than $\frac{1}{3}$).

The behaviour exhibited even in the simple setting of this experiment is incompatible with the idea that agents have probabilistic beliefs. The main reason for this is that subjects lack any precise probabilistic information on the number of yellow and black balls. Bayesian theory implies that this lack of 'objective' knowledge is immaterial, in the sense that agents should have probabilistic beliefs regardless of the information at hand. Ellsberg experiments suggest that subjects are reluctant to do so. Furthermore, it is not *a priori* obvious that this reluctance should be considered 'irrational', and hence discarded on normative grounds. On the contrary, one could argue that in this case the only information at hand takes the form of a set of probability distributions and should be taken as such by the decision maker, thus possibly making a behavioural difference compared to a situation in which this set is reduced to a singleton.

What this discussion suggests is that there is some latitude in modelling beliefs in a one-shot, static decision problem. Certain models take beliefs to be non-probabilistic and represent a kind of behaviour which, though violating the *Sure-thing principle*, is difficult to consider irrational.[1]

Things become slightly more complicated when we move to dynamic decision problems, as argued in Hammond (1988 and 1989).[2] He argues that 'weak' rationality requirements imply that beliefs in dynamic choice problems have to be probabilistic or decision makers will behave inconsistently. Thus, one of the requirements is that chosen behaviour be dynamically consistent. Though we shall examine the precise meaning of this statement later in this chapter, loosely speaking we can say that dynamic consistency requires agents to be able to implement *ex ante* choices (i.e. made prior to receiving any information) dynamically. In other words, if a certain course of action is judged *ex ante* to be optimal, the same course of action should be implemented following receipt of information. Hammond's conclusion is that the expected utility model put forward by Savage (1954) combined with Bayesian updating satisfies his rationality requirement.[3] In fact, the result is even stronger: Hammond argues that any model representing behaviour that does not respect the *Sure-thing principle* lends itself to the criticism that it is not dynamically consistent.

In this contribution we put forward a modified version of Hammond's argument. After reviewing the argument more formally, we propose a weaker notion of dynamic consistency. We observe that this notion does not imply a fully-fledged *Sure-thing principle*, thus leaving some room for models that are not based on expected utility maximization. However, we argue that these models still fail to account for 'imprecision averse' behaviour, such as the one exhibited in the Ellsberg experiment, captured by non-Bayesian models, such as the multiple-prior model of Gilboa and Schmeidler (1989). We go on to establish that such non-Bayesian models present a weak form of dynamic consistency when the information considered reduces imprecision (in the Ellsberg example that would, for example, be information about the relative proportions of black and yellow balls).

7.2 A PRELIMINARY EXAMPLE: ON THE CORRECT USE OF THE BAYESIAN UPDATING RULE

Our aim in this section is to show, through a simple example, that the description of the sources of uncertainty is as important as the ability to assign probability weights to them. Indeed, 'well-behaved' Bayesian decision makers might act in a non-Bayes rational way if they fail to correctly represent the states of nature describing the uncertainty they face and the arrival of information.

There are many versions of the example we are about to put forward but we have deliberately chosen a 'dramatic' one. Say there are three prisoners, a, b, and c in a cell; one of them has been sentenced to death and all three know this fact. However, they do not know which of the three has been sentenced. Suppose now that prisoner a has managed to ask the warden which of the other two prisoners has not been sentenced and has been told that b is innocent. How does this information affect a's prior beliefs (that are realistically assumed to be uniform $(\frac{1}{3}, \frac{1}{3}, \frac{1}{3})$) on who the sentenced prisoner is?

A quick (and Bayesian-like) reasoning would be to update beliefs by saying that the probability is now $\frac{1}{2}$ that a is the convicted prisoner. However, this reasoning is based on a misrepresentation of what the states of nature (i.e. the full description of all sources of uncertainty) are. In this example, the prisoner fails to understand that the messages that the warden can give are actually constrained. Indeed, a state of nature in this problem has to be given by a couple (sentenced prisoner, announcement of the warden). Thus, the possible states are $\{(a, b), (a, c), (b, c), (c, b)\}$. Prior beliefs of a over this set are $(\frac{1}{6}, \frac{1}{6}, \frac{1}{3}, \frac{1}{3})$ (assuming that he believes that the warden has an equal chance of saying b or c if he (a) is the one sentenced to death). If the warden says b is innocent, i.e. that the state is not (a, c) or (b, c), then Bayesian revision yields a's new beliefs: with probability $\frac{1}{3}$ he is the sentenced prisoner, with probability $\frac{2}{3}$ c is the sentenced prisoner. So, in this case, the information revealed by the warden is not informative as to a's probability of being convicted but teaches a lot about c's probability.

The upshot of this example is simple: the description of what uncertainty really is, that is, the description of the space of states of nature, is crucial. While deceptively simple, this remark points to the fact that, in decision problems involving the potential arrival of new information, the description of a state must include all the possible messages.

This example can also be turned into a decision problem. Another version of the same example is that of a TV game-show. The host shows three doors to a player. There is, say, a car behind one of these doors. He then asks the candidate to pick one of the doors. If the car is behind it, he wins it, otherwise he loses. After the candidate has announced which door he has picked (say door a), the host tells him that he is going to open one of the remaining two doors, behind which there is no car, say door b. He then asks the candidate if he wants to change his choice and now pick door c, or if he wants to stick to his original choice. Bayesian revision, as presented above, requires the candidate to pick door c at this stage.

Moreover, the candidate should be able to announce all his strategies *ex ante*, as a function of which door is opened. In other words, he should be able to plan in advance that if the host opens door b he should switch to door c and *vice versa*. An important property of probabilistic beliefs, coupled with a Bayesian revision rule, is that the *ex ante* plan and the choice that the decision maker actually makes after receiving the information dictate the same thing. This, loosely speaking, is the property of dynamic consistency that was put forward by Hammond (1988) as a justification for expected utility theory. We now turn to a more formal discussion of this principle.

7.3 STRONG DYNAMIC CONSISTENCY IMPLIES BAYESIANISM

In this section, we examine the dynamic consistency argument in favour of Bayesian decision theory more systematically, using conditional preferences to represent dynamic choice situations. We will illustrate the abstract discussion by taking the value of information as an example and explaining it by using a dynamic representation of choices (decision trees) and an 'equivalent' representation, cast in the language of static preferences over acts and associated with one-shot decisions.

We start with some notation. Let us consider Savage's (1954) familiar framework, where Ω is the set of states of nature, A is the set of acts or decisions which are functions from Ω into X, the set of consequences. An act then specifies the 'gain' of a decision in each state of nature: act f has pay-off $f(\omega)$ in state $\omega \in \Omega$.

In this setting, information is captured by the fact that the agent might be told that a specific event has occurred. An event is a set of states of nature. Hence, the knowledge of an event enables the decision maker to disregard the complement event as being impossible. The preference-based approach to belief revision postulates that for any event $E \subseteq \Omega$, the decision maker has a preference relation conditional on this event.[4] A conditional preference relation of this kind is denoted $\geq$ and is interpreted in the following way: $f \geq_E g$ means that if event E were true, then the agent would prefer act f to act g. What we are interested in is $\geq_\Omega$, which is the *ex ante* preference relation for which we want to examine whether rationality arguments force an expected utility type of preference. The relation $\geq_E$ can be seen as a potential *ex post* preference relation in the case where event E is true. Denoting by E^c the complement of E, that is, the states that are not in E, one can also define a preference relation conditional on that event, $\geq_{E^c}$. The following axiom captures some consistency requirement about how the *ex ante* preference relation relates to possible *ex post* preference relations, that is, the agent's preferences after he receives some information. This axiom is at the heart of Hammond's defence of expected utility based on dynamic principles.

Axiom (Strong Dynamic Consistency of Preference)

$\forall E \subseteq \Omega, \forall f, g \in A,$
- if $f \geq_E g$ and $f \geq_{E^c} g$ then $f \geq_\Omega g$,
- if $f \geq_E g$ and $f \geq_{E^c} g$ and at least one preference is strict (i.e., $f >_E g$ or $f >_{E^c} g$) then we have $f >_\Omega g$.

This axiom relates the *ex ante* preferences $\geq_\Omega$ to possible *ex post* preference pre-orders (conditional on E and E^c). It says that if f is preferred to g conditionally, both when E and E^c, this should also be the case unconditionally. This axiom can be seen as a dominance axiom, preventing situations where we could have $f >_E g$ and $f >_{E^c} g$ while $f <_\Omega g$. Indeed, in such a case, there would be a clear contradiction between *ex ante* and *ex post* preferences leading potentially to dynamic choice problems: the agent may have some difficulty in carrying out a particular decision plan if his initial preferences and the final ones are contradictory in any way.

Let us now examine the problem of dynamic choice more precisely, by looking at a specific case, namely the acquisition of information. Consider the situation where an agent is offered the possibility of postponing his choice after he receives some free information. It seems intuitive that in a pure decision problem the agent should not refuse such information, thus demonstrating the 'positive value of information'. To formalize this intuition, consider the following decision tree (Figure 7.2), which represents the situation where an agent has to choose between f and g and can learn whether E or E^c is true before he chooses (as usual, squares represent decision nodes while circles represent chance nodes). If the decision maker chooses to go up at the beginning of the tree, this means he will first learn whether E or E^c occurred and then make a choice between f and g. On the other hand, if he chooses to go down, this means that he will choose between f and g without having any information on event E.

Observe that the two branches of the tree in Figure 7.2 that start from the origin are equivalent to the two trees in Figure 7.3. The left part of Figure 7.3 depicts the simple choice between f and g without any information. The right part represents the equivalent strategic form of a tree in which the decision maker has the possibility of getting informed and more specifically of learning whether E has occurred or not. The act $f_E g$ should be read as follows: if the true state is in E then get $f(\omega)$, while if it is in E^c then get $g(\omega)$. Hence, $f_E g$ is the act that yields f if E and g if E^c.

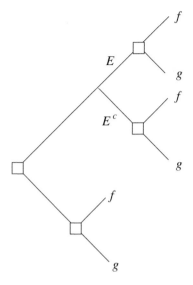

Figure 7.2   Choosing to get informed

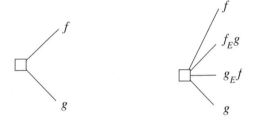

Figure 7.3

The obvious advantage of receiving this information is that the decision maker can condition his choice on the realization of E. In other words, when comparing the two decision trees of Figure 7.3, the decision maker will always prefer to act on the right-hand-side tree, as the strategies it offers include all the ones available on the left-hand-side tree.

In the choice situation just described, an agent satisfying the *Strong dynamic consistency axiom* will be willing to accept the information, which, as argued above, is a sensible choice (if not the only sensible choice). Indeed, consider the case where $f >_E g$ while $g >_{E^c} f$. If the agent chooses to go up in the tree of Figure 7.2, he will choose f conditionally on E, and g conditionally on E^c. Therefore, going up is equivalent to getting the act $f_E g$. Yet, since $f_E g \sim_E f$ and $f_E g \sim_{E^c} g$ we have $f_E g \sim_E f >_E g$ and $f_E g \sim_{E^c} g >_{E^c} f$.[5]

Therefore, the *Strong dynamic consistency axiom* implies that $f_E g >_\Omega f$ and $f_E g >_\Omega g$, and thus the agent should find this information valuable.

More systematically, it can be shown that the agent should always accept the information. If this were not the case, there would be instances where $f_E g \sim_E f >_E g, f_E g \sim_{E^c} g >_{E^c} f$, while $f >_\Omega f_E g$ which constitutes a violation of the *Strong dynamic consistency axiom*. Just as before, going up the tree in Figure 7.2 means getting the act $f_E g$ but in this case the perspective is negative, since by going down the tree the agent could get f. The agent should, therefore, refuse the information exhibiting a negative value. This phenomenon might happen in non-expected utility models like the one put forward by Gilboa and Schmeidler (1989). We provide an example of this kind in the Appendix.

We now turn to the restrictions that the *Strong dynamic consistency axiom* places on preferences, focusing on its implications on a cornerstone of Bayesian decision theory, the *Sure-thing principle*, which we now recall.

Axiom (Sure-thing Principle)

$\forall E \subseteq \Omega, \forall f, g, f', g' \in A$. If $f = f'$ and $g = g'$ on $E, f = g$ and $f' = g'$ on E^c then $f \geq_\Omega g$ if and only if $f' \geq_\Omega g'$.

This axiom can be explained on the Ellsberg experiment presented in the introduction. Take the event E to be the event $\{Black, Red\}$. Then, on this event, act f and act f' are the same, and act g and act g' are the same. On E^c, that is on $\{Yellow\}$, f and g are equivalent, and f' and g' are equivalent. The *Sure-thing principle* then states that if f is preferred to g then f' should also be preferred to g': indeed the only difference between the comparison of f to f' and the comparison of g to g' is to be found in the column *Yellow*, i.e., in the event the ball drawn is yellow. However, conditionally on this event, f and g are the same and f' and g' are the same. Hence, concludes the *Sure-thing principle*, the choice should not depend on the pay-off for this event, as long as it is the same for f and g, and for f' and g'. Obviously, the choice pattern observed in the Ellsberg experiment violates this principle.

Now, it can be shown that the *Sure-thing principle* is a consequence of the *Strong dynamic consistency axiom*. Hence, adhering to the *Strong dynamic consistency axiom* prevents Ellsberg type behaviour.

Proposition: *Strong dynamic consistency of preference implies that* $>_\Omega$ *satisfies the Sure-thing principle.*

As previously mentioned, the *Sure-thing principle* is at the heart of the subjective expected utility model. Conversely, note that if we update subjective probabilities according to the Bayes rule, then the subjective expected utility model satisfies the *Strong dynamic consistency axiom*. Therefore, if we accept the *Strong dynamic consistency axiom* then we do not have much latitude in terms of the kind of preferences we can consider: they essentially have to conform to the subjective expected utility model. However, as we will see in what follows, this axiom is slightly too strong and there is scope for its relaxation.

7.4 WEAK DYNAMIC CONSISTENCY OF PREFERENCE

We saw in the previous section that the rationale for the *Strong dynamic consistency axiom* was to ensure that an agent did not fear preference conflicts when faced with certain dynamic choices and, particularly, that he would attribute a positive value to information. Let us now turn to the following weaker axiom.

Axiom (Weak Dynamic Consistency of Preference)

$\forall E \subseteq \Omega, \forall f, g \in A$. If $f \geq_E g$ and $f \geq_{E^c} g$, then $f \geq_\Omega g$.

This axiom is weaker than the *Strong dynamic consistency axiom* in the sense that this axiom allows for the situation where $f \sim_E g, f >_{E^c} g$ and $f \sim_\Omega g$. It seems that this axiom could do the job as well. Indeed, this axiom also prevents the kind of reversal where $f >_E g$ and $f >_{E^c} g$ while $f <_\Omega g$ that we previously identified as being problematic.

It is worth noting that in the particular case of the information acquisition problem, this axiom is actually sufficient to guarantee that the agent values information positively. Indeed, in the situation where $f >_E g$ while $g >_{E_c} f$, the *Weak dynamic consistency axiom* implies that $f_E g \geq_\Omega f$ and $f_E g \geq_\Omega g$, and thus that the agent will find this information valuable.

One could argue that this is a rather weak departure from the strong form of dynamic consistency: playing on weak and strict preferences might appear somewhat anecdotal. Note, however, that an important consequence of this apparently mild weakening is that the *Sure-thing principle* cannot be deduced from the *Weak dynamic consistency axiom*. Hence, it opens the door to a weakening of the *Sure-thing principle* that might be of interest if one wants to be able to accept preferences that do not belong to the subjective expected utility class. More precisely, consider the following weakening of the *Sure-thing principle*.

Axiom (Weak Sure-thing Principle)

$\forall E \subseteq \Omega, \forall f, f', g, g' \in A$, if $f = f'$ and $g = g'$ on E, $f = g$ and $f' = g'$ on E^c
then $f >_{\Omega} g$ if, and only if, $f' \geq_{\Omega} g'$.

It can be shown that the *Weak sure-thing principle* is a consequence of the *Weak dynamic consistency axiom*.

Proposition: *Weak dynamic consistency of preference implies that $>_{\Omega}$ satisfies the Weak sure-thing principle.*

So far, we have weakened dynamic consistency in a rather mild way and shown that it leads to a weak version of the *Sure-thing principle*. This would not be of much interest if the preferences that satisfy the *Weak sure-thing principle* but not the fully-fledged *Sure-thing principle* were of little interest. We now want to argue that this is not the case and that they include an interesting set of preferences, in which the decision maker treats the information in a purely qualitative way. We present this class of models in the following section.

7.5 POSSIBILISTIC DECISION MODEL

Zadeh (1978) introduced a representation of uncertainty based on possibility measures in the field of artificial intelligence (see also Dubois and Prade 1985). This work has been extended to a decision theoretic setting by Dubois et al. (2000). Possibility measures were introduced to represent situations in which the information is qualitative as opposed to probabilities that are by nature quantitative. This notion of qualitative information can be seen as the formal representation of ideas introduced into economics by Shackle (1952).

Definition (Possibility Measure)

A possibility measure is a set function $\Pi: 2^{\Omega} \rightarrow [0,1]$, such that $\Pi(\emptyset) = 0$, $\Pi(\Omega) = 1$ and $\forall A, B \subseteq \Omega, \Pi(A \cup B) = Max(\Pi(A), \Pi(B))$.

The interpretation of the possibility of event A is essentially an assessment of the degree to which the event is considered possible. It is qualitative in the sense that statements like 'this event is twice as possible as that event' do not have a well-defined meaning. Indeed, the definition makes it clear that the union of two events is 'as possible as' the most possible of the two events. Observe that many events could be assigned the maximal possibility, i.e. 1, without any contradiction. In particular, for any event E, it must be the case that E or E^c has possibility 1, since $E \cup = E^c = \Omega$. Possibility measures can be used in decision problems if one manages to come up with a decision criterion that is based on such objects. In much the same way as probabilities are naturally combined with utilities in the expected utility model, possibility measures can be combined with utility via the so-called Sugeno integral. Let $u:X \to [0,1]$ be a utility function. It is possible to axiomatize a decision criterion that is based on the combination via minimal and maximal operations of the possibilistic representation of uncertainty and the utility of the consequence of an act. More precisely, an act f is evaluated by

$$\max_{\omega \in \Omega} \left[\min \left(\Pi(\omega), u(f(\omega)) \right) \right].$$

The Sugeno integral, which is a generalization of the above formula, can be seen as a 'regular' integral in which the minimal operator replaces the product operator while the maximal operator replaces the sum operator. If we consider simple acts like bets, it is easy to see that betting on the event A (i.e. win if A is observed, lose if not), is simply evaluated by the possibility of A, $\Pi(A)$.

One can check that the Sugeno integral with possibility satisfies the *Weak sure-thing principle*. Furthermore, if the possibility measure is updated according to the following rule called the non-normalized Bayes rule

$$\Pi(A \mid E) = \Pi(A \cap E)$$

then it can be checked that this model satisfies the *Weak dynamic consistency axiom* as well, and hence will never be subject to problems such as negative information value.

More generally, it is possible to extend this model in order to mix the expected utility model and the Sugeno integral in a general criterion which also satisfies the *Weak sure-thing* principle. However, this kind of model, while generalizing the expected utility model, still fails to explain the Ellsberg paradox as the latter constitutes a violation of the *Weak sure-thing principle* as well. Given that, as we mentioned in the introduction, the Ellsberg paradox is one of the main reasons for looking for non-Bayesian models, it might appear that the kind of possibilistic models we have just examined, while of theoretical interest, are somehow missing an important point of what imprecise information, as captured by the Ellsberg experiment, is all about.

7.6 THE CONTENT OF INFORMATION

In this section, we explore the *Weak dynamic consistency axiom* properties further, especially when coupled with information of a different kind from the one we have dealt with so far. We do so by going back to the original motivation we gave for looking at non-Bayesian models, namely to capture imprecision or ambiguity in the data provided to the decision maker. For instance, in the Ellsberg paradox, the urn's content is incompletely described: there is a set of probability distributions that are compatible with the objective data.

Now, the previous sections showed that we can run into trouble, with respect to the dynamic consistency requirements of non-Bayesian decision models, when the decision maker is in a position to learn whether the ball which was drawn was yellow or not. Arguably, non-Bayesian models are not meant to deal with this type of learning. Indeed, it is easy to imagine other types of information that would lead to other kinds of learning. For instance, the decision maker might learn that there are fewer than 20 yellow balls in the urn. This operation would amount to a decrease of the imprecision in the data the agent has.

A different, though related, kind of learning, which fits well with non-Bayesian models, is sampling. Suppose the agent is allowed to sample the urn before he makes his choice and the final draw is made. For instance if he observes 2 red balls, 7 black balls and 1 yellow ball, he will learn something about the urn. Intuitively, this kind of learning, which reduces the imprecision about the probabilistic data, will probably be valuable to a decision maker who is averse to such imprecision.

In the remainder of this section, we put forward a rather abstract argument in order to establish that in these situations the *Weak dynamic consistency axiom* can be satisfied. Since we want to consider information that bears on the imprecision of probabilistic data, it is convenient to broaden the description of the states of nature in order to explicitly capture this dimension. For instance, assume that the set Ω is the cross product of two sets: $\Omega = \Theta \times S$. Then, further assume that the objective datum about this problem is that, conditionally on a realization of $\theta \in \Theta$, there is a probability distribution p_θ over S although there is no available probability distribution over Θ. Loosely speaking, this represents a world with two layers of uncertainty: a first layer, on which one has very few data or information, is given by the set Θ, which captures general features about the world, and a second layer, S, on which, conditionally on the realization of a general feature θ, there exists a probability distribution. For instance, in the Ellsberg urn example, an element $\theta \in \Theta$ is the description of the content of the urn while $s \in S$ is the colour of the ball drawn.

Beyond the anecdotal problems posed by the Ellsberg experiment, this formalization also captures features of problems relating to scientific uncertainty. For instance, in the climate change problem, Θ can be understood as a list of hypotheses and predictions provided by the scientific community. In this case, $\theta \in \Theta$ could be the level of temperature increase in 50 years' time. S is the description of natural catastrophic events such as storm, flood etc. Conditionally on θ we may know p_θ, which gives the frequency of catastrophic events if temperature increases by a given amount: for example, if the temperature rises by 2°C, then a type of storm that occurred every 100 years in the past will now occur every 10 years.

Consider now the following (non-Bayesian) decision criterion, known as the multiple-prior model, which was axiomatized by Gilboa and Schmeidler (1989).[6] An act f, which is a mapping from $\Theta \times S$ to the space of consequences X, is evaluated by

$$\min_{\theta \in \Theta} \left[E_{p_\theta} u\big(f(\theta, s) \big) \right].$$

The distinction between the two kinds of learning we suggested can easily be embodied in this formalization. Indeed, one can oppose learning about S (learning about the colour of the ball) and learning about Θ (learning about the content of the urn). To learn about S is to consider an event $E \subseteq \Omega$ of the form $E = \Theta \times F$, where $F \subseteq S$. The multiple-prior criterion clearly does not satisfy the *Weak sure-thing principle* with respect to such an event. However, if we consider an event $E \subseteq \Omega$ of the form $E = \Phi \times S$, where $\Phi \subseteq \Theta$, then the multiple-prior criterion satisfies the *Weak sure-thing principle*.

Moreover, if we suppose that $f \geq_\Phi g$ if and only if

$$\min_{\theta \in \Theta} \left[E_{p_\theta} u\big(f(\theta, s) \big) \right] \geq \min_{\theta \in \Theta} \left[E_{p_\theta} u\big(g(\theta, s) \big) \right]$$

one can easily check that the *Weak dynamic consistency axiom* can be satisfied. In this sense, no dynamic consistency problems arise for the type of learning we have introduced and that we could call *reduction of imprecision*. Thus, one is led to conclude that when modelling the arrival of information, one should be careful to distinguish what type of information this is, and whether the underlying decision model is adapted to treat that particular

type of information. We can now also review Hammond's result and read
it as saying that the type of information considered is appropriate to the
expected utility criterion. The result of this section, on the other hand,
leads to the conclusion that non-Bayesian decision models, such as the
multiple-prior model, are tailored to treat the arrival of information that
leads to a refinement of the initial non-probabilistic data and to a reduction
in imprecision.

It should also be noted that when formalizing scientific uncertainty, the
reduction of imprecision could be interpreted as the normal evolution of
science. It does not make sense to attribute a probability to the validity of
a scientific hypothesis, whose refutation leads to the removal of the theory
resting on it from the corpus of scientific knowledge.

7.7   CONCLUSION

In this contribution, we reviewed Hammond's argument that bases expected
utility on a dynamic consistency principle. We weakened Hammond's
Strong dynamic consistency axiom and showed that this weakened version
is compatible with a qualitative treatment of uncertainty coupled with the
use of a possibilistic decision model. However, we found that this model
still failed to account for the type of imprecision-averse behaviour that we
discussed in the introduction. We therefore broadened the discussion and
showed that non-Bayesian representations of imprecision-averse behaviour
admit a form of dynamic consistency property with respect to the arrival
of a particular type of information. Indeed, reduction in imprecision (such
as the rejection of a scientific hypothesis) will not lead to dynamically
inconsistent behaviour in these models, even though the *Sure-thing principle*
is not satisfied.

Another stream of research that we will simply mention here has
questioned another aspect of Hammond's 1988 and 1989 argument. Indeed,
our discussion implicitly[7] embodied another principle put forward by
Hammond (1988), namely consequentialism. Consequentialism, loosely
speaking, is a separability principle that states that the decision maker's
choice at a given decision node in a tree should depend only on the
continuation of the tree from that node on. The part of the tree that has
not been reached (and can no longer be reached) can simply be dropped
without leading to any change in the decision maker's choice.

This principle, which allows the performance of backward induction and
dynamic programming, was kept to in the approach we followed here. Had we
dropped it, we would have broken the link between the dynamic consistency
requirement and the *Sure-thing principle* and hence would have considered

non-Bayesian models. However, if one were to drop consequentialism, as some authors like Machina (1989) or MacClennen (1990) did, one would have to specify how the decision maker analyses the decision tree. One way that has been explored in the literature is to assume that the decision maker is resolute enough to follow his initial intentions. Hence, the equivalence between the optimal choice in the reduced strategic form of a tree and the choice operated in the dynamic decision tree is postulated. If such a postulate is taken for granted, dropping the *Sure-thing principle* is of no real consequence as far as the dynamic properties of choices are concerned. Machina (1989) and MacClennen (1990) propose different ways of doing so.[8] Another approach to this problem is to consider that the decision maker is composed of different selves (one at each point in time and for each realization of uncertainty): in this case the final outcome is some sort of Nash equilibrium of the game played by the different selves. This so-called 'sophisticated behaviour' was introduced by Strotz (1955) and has been compared to the resolute choice approach by Machina (1989). In this paper, we have taken a different route to the problem posed by dynamic inconsistency, arguing that it might be the consequence of an inappropriate way of modelling information in various contexts.

APPENDIX 7.1

Negative Value of Information with the Multiple Prior Expected Utility Criterion

A non-Bayesian decision criterion might lead to negative information value when coupled with the idea that agents analyse trees by backward induction and use a revision rule to determine their beliefs at each point in the tree.[9] This is, for instance, the case in the so-called multiple-prior model put forward by Gilboa and Schmeidler (1989). In this model, the agent's beliefs are given by a set of probability measures. The decision criterion is then to choose the act that gives the highest minimal expected utility (where the minimum is taken over the set of probabilities representing the agent's beliefs). In what follows we present a slightly more complicated version of the type of behaviour exhibited in Ellsberg experiments.

There are 100 balls in an urn and the decision maker is given the following information: 60 balls are marked A or D in an unknown proportion, while 20 are marked B and 20 are marked C. Thus, the set of probability measures (p_A, p_B, p_C, p_D) representing the decision maker's beliefs is given by $\{(p, .2, .2, .6 - p) \mid p \in [0, .6]\}$.

Assume that the decision maker's set of available actions is $\{f_{A\cup D}, f_B, f_C\}$, i.e. bet on A or D, bet on B, bet on C with the following pay-offs:

	A	B	C	D
$f_{A\cup D}$	1	0	0	1
f_B	0	1	0	0
f_C	0	0	1	0

Figure 7.4

Now assume that the decision maker has access to some information that will tell him whether the ball is marked A or B, or whether it is marked C, or whether it is marked D. Formally, the decision maker is told whether $\{A,B\}$, or $\{C\}$ or $\{D\}$ occurred. Using this information, the decision maker has now access to a richer set of strategies if he conditions the available bets on the information received. For instance, the strategy, bet on B if told $\{A,B\}$, bet on C if told $\{C\}$, bet on D if told $\{D\}$ will amount to $f_{B\cup C\cup D}$. One can check that the set of available choices with information in the strategic form decision tree is:

$$\{f_{A\cup D}, f_B, f_C, f_{A\cup C\cup D}, f_{B\cup C\cup D}, f_{C\cup D}, f_{B\cup D}, f_{B\cup C}\}.$$

When asked for his optimal choice in this set, the decision maker will say $f_{A\cup C\cup D}$. Indeed, this bet gives him an 80 per cent chance of winning. The other bets have smaller chances of winning, when evaluated by the minimal probability. For instance, $f_{B\cup C\cup D}$ has only a minimal 40 per cent probability of winning. Hence, the decision maker will want to use the information, in the sense that he will choose a bet that is contingent on the information received.

Let us now look at the dynamic choices associated to this story. Assume that the decision maker revises his beliefs by updating in a Bayesian fashion all the probability measures in his sets of priors. For instance, conditionally on the fact that the ball is marked A or B, the decision maker's beliefs will be given by the set

$$\left\{ \left(\frac{p}{.2+p}, \frac{.2}{.2+p}, 0, 0 \right) \mid p \in [0,.6] \right\}$$

of probability distributions over $\{A,B,C,D\}$.

Hence, at the node where he receives the information $\{A,B\}$, the decision maker, having to choose among $\{f_{A\cup D}, f_B, f_C\}$, will choose f_B, since its minimal expected value (with respect to the set of updated priors) is .8, while $f_{A\cup D}$ yields a minimal expected value of 0. Trivially, when the information is $\{C\}$, the decision maker will have (revised) beliefs given by $(0, 0, 1, 0)$, and will choose f_C, while if given the information $\{D\}$, the revision of beliefs would lead to the beliefs $(0, 0, 0, 1)$, and the act $f_{A\cup D}$ would then become optimal. Hence, the optimal choice is:

$$
\begin{bmatrix}
\text{If } \{A, B\}, & \text{choose } f_B \\
\text{If } \{C\}, & \text{choose } f_C \\
\text{If } \{D\}, & \text{choose } f_{A\cup D}.
\end{bmatrix}
$$

This choice amounts to choosing $f_{B\cup C\cup D}$ in the equivalent strategic form. Hence, the choice the decision maker would make in the dynamic decision tree when he decided to acquire the information would be $f_{B\cup C\cup D}$, which is dominated in the equivalent strategic form by $f_{A\cup C\cup D}$. Furthermore, if the decision maker were to refuse the information (i.e., go down the tree in Figure 7.2 for the case at hand), his optimal choice would be $f_{A\cup D}$.

To conclude the argument, observe that $f_{A\cup D}$ gives a 60 per cent chance of winning, while the minimal probability of winning with $f_{B\cup C\cup D}$ is only 40 per cent. Hence, according to the maximal/minimal expected utility criterion, $f_{A\cup D}$ is preferred to $f_{B\cup C\cup D}$. Thus, the decision maker will prefer to remain uninformed, whereas the information is potentially useful in the sense defined in section 7.2 (i.e. the decision maker would indeed condition his choice on such a piece of information in the equivalent strategic forms). The information can then be said to have a 'negative' value for him.

NOTES

1. See for instance Schmeidler (1989) and Gilboa and Schmeidler (1989). For a survey, see Karni and Schmeidler (1991) and Cohen and Tallon (2000).
2. For a recent review, see Hammond (1998a) and (1998b).
3. For a somewhat different argument, see Epstein and LeBreton (1993).
4. For a general approach to belief updating based on conditional preferences, see Wang (2002).
5. There is a hidden assumption behind the fact that $f_E g \sim_E f$, namely that the decision maker, when informed that E has occurred, considers that what might have happened had E^c occurred is irrelevant. This is a form of separability of preferences, which we take for granted throughout this contribution and on which we shall comment briefly in the conclusion.
6. This model is used in the Appendix to illustrate how information, as modelled in the previous sections, might assume a negative value for non-Bayesian decision makers.
7. Although see remark in note 5.

8. For yet another approach, see Gul and Pesendorfer (2001).
9. Several revision rules can be introduced in non-Bayesian models. We focus on one such rule though, essentially, a similar argument could be made for any rule.

REFERENCES

Allais, M. (1953), 'Le comportement de l'homme rationnel devant le risque: critique des postulats de l'école américaine', *Econometrica*, **21**, 503–46.
Cohen, M., and Tallon, J.-M. (2000), 'Décision dans le risque et l'incertain: l'apport des modèles non-additifs', *Revue d'Economie Politique*, **110**, 631–81.
Dubois, D., and Prade, H. (1985), *Théorie des Possibilités*, Masson: Paris.
Dubois, D., Prade, H. and Sabbadin, R. (2000), 'Qualitative decision theory with Sugeno Integrals', in M. Grabisch, T. Murofushi and M. Sugeno (eds), *Fuzzy Measures and Integrals: Theory and Applications*, Physica-Verlag, pp. 314–22.
Ellsberg, D. (1961), 'Risk, ambiguity, and the Savage axioms', *Quarterly Journal of Economics*, **75**, 643–69.
Epstein, L. and LeBreton, M. (1993), 'Dynamically consistent beliefs must be Bayesian', *Journal of Economic Theory*, **61** (1), 1–22.
Gilboa, I. and Schmeidler, D. (1989), 'Maxmin expected utility with a non-unique prior', *Journal of Mathematical Economics*, **18**, 141–53.
Gul, F. and Pesendorfer, W. (2001), 'Temptation and self control', *Econometrica*, **69**, 1403–35.
Hammond, P. (1988), 'Consequentialist foundations for expected utility', *Theory and Decision*, **25**, 25–78.
Hammond, P. (1989), 'Consistent plans, consequentialism, and expected utility', *Econometrica*, **57** (6), 1445–9.
Hammond, P. (1998a), 'Objective expected utility: a consequentialist perspective', in S. Barbera and C. Seidl (eds), *Handbook of Utility Theory*, Kluwer, Chapter 5.
Hammond, P. (1998b), 'Subjective expected utility', in S. Barbera and C. Seidl (eds), *Handbook of Utility Theory*, Kluwer, Chapter 6.
Karni, E. and Schmeidler, D. (1991), 'Utility theory with uncertainty', in W. Hildenbrand and H. Sonnenschein (eds), *Handbook of Mathematical Economics*, North-Holland, vol. IV, pp. 1763–831.
Keynes, J.M. (1921), *A Treatise on Probability*, London: Macmillan.
Knight, F. (1921), *Risk, Uncertainty and Profit*, Boston, MA: Hart, Schaffner & Marx; Houghton Mifflin Company.
MacClennen, E. (1990), *Rationality and Dynamic Choice: Foundational Explorations*, Cambridge University Press.
Machina, M. (1989), 'Dynamic consistency and non-expected utility models of choice under uncertainty', *Journal of Economic Literature*, **28**, 1622–68.
Savage, L. (1954), *The Foundations of Statistics*, New York: John Wiley.
Schmeidler, D. (1989), 'Subjective probability and expected utility without additivity', *Econometrica*, **57** (3), 571–87.
Shackle, G. (1952), *Expectation in Economics*, Cambridge University Press.
Strotz, R. (1955), 'Myopia and inconsistency in dynamic utility maximization', *Review of Economic Studies*, **23**, 165–80.
Wang, T. (2003), 'Conditional preferences and updating', Discussion Paper, University of British Columbia, *Journal of Economic Theory*, **108**, 286–321.
Zadeh, L. (1978), 'Fuzzy sets as a basis for a theory of possibility', *Fuzzy Sets and Systems*, **1**, 3–28.

8.   Utility or rationality? Restricted or general rationality?

Raymond Boudon

8.1   INTRODUCTION

Two eminent Nobel Prize-winning economists, Herbert Simon and Gary Becker, have made important contributions that extend the explanatory power of the Expected Utility Model (EUM). Simon suggested decision makers will accept decisions they perceive to be satisfying, relegating the search for optimal decisions only to particular situations. Given that information is generally costly, rather than aiming to gather all the information required to make a fully rational decision, decision makers make use of a bounded rationality approach. This idea has deeply influenced the social sciences.

Moreover, Gary Becker showed that actors' preferences can be treated as endogenously generated by earlier behaviour rather than be taken as given. In his *Accounting for Tastes* (1996, Chapter 1, paras 1, 3–4), he claimed that the EUM was an alternative to the causal approach used in the social sciences, and one in which behaviour was explained by psychological, cultural or biological forces. He also contended that this alternative approach had much greater explanatory power than its causal counterpart.

While I agree with this latter point, I will try to show that the EUM and the causal approach do not exhaust all the possible ways of explaining individual behaviour. A third approach puts forward the idea of seeing individual behaviour as basically rational, while at the same time broadening the definition of rationality used by the EUM. This approach has a greater explanatory power than the EUM and will be the focus of my discussion in the text that follows.

At any rate, it should be recognized that Simon's and Becker's works owe their exceptional importance to the fact that they raise a question essential to all the social, and possibly all the human, sciences: the question regarding which principles should be used to explain individual behaviour.

8.2 THE REASONS FOR THE INFLUENCE OF THE EUM

An essential reason for the influence of the EUM was identified by Coleman (1986, p. 1), who stated that the 'rational action of individuals has a unique attractiveness as the basis for social theory'. Hollis (1977) had already expressed the same idea earlier: 'rational action is its own explanation'. In these statements, the notion 'rational action' means 'action aiming at maximum utility'; in other words 'action inspired by the comparison between costs and benefits of alternative means'. The EUM is, in fact, often called the 'Rational action theory' or referred to as the 'Rational Choice Model' (RCM). These quotations reveal one of the main reasons for the scientific appeal of the EUM: as soon as one has been able to explain that actor X has done Y rather than Y' because, given his objectives, the cost–benefit balance of Y was better, the explanation becomes self-sufficient. Even if biologists were able to describe the electrical and chemical phenomena occurring in an agent's brain while he tried to decide whether to choose Y or Y', this would add nothing to the explanation. In other words, the EUM can produce explanations without recourse to black boxes.

This property, i.e. the ability to produce self-sufficient explanations, gives the EUM, as Gary Becker rightly states, an unquestionable superiority over alternative explanations that make behaviour an effect of *biological, cultural* or *psychological* forces. It is also true that sociobiological explanations, such as those put forward by Wilson (1993) or Ruse (1993), which see moral sentiments as the effects of biological evolution, are purely conjectural. Moreover, this type of theory is unable to explain the variation of moral sentiments over time and space (Boudon 1999, 2001). On the side of cognitive psychologists, Kahneman and Tversky (1973) have shown that people can estimate frequencies, probabilities and other data in a biased way. However, they have not explained how such biases arise, and consequently they provide no clear vision of the conditions that make people's estimations biased or unbiased. Their experiments may be fascinating, but no clear prediction can be derived from them as to whether, for example, the estimation of a particular subject's probability estimate will, in given conditions, be biased or not. The cultural forces evoked by some sociologists and anthropologists also provide unsatisfactory explanations.

Let us assume that socialization means that people internalize some values. Given, however, that the mechanisms underlying socialization are to a large extent unknown, it is impossible to predict, for example, whether some value will hold in the mind of a social subject when he moves to another social context, meets a friend who has endorsed other values, etc.

Most people educated in a social context that makes criminal behaviour more likely actually commit no crime.

This is not to say that socialization is an empty notion, only that it is descriptive rather than explanatory. It draws attention to the fact that being raised in a given context makes certain types of behaviour more likely. It does not explain why this is the case, whether the correlation will last over time, or whether some categories of people will not contradict the correlation. Roman soldiers and civil servants, states Max Weber ([1920–21] 1999), were educated in the traditional polytheistic Roman religion. However, they very frequently endorsed monotheistic cults, such as that of Mithra. Socialization clearly fails to explain the phenomenon: though these people were brought up in a particular cult, they later adopted a different one. Given that conversions were sufficiently frequent to explain the implantation of Christianity in the Roman Empire, there must be some underlying causes that can help explain them. The psychological forces summarized by the word 'socialization' are certainly not a good candidate in this respect.

So, Becker is right: biological, psychological or cultural forces provide unsatisfactory explanations of behaviour. However, where do the cognitive biases detected by Kahneman and Tversky come from? Under which conditions do they operate? Many Roman soldiers remained faithful to the old Roman polytheistic religion because they had been socialized in this cult; many others endorsed the monotheistic Mithra cult and later Christianity, although they had been socialized in the same traditional polytheistic religion. Why did this happen? Cultural forces do not explain the difference or the major macroscopic fact that the conversion process of many Roman soldiers and civil servants meant that the Roman Empire was eventually Christianized, so that today in Paris, London and New York we find ourselves in a Christian environment. Concepts such as socialization, *habitus*, social representation, instinct etc. label questions rather than provide a genuine explanation of the phenomena they describe. At least, they provide no self-sufficient explanation. Unlike explanations based on the EUM, they create black boxes. Viruses were also originally black boxes, hypothesized long before they were actually observed. However, they were finally observed, whereas the cultural, biological and psychological forces evoked by Becker seem to be doomed to keep their status of black boxes for ever.

Explanations of behaviour which rely on cultural, biological and psychological forces owe their prominence to the broad and lasting influence of Positivism. A core idea of Positivism – in the broad sense – is that a scientific explanation should eliminate unobservable and in particular subjective factors. This explains the current interest for Davidson's thesis that reasons can be granted the logical status of causes: the idea that subjective reasons can be seen as the cause of behaviour contradicts the positivistic postulate that genuine causes should be 'material'. Many sociologists, anthropologists and psychologists consider it evident that subjective reasons cannot be held as genuine scientific causes of behaviour. This postulate, which was adopted by behaviourism in psychology and by dominant forms of Structuralism and Functionalism in anthropology and sociology, explains to a large extent the great divide between economists and the other social scientists. Its influence explains why the latter often appear unaware of the fact that explaining behaviour by forces is deeply unsatisfactory.

However, the influence of the EUM is not only due to the fact that, by contrast with the explanations which rely on forces, it provides self-sufficient explanations, but also due to its unquestionable scientific achievements. The model has succeeded in providing an explanation for many puzzles, not only in the field of economics, but of other social sciences as well.

Rousseau's political theory provides *ante literam* testimony of the explanatory power of the EUM. In the 'state of nature', where neither moral nor legal pressure is available, cooperation may appear impossible: each actor will be tempted to take insurance against the risk that his partner will fail to keep his promise of cooperation by defecting. Rousseau was right when he observed that cooperation is guaranteed only if moral or legal constraints make defection costly. In other words, he discovered the suboptimal outcome of what game theorists call *the insurance game*. This classical game theoretical structure constitutes the logical core of Rousseau's *Social Contract*. As game theory rests upon EUM axioms, this example shows that a great work in political theory instinctively made use of the EUM.

The EUM was successfully applied to political theory in many works that appeared mainly in the US during the 1950s and 1960s. The names of Downs, Buchanan, Tullock and Olson can be mentioned here as prominent examples. The achievements of the EUM outside the field of economics, in political theory, may have led social scientists such as Becker or Coleman to think that it provides a general theoretical framework for all the social sciences.

The EUM was also successfully applied in history. Tocqueville intuitively discovered its importance, as shown by Boudon ([1979] 2001). Root (1994) follows in his footsteps. He wonders, for instance, why, during the whole eighteenth century, politics served the interests of the producers of cereals in Britain and of the consumers in France. Root suggests that this macroscopic and lasting difference between France and Britain was a consequence of what Tocqueville had called the 'centralisation administrative' (*centralized administration*) which was characteristic of France. French consumers understood that they could easily protest publicly against a rise in the price of bread, because the price was fixed by the bureaucratic government of an absolute monarchy. It was, therefore, worthwhile to protest loudly under the windows of the officials responsible for the price of bread. British consumers, by contrast, understood that it would have been useless to organize a public protest under the windows of Westminster, since members of parliament were elected mainly by corn producers living far from London. Similarly to Tocqueville, Root explains a number of macroscopic differences between Britain and France using the postulates of the EUM.

Among sociologists, Marx, Sombart, Simmel, Max Weber, Tarde and even Durkheim have proposed numerous analyses which *implicitly* make use of the EUM (Boudon 1998–2000, 2003a); I say *implicitly*, since the EUM was given a name well after their time. Of the modern sociologists, Oberschall (1973, 1994), Kuran (1995) and Hardin (1995), among others, illustrate the importance of the EUM in the analysis of sociological phenomena. On the whole, the EUM has been used successfully in the analysis of many puzzling phenomena in various different fields: crime, public opinion, social movements, politics, and organization.

However, while the EUM has explained many phenomena successfully, it is easy to list a number of other phenomena which it appears unable to explain.

8.3 THE SHORTCOMINGS OF THE UTILITARIAN VERSION OF RATIONALITY

The 'paradox of voting' has been given this name because, despite the EUM's prediction that people should not vote, they actually do. The effect of any single vote on any electoral outcome is so small, the EUM claims, that rational actors should refrain from voting: the costs of voting will always be higher than the benefits. As one of these voters, I should prefer resting, walking, writing an article, even using my vacuum cleaner to voting. Still, I vote. The paradox has been 'solved' in many different ways: people like to vote, says a first theory. Like Pascal's Christians, a second theory has it, the infinitesimal chance of a vote making a difference is sufficient to motivate voters (Ferejohn and Fiorina 1974). More recently, a solution was put forward which turned the problem into a reputation issue: people vote in order to avoid a loss of good repute (Overbye 1995). This 'solution' to the paradox implies, however, that people are generally convinced that one should vote, and therefore implies that people are irrational in the EUM sense. So, this 'solution' to the paradox fails to save the EUM. Other solutions have also been, or could easily be, imagined.

Sometimes, the EUM is made more flexible through the use of the notion of 'cognitive frames' (Quattrone and Tversky 1987). Applied to the present case, the notion would, for instance, suggest that some particular 'frame' would lead people to overestimate the influence of their ballot. Though such 'frames' are often present, they are not only *ad hoc*, but typically are black boxes as well.

At any rate, none of these 'solutions' has been universally accepted. Though some, as in the case of Ferejohn and Fiorina, display a high intellectual virtuosity, they have failed to solve the 'paradox of voting'.

Besides voting, there are other classical 'paradoxes'. The Allais 'paradoxes' show that, when people are called upon to play certain types of lotteries, their choices fail to conform to the predictions of the expected utility maximization model. Some of the experimental lottery situations considered by Allais are variations of the basic observation that, when playing the lottery, people normally prefer the certainty of earning a particular sum X to the mathematical expectation of X plus H (H being some positive quantity), even when they can play as long as they wish (Allais 1953, Allais and Hagen 1979, Hagen 1995). In other words, they prefer less to more. This finding has been confirmed by experimental psychology. If we want to stick to the RCM, we have to introduce the idea that economic subjects are risk averse. This kind of assumption, however, introduces a typical black box, so that the main benefit of the EUM, the avoidance of black boxes, is lost.

Psychologists have produced many other observations challenging the EUM. In a classical experiment, subjects are asked to play a game called the 'ultimatum game' (Wilson 1993, pp. 62–3, Hoffman and Spitzer 1985). At the beginning of the game, the experimenter asks subject A to suggest a way of sharing €100 between himself and another subject, B. B can either accept or reject A's proposal. If the proposal is rejected the experimenter keeps the cards; if it is accepted, B gets the sum allocated to him by A. The EUM, according to which people are exclusively concerned with maximizing the difference between benefits and costs, would predict that A would make proposals of the type '€99 for me (A), €1 for him (B)', since B would not refuse the proposal and A would maximize his gains. A more sophisticated version of the EUM would predict proposals of the type '€70 for me (A), €30 for him (B)'. In fact, the most frequent proposal is equal sharing. This outcome contradicts the utilitarian axioms of the EUM.

Sociology has also produced many observations that can be read as challenges to the EUM model. The negative reaction of social subjects to some given state of affairs is often unrelated to the costs they are exposed to by the state itself. On the other hand, actions that bring no benefit or are even detrimental to the actor are often observed. Famously, Kleist's Michael

Kolhaas accepted a settlement that bore no relation to the damages he had suffered. There are many Michael Kolhaases among us.

Mills (1956) in his *White Collar* identified what could be called the 'over-reaction paradox'. He described women clerks working in a large room, at identical desks, carrying out the same tasks. In this context, violent conflicts frequently occurred on issues any observer would normally consider as 'minor', such as sitting closer to a source of heat or light. An external observer would normally think of such conflicts as irrational, implicitly using the EUM to reach this conclusion. Why, the argument would go, should such a minor issue cause such a violent reaction? The most likely interpretation, such as childish behaviour, would rely on a concept of irrationality. An explanation of this kind however is equivalent to stating that the EUM cannot easily explain the 'overreaction paradox' observed by Mills.

Many other observations could lead us to the conclusion that neither irrationality nor the EUM provides a satisfactory explanation of the issues at hand. People queuing at an airport, waiting to show their passport to the immigration officer, can easily be exasperated by a person jumping the queue. Though the cost of queue jumping is negligible to the other passengers, their exasperation can be significant and is usually shared by all those present. We generally find that the longer a queue is, the more severe the reaction to anyone jumping it is likely to be, despite the fact that a longer queue implies a smaller cost for each individual passenger. Why is the reaction disproportionate to the cost and why is it contrary to the predictions of the EUM?

When the phenomenon of optical interference was first observed, Fresnel concluded correctly that it was incompatible with the Cartesian representation of light. Economists, psychologists and sociologists have produced a substantial number of observations that are difficult to explain within the EUM framework. It may well be time then to consider the possibility that an alternative theory of rationality is necessary to explain the paradoxes generated by the EUM.

The current situation raises three questions. First, why is the EUM so popular despite the fact that it fails to explain many familiar social phenomena and the findings of psychological and sociological research? I have already sketched out an answer to this question and it is that the model has proved successful in explaining many puzzles without having to make use of black box theories. Secondly, why does the EUM fail so often? Thirdly, is there a model that could save the EUM's scientific ambition of providing black-box-free theories, while at the same time overcoming its major defects?

8.4   THE SOURCES OF WEAKNESS OF THE EUM

Why do I look around me before crossing a street with heavy traffic? The EUM provides an immediate explanation for this trivial observation, namely that the cost–benefit balance of this behaviour is positive. The cost, in this case, is the delay whereas the benefit is that I reach the other side of the street alive. Clearly, the EUM's explanation of my actions is a bit telegraphic. A more complete explanation would include cognitive statements such as 'I believe that, if I cross the street blindly, I run the risk of being hit by a car'. It would also include normative statements, such as 'staying alive is a good thing'. In this case, the statements are trivial, so it is unnecessary to mention them when attempting to explain my actions when crossing the street.

However, in many other cases, the cognitive and normative statements are far from trivial; indeed they become a core part of the explanation. For example, when observing a tribal rite carried out in the belief that it will produce rain, the analysis does not focus on why it is the tribesmen would wish it to rain, but on why it is they believe that their ritual leads to rainfall. In this example, the 'utilitarian' statements of the type 'tribesmen wish to survive', 'tribesmen want rain to fall on their fields' are trivial, while 'cognitive' statements of the type 'this type of ritual helps my crops grow' (or induces rainfall) become the *explanandum*.

The same applies to normative statements. When the explanation of some phenomenon includes statements of the type 'the people observed believe that X is good' (or legitimate, fair, unfair, etc.), the analyst cannot avoid the task of explaining why the observed people believe a particular normative statement if it is not trivial.

The EUM has little to say about beliefs. More precisely, it has almost nothing to say about beliefs regarding the *nature* of a state of the world (positive beliefs). I have already mentioned that EUM theorists rely on the notion of 'frames' when having to deal with beliefs they cannot ignore. Particular beliefs held by actors are attributed to frames the actors have in mind. These are generally *ad hoc*, and are therefore black boxes. It would be a lot more interesting to suggest that such beliefs are the effects of a 'cognitive rationality': when social actors need to understand a particular state of the world, they mobilize alternative theories available to them and try to maximize the credibility of the answer. The process is clearly illustrated when considering scientific theories. The notion of 'cognitive rationality' postulates that the same process is at work in ordinary knowledge, though obviously less clearly and less consciously.

Some sociologists have sought to reduce cognitive rationality to instrumental reality. Thus, Radnitzky (1987) suggests that even the endorsement of a scientific theory could be the result of a cost–benefit analysis, and puts forward an EUM-based explanation of scientific beliefs. A scientist stops believing in a theory, writes Radnitzky, as soon as the objections raised against it make it too costly to defend. It is, indeed, difficult to explain why a ship's hull disappears from the horizon before its mast or why the moon takes the shape of a crescent or why a ship sailing in a particular direction eventually returns to its starting point, if we accept the theory that the earth is flat. However, what is the advantage of replacing the word *difficult* with the word *costly*? Defending the theory is more costly precisely *because* it is more difficult and in order to explain this we move from instrumental to cognitive rationality.

The situation is more complicated with respect to beliefs about how some state of the world *should be* (normative beliefs). In some cases, people believe X to be good because it eliminates undesirable outcomes. Thus, traffic lights are unpleasant but good, because they make driving easier. The EUM can often provide adequate explanations for normative beliefs grounded in consequential reasons, such as the one just outlined.

However, many other normative beliefs cannot be explained in this way. EUM theorists themselves would have no difficulty in recognizing this fact, as the economic tradition has always attributed the choice of means to 'rationality' (in the economic sense) but never the choice of ends. There are also events that give rise to strong reactions which are not dictated by their consequences: the public will always believe that Antigone was right to bury her brother and that Creon acted despicably. Why should this be the case? We can certainly not explain the reaction in terms of consequences, but can see that the public would have strong reasons to approve of Antigone's behaviour and to disapprove of Creon's.

On the whole, the EUM has little to say about opinions in general and public opinion, a major subject in the social sciences, in particular. Though Kuran (1995) used the EUM to explain why people *express* their opinions on given issues, he failed to explain why they *held* these opinions in the first place. It is not enough to argue that the economic theory of rationality is interested in action, not opinion. Many actions become unintelligible if one is unable to understand the beliefs they rest upon. This is particularly the case for political decisions, which are influenced by the potential reaction the public will have to them. No realistic theory of rationality can afford to ignore cases in which beliefs are an ingredient of the decision-making process.

It is, therefore, a major weakness of the EUM that it has little to say about beliefs that are normal and essential ingredients of many social actions. This is perhaps the main reason why the model and its ambition to become a general paradigm of black-box-free explanations remain controversial. In particular, the EUM is incapable of handling any phenomenon that is the outcome of actions involving non-trivial 'positive' beliefs or normative beliefs that cannot be accounted for consequentially.

8.5   THE GENERAL RATIONAL MODEL (GRM)

A further contention of this chapter is that the following two EUM postulates should be abandoned: (1) an actor is always essentially interested in the consequences of a given action with respect to his own well-being (*egoism*) and (2) behaviour should always be explained by the consequences it generates in the mind of the actor (*consequentialism*). If these two postulates are eliminated we are left with the ideas that social phenomena are the outcome of individual actions (*individualism*) and that an action can always be understood in principle (*comprehension*) and with the somewhat narrowed-down idea that actors have reasons to do what they do and that these reasons are the causes of their actions (*rationality*).

Let us call this model the 'General Rational Model' (GRM). Actors here are generally assumed to have strong reasons for doing what they do. They may, at times, be concerned about the consequences of their actions for themselves, at others they may be interested in the social system and on yet other occasions they may have strong reasons for doing something regardless of its consequences to themselves or anyone else. An actor may thus do X because X is the consequence of a theory the actor believes to be true or fair. For example, an actor may endorse a scientific theory because he believes it to be true, not because of the consequences of endorsing it. In many cases the actor may even ignore the possible consequences of the theory.

The GRM is compatible with the classical philosophical definitions of rationality. Rescher's idea that 'rationality is in its very nature teleological and ends-oriented' (Rescher 1995, p. 26) makes it immediately clear that for Rescher 'teleological' does not mean 'instrumental'. In the same passage, he goes on to say that 'cognitive rationality is concerned with achieving true beliefs. Evaluative rationality is concerned with making correct evaluation. Practical rationality is concerned with the effective pursuit of appropriate objectives.'

This definition of rationality is in line with the definition used by classical sociologists. It was Max Weber who introduced the crucial distinction between 'instrumental rationality' and 'axiological rationality'. He argued that though a combination of both forms was to be found in most concrete actions, the two concepts were analytically distinct. In other words, the existence of a non-instrumental form of rationality had to be recognized. In simple terms, this means that I may do X because I judge X to be fair (or fine, legitimate etc.) according to a system of reasons I believe to be convincing, in the same way that I believe 'Y is true' if I find Y to have been derived from what I believe to be a strong system of reasons. In other words, 'instrumental rationality' should be distinguished from the 'non-instrumental' rationality that comes into play when we are called to judge the value of a scientific theory. Let us call this kind of rationality 'cognitive rationality' and, following Weber, speak of 'axiological rationality' when a system of reasons tells me that 'Y is fair, legitimate, etc.'.

Why does an actor consider a system of reasons to be good? Is his evaluation not subjective? If so, is not the very notion of rationality introduced by the GRM fuzzy and undefined? These are common objections to the GRM. For reasons of space I shall only sketch out an answer in this context (for a more detailed account see Boudon 2003b). As Kant pointed out a long time ago, looking for general criteria of truth is like trying to milk a billy goat. There are no general criteria on the basis of which a theory can be considered to be true. More generally, no criteria can guarantee the validity of a system of reasons. However, criteria on the basis of which a theory can be considered to be *better* than another *can* and in many cases *do* exist. Thus, Torricelli–Pascal's theory that was later to give birth to the invention of the barometer is better than the theory of Aristotelian inspiration, not only because it reproduces the behaviour of barometers correctly, but also because it avoids the Aristotelian idea that nature abhors a vacuum and substitutes for it the much more acceptable notion of the weight of the atmosphere.

A theory T1 can be preferred to a theory T2 on the basis of a well-defined set of criteria, though a different set is applied when comparing T3 to T4. Briefly, comparative statements of the type 'T1 is better than T2' can be grounded on unambiguous criteria, while this is not the case for statements of the type 'T1 is true'. The same can be said of other predicates: there are no general criteria on which a system of reason can base statements asserting not only that something is true, but that, say, some action is legitimate or fair, etc. There can, however, be convincing criteria that allow us to decide whether an action is fairer than another, so that we can have clearly grounded comparative evaluative statements. What we cannot have are absolute evaluative statements. More precisely, absolute evaluative statements can only be provisional statements resulting from a set of comparisons. If T1 is better than T2, T3, ..., Tn and if I am unable to imagine an alternative theory, I will provisionally consider T1 as true (or worth some other evaluative predicate).

Let us consider 'axiological rationality' to be a particular case of 'cognitive rationality'. 'Cognitive rationality' refers to the process that leads me to conclude that 'X is true'. 'Axiological rationality' instead refers to the process that leads me to conclude that 'Y is fair', (or legitimate, etc.). The procedures followed are the same in both cases: I believe that 'X is true' or that 'Y is fair' based on a system of reasons which I endorse having compared it with alternative systems of reasons. Clearly, these comparisons are context-dependent in most cases: before Torricelli suggested that the level of mercury in a tube varies according to the weight of the atmosphere, it is understandable that scientists attributed the phenomenon to *horror vacui*. In the absence of an alternative, the Aristotelians had strong reasons to believe in their explanation. However, the reasons became weak once confronted with Torricelli's.

The fact that no general criteria exist that can establish the truth of a scientific theory does not mean that scientists' preferences are arbitrary. No basic distinction is made in the GRM between the processes leading to a belief of the form 'X is true' and those leading to a belief of the form 'Y is good' (or fair, legitimate, etc.) – and this is what makes a system of reasons appear *strong* to the eyes of an actor. I believe that 'Y is good' (or fair, legitimate, etc.) on the basis of strong reasons, exactly as I judge that 'X is true'.

An objection is sometimes raised against the idea of seeing in axiological rationality a special case of cognitive rationality. This is based on Hume's theorem, according to which a prescriptive-normative conclusion cannot be derived from a set of descriptive-factual statements. It should be noted, however, that the exact formulation of the theorem is: a prescriptive conclusion cannot be derived from a set of statements which are *all* descriptive. In other words, a prescriptive conclusion *can* be derived from a combination of prescriptive and descriptive statements. A single prescriptive statement among the premises is sufficient to make a normative conclusion possible. In Weber's parlance, axiological and instrumental reasons are both distinct from one another and always combined with one another in practice. This also means that normative statements can be criticized on the basis of the refutation of descriptive statements. Thus, the belief in the legitimacy of the death penalty was weakened once it was shown that it did not act as a deterrent and the opposition to universal voting was weakened once it became clear that it did not lead to political chaos (Boudon 2001).

8.6   PHENOMENA EXPLAINED BY THE GRM THAT ARE NOT EXPLAINED BY THE EUM

There are many phenomena that can be explained using the GRM that do not fit the EUM framework. Let us take the example of political decisions. A rational decision maker will usually believe that a particular decision is good or otherwise on the basis of a set of reasons. His belief will, therefore, be rational though not in the EUM sense. A decision maker will, for instance, try to impose a certain measure if he believes that its consequences will be perceived to be good. This means he also has an idea of what the public's reaction will be. In other words, both descriptive and normative beliefs and the public's reaction will affect the decision maker's choice. All these actions and reactions can be rational, but they cannot be so in the EUM sense. People do what they do and act and react the way they do on the basis of what they believe are strong reasons. They are therefore rational, but in the GRM rather than the EUM sense.

I will illustrate this point by presenting three examples which can be explained using the GRM, but where the EUM is of little help. The EUM can only explain public opinion in the case of political decisions that have a direct impact on the personal interests of the majority of the people. However, many political decisions that have no direct bearing on the interests of the majority will raise reactions from people who may have strong reasons to approve or reject a particular decision. In such cases, the postulates of the EUM, according to which people are essentially interested in the consequences (*consequentialism*) particular actions and/or reactions will have on them (*egoism*), would appear to be inadequate. By contrast, the more limited set of postulates (*individualism, comprehension* and *rationality* in the cognitive sense) offer a more adequate framework.

Let us concentrate on explaining public reaction to political decisions. The following examples are a good illustration of the strengths of the GRM as an analytical tool. They also provide a concrete illustration of the variety of cases that can arise when attempting to explain public reaction to a political decision. According to the case at hand, public reaction can be motivated by consequential reasons but also by universal or contextual reasons.

Example 1: Public Reaction Grounded on Consequential and Contextual Reasons

The first example is drawn from a study made by Inglehart (1998). People in different countries were asked whether they would approve of two measures aiming at the reduction of unemployment: (1) lowering the age of retirement, and (2) closing the borders to immigrants. Affirmative answers to the first question varied widely across countries (Table 8.1). Whereas the EUM would have little to say by way of an explanation, the GRM would be able to provide a reason. According to the GRM people answering positively would have strong reasons to believe that the measure would be efficient. Moreover, the variation would be explained by stating that the proportion of those holding the belief varied with context. In some contexts the reasons would seem strong while in others they would appear weak, exactly as in some contexts the *horror vacui naturae* seemed an acceptable explanation of the 'barometer effect', while in others it did not. The GRM, therefore, provides a clue as to the explanation underlying the complex variations of answers given in different contexts.

Table 8.1   Forced retirement

'When jobs are scarce, people should be forced to retire early' (percentage of those who agree)

Spain	62
(West) Germany	50
France	49
England	43
USA	16
Sweden	9

Source: Inglehart et al. 1998.

The findings of Inglehart's study (Inglehart et al. 1998) suggest that the proportion of positive answers to the first question varies from country to country. A positive answer supposes that the respondent has a *theory* (a system of reasons) in mind, which states that as the number of jobs is constant, excluding people beyond a given age will increase the number of available jobs. Clearly, the positive answer rests upon a simplistic understanding of what is in fact a more complex economic phenomenon. For example, when a senior worker is forced to retire, an employer may decide to increase productivity and not replace him; if the job is highly specialized, it is also possible that the market may not offer suitable replacements. In other words, in this case, a negative answer may reveal a greater awareness of the complexity of economic phenomena than an affirmative one.

Does this mean that the public is better trained to analyse economic phenomena in some countries than in others? This seems quite plausible. If these percentages were simply a reflection of the extent to which 'neo-liberal culture' has permeated these different countries, it would be incomprehensible that Sweden, a country with a particularly long-standing and influential social-democratic tradition, should have a lower score than the USA.

However, the main argument confirming the interpretation that international variation in the answers is essentially due to the fact that in some national contexts people are less likely to see the frailty of the 'finite cake' assumption than in others is that when the proportion of yes/no answers is correlated with other variables (age, sympathy for left- or right-wing political parties, materialist/post-materialist values, socio-economic status, gender, etc.) within any given country, the only variable that appears to be strongly correlated with the proportion of yes/no answers is the level of education. In all countries, the correlation with political and ideological affiliation, with values, gender, socio-economic status, etc. is weak. Age is also correlated with the proportion of yes/no answers to the question, but more weakly than the level of education. Moreover, some of the correlation between age and the proportion of yes/no answers reflects the effect of the level of education, since, for all countries, the younger the age the greater the frequency of those with a higher level of education. The reaction of the public to the proposal is thus satisfactorily explained using the principles of the GRM: it is due to the fact that the evaluation of the proposed measure is based on a system of reasons people have in mind. Depending on the level of education, a more or less sophisticated system of reasons is likely to appear. This explains the main features of the statistical distributions.

If the 'job cake' is finite, another way of reducing unemployment, one could think, would be to reduce the number of job candidates by excluding immigrants. In this case, we have a combination of two oversimplified prerequisites: the finite nature of the job cake and the infinite interchangeability of job candidates (see Table 8.2).

Table 8.2   Job preference to one's own nationality

'When jobs are scarce, employers should give priority to their own nationality over immigrants' (percentage of those who agree)

Spain	75
(West) Germany	62
France	63
England	51
USA	51
Sweden	35

Source: Inglehart et al. 1998.

Though country rankings are similar for both questions, the percentages are all higher in this second table. A plausible explanation is that the reactions of the respondents were dictated by a system of reasons that led them to judge the proposed measure not only in terms of its efficiency but also normatively. It is easier to close the barriers to immigration than to change the age of retirement. Indeed, whereas the latter, under normal circumstances, involves a breach of contract entailing social, economic and ethical costs, the former simply implies the refusal to allow entry into a contractual relationship. Normatively speaking, a breach of contract is less acceptable than the alternative (Kahneman et al. 1986).

Overall, we have seen that the GRM helps explain not only the main properties of the statistical distributions of the two tables but also the variety of reactions to the two proposed measures.

Example 2: Public Reaction Grounded on Non-consequential Reasons

My second example is drawn from Adam Smith. While it is recognized that Smith's *Theory of Moral Sentiments* does not rest on the EUM, it is sometimes believed that his better-known work, the *Wealth of Nations*, does. The following example shows, however, that this is not the case. Despite the book's tremendous influence on economic theory, Smith does not use the EUM, but relies instead on the GRM when dealing with issues involving reactions steeped in beliefs. Smith sees very clearly that certain beliefs cannot be explained in purely consequential or egoistic terms.

Why, asks Smith, do we (i.e. eighteenth-century Scotsmen) consider it normal that soldiers be paid less than miners? The methodology Smith uses to answer the question could be applied to many similar questions of our time: why do we think it fair that a particular occupation be better remunerated than another (Smith [1776] 1976, Book 1, Chapter 10)? Why do people consider, say, pay strikes by pilots working for commercial airlines to be illegitimate? (Boudon 1999). Such normative beliefs do not appear to rest on consequential reasons: I would be neither better nor worse off if pilots were paid less or more than they currently are; the nation itself would be neither better nor worse off if many income differentials were to change. Still, we believe some differentials to be fair whereas we think of others as unfair.

Smith sets out the following argument to explain why we feel miners ought to be paid more than soldiers:

1. A salary is the retribution for a contribution.
2. Equal retributions should correspond to equal contributions.
3. Several components enter into the value of a contribution: the investment required to produce a given type of competence, the risks involved in the realization of the contribution, etc.
4. The investment time is comparable in the case of the miner and of the soldier. It takes about as much time and effort to make a soldier as it does to make a miner. The two jobs are characterized by similar risks, as both include a high risk of death.

5. Nonetheless, there are important differences between the two types of jobs.
6. A soldier serves a central function in society. He preserves the identity and the very existence of the nation. The miner merely fulfils an economic activity among many others. He is not more central to the society than, say, the textile worker.
7. Consequently, the deaths of the two men have different social meanings. The death of the miner will be identified as an accident, the death of the soldier on the battlefield as a sacrifice.
8. Because of this difference in the social meaning of their respective activities, if the soldier dies on the battlefield, he will be entitled to symbolic rewards, prestige, distinctions and even funeral honours.
9. The miner is not entitled to the same symbolic rewards.
10. As the contribution of the two categories in terms of risk and investment is the same, the equilibrium between contribution and retribution can only be restored by making the salary of miners higher.
11. This reasoning is responsible for our *feeling* that the miner should be paid a higher wage than the soldier.

First of all, Smith's analysis (which I have rendered more explicit than it actually is in the book) does not rely on the EUM. People do not believe what they believe because this would maximize some cost–benefit difference. They have strong reasons for believing what they believe and these reasons are not of the cost–benefit type. In fact, they do not simply fail the *utilitarian* criterion, they also fail the *consequential* one. The argument never evokes the consequences of miners being paid less than soldiers. Instead, Smith's argument reads like a deduction from principles: people feel that it is fair to pay higher salaries to miners on the basis of strong reasons derived from strong principles. Smith never states that these reasons are consciously known to all, but assumes that they are intuitively responsible for the beliefs people hold.

It is possible that Weber was thinking of precisely this kind of case when he introduced his famous and often misunderstood distinction between instrumental and axiological rationality (my translation of *Zweck* and *Wertrationalität*).

A contemporary theorist of ethics has also put forward an analysis of some of our moral sentiments that is similar to Smith's (Walzer 1983). Why do we consider conscription to be a legitimate recruitment method in the case of soldiers but not of miners? he asks. Once again, the answer lies in the centrality of the function of soldiers. If conscription were to be applied to miners, it could be applied to any, and eventually to all, kinds of activities. This would lead to a regime that is incompatible with the principles of democracy. Similarly, it is generally acceptable for soldiers to be used as dustmen in emergencies, whereas this is not the case under normal circumstances. In all these examples, just as in Smith's example, the collective moral feelings are grounded on solid reasons, though not EUM reasons.

Example 3: Public Reaction Grounded on a Combination of Consequential, Non-consequential, Contextual and Non-contextual Reasons

People will often tend to follow the opinions of some concrete or notional 'community' to which they believe they belong out of interest and not simply due to a need to conform. For instance, opinion polls indicate that socialist sympathizers were shocked by the way the highly controversial trial that followed the contaminated blood scandal was conducted in France in early 1999. The trial saw three socialist ministers in the dock.

Like any other ordinary citizen, socialist sympathizers were probably disturbed by a number of facts: the ministers were judged by a special court; this is a court (*Cour de Justice de la République*) that tries government officials for crimes committed while in office; it follows special rules and includes members of parliament as well as professional judges; its debates are not adversarial; private claimants are not heard by the court, etc. As a result, although the trial may not have violated the letter of the law, it certainly violated the basic principles of law, justice and morality. At the same time, according to the polls, socialist sympathizers were also more indulgent towards the ministers than right-wing voters, because of 'communitarian' considerations. When the poll was conducted, the prosecutor had already suggested that he considered the ministers to be not guilty and that he was going to call for their acquittal. Sympathizers were thus led to soften their stance towards the trial: despite being unpalatable, the court had taken a good decision in their eyes by finding the ministers to which they were sympathetic not guilty. Conversely, the severity of right-wing sympathizers was also partially prompted by considerations of their own 'community'. Supporters of the extreme-right despised socialist governments and, as such, had general objections against the court. In particular they believed it would be lenient towards personalities they disliked.

On the whole, the findings of the BVA poll on the contaminated blood trial are much easier to understand if we assume that the reactions of those questioned followed the principles set out in the GRM. In practice, the results show a general rejection of the special court in the name of universal values and specific differences attributable to adherence to different community values (see Table 8.3). 'Community' considerations meant the prospect of an acquittal made socialist sympathizers less vehement in their criticism of the court. Conversely National Front (FN) sympathizers were particularly severe in their criticisms for exactly the same reasons. Whereas the criminal responsibility of government members is widely acknowledged, greater hesitation is found when the incriminated ministers belong to the same political 'community' as the person questioned.

Table 8.3   Confidence in the special Court of Justice of the Republic

'Are you confident that the Court of Justice of the Republic, composed of elected officials and senior magistrates, will judge the three former ministers, L. Fabius, G. Dufoix and E. Hervé equitably? (A) confident or relatively confident, (B) not confident or relatively not confident'

	Total (%)	PC	PS	Ecologists	UDF-DL	RPR	FN	None
				Sympathizers				
A	38	45	53	37	34	37	12	30
B	57	55	44	63	63	62	88	58
Don't know	5	–	3	–	3	1	–	12

Source: BVA poll, 18 February 1999.

Note how the differences virtually disappear when the question does not specify that legal responsibility of ministers will be determined by a special court. Community considerations do not affect the reactions of the respondents when asked whether ministers should be treated as ordinary citizens and judged by ordinary courts in cases of misbehaviour (see Table 8.4).

Table 8.4   Opinions on the criminal responsibility of ministers

'In your opinion, is the fact that a minister may be brought to court for decisions made in the course of his or her duties (A) a relatively good thing, since political leaders are not above the law, (B) a relatively bad thing, since it may make being a minister an almost impossible job?'

	Total (%)	PC	PS	Ecologists	UDF-DL	RPR	FN	None
				Sympathizers				
A	85	78	81	91	90	88	85	84
B	11	22	15	9	7	10	12	9
Don't know	4	–	4	–	3	2	3	7

Source: BVA poll, 18 February 1999.

On the whole, the GRM provides a satisfactory explanation of the structure of Tables 8.3 and 8.4 and their complex two-level interaction effects (in the statistical sense): all answers are grounded in a set of reasons. The non-contextual and non-consequential reasons lead to the conclusion that the court should not contradict basic principles of law, justice and morality. The contextual and consequential reasons explain why socialist sympathizers are happy to know that ministers belonging to their 'community' in the broad sense are going to be considered not guilty, while extreme-right FN sympathizers are unhappy for exactly the same reasons and sympathizers of the moderate parties give more weight to the non-consequential reasons.

8.7   THE PARADOXES EXPLAINED

In the concluding part of this chapter I want to return to the paradoxes I mentioned earlier. The examples are paradoxical in the sense that they cannot be dealt with within the EUM framework while they can be easily treated in a GRM context.

The Wright Mills Paradox

The women Mills describes all carry out the same tasks in similar work conditions. As such, they spot any departure from the contribution–retribution equality immediately and also find it intolerable. In this context, white-collar workers are all equal in the sense that they are all set the same tasks. Any minor advantage comes to be perceived as an illegitimate privilege. From a strictly utilitarian viewpoint, it matters little whether I sit close to the window or not. However, as soon as this advantage benefits another party and results from a supervisor's decision, I will immediately perceive it not as unpleasant but as unfair. If I am here to get some retribution from my contribution and have a social contract with the firm, any unjustified advantage in favour of another worker, however minor, becomes a violation of this basic contract and consequently morally intolerable, even if fairly irrelevant materially. Any irrational analysis fails to account for the apparent disproportion between cause and effect and EUM analysis fares no better. Irrational analysis does not account for the fact that the conflict occurs independently of personal idiosyncrasies. EUM analysis fails to account for the disproportion between the importance of the issue and the strength of the reaction.

The Voting Paradox

Given that I have already discussed the various solutions to the 'voting paradox' elsewhere (Boudon 2001, 2003a), I will not engage in a detailed discussion of the critical side of the analysis here. The analysis leads to the conclusion that the various 'solutions' to the paradox are all based on strong assumptions and fail to reproduce observations correctly. As a result, they can be considered weak on Popperian and non-Popperian grounds alike. By contrast, a theory that takes axiological rationality along the GRM lines seriously meets both set of criteria easily. People vote because they have strong reasons to believe that democracy is a good regime. Elections are an essential part of the democratic system. So, they conclude that one *should* vote on the basis of a practical syllogism with strong premises: even if voting is boring, I should still vote. Of course, in some cases, people may be unable to choose between candidates or be convinced of their inadequacy, thus refraining from voting. On the whole, however, many people vote. The GRM is able to explain why people vote and also why they vote more or less depending on the issues at stake.

Despite its simplicity (why should simple explanations be wrong?), this explanation appears to be a lot more acceptable than others according to the criteria generally used to evaluate scientific theories. It is consistent with the fact that people vote. It is also consistent with the subjective explanation people usually give of their voting behaviour. In most cases people feel and say that they vote because one should vote, not because they like to vote or because they feel constrained to, as strict Durkheimian sociologists would maintain. Why should we ignore these subjective facts? Despite being subjective, they are still facts to all but hard-core positivists. It is a basic rule that a scientific theory should try to explain all relevant facts without arbitrarily omitting any of them. If a theory claims that people *like* to vote or *feel constrained* to vote, it should explain why people feel that they *should* vote. In other words, it should explain the causes of this *false consciousness*. Should false consciousness be taken for granted, then the theorist should explain why he himself has not been subjected to the same fate.

The Ultimatum Game

The subject in the ultimatum game acts against his interest because he is applying a theory. He does not propose to share the sum equally because he is attempting to ensure a prosperous future for himself in a one-shot game. Instead, he acts on the theory that one should not profit from unexpected good fortune at another's expense. He thus acts against his interest and applies an axiological theory that derives from the principle of respecting others. Numerous social psychology studies have confirmed this axiological-reasoning interpretation (Kahneman and Tversky 1973).

The person who is in no way hurt by corruption is, nevertheless, profoundly irritated by it. In fact, the fight against corruption is one of the main criteria used to judge those governing him. By definition, his reasons are neither self-interested nor end-oriented. They derive from the theory that an advantage is not justified if it is not obtained in return for a contribution. He finds corruption unbearable not because he is in danger of suffering from its consequences, but because it contradicts principles he considers important. Likewise, the voter votes as soon as she judges herself capable of expressing a preference because she believes in democracy and thinks it normal to participate in the functioning of its institutions.

Frey's Paradox

People will often consent to undesirable situations (such as the acceptance of radioactive waste in the vicinity of their homes) more easily when they are not compensated for their efforts. The paradox has no solution in the EUM framework, though it is solved by the GRM: if no compensation is proposed, I will consider the proposal as an opportunity to pay a service to the national community and might accept; if compensation is proposed, I will simply consider it a bad bargain and will in all likelihood reject it. The theorization of the situation created by the proposal shifts from a system of reasons T1 to a system T2 as soon as compensation is proposed. Frey's paradox (Frey 1997) is particularly important: it shows that *egoism* is a variable, not a constant. This is one of the reasons why the EUM cannot be generalized. Generally speaking, the difference between the EUM and the GRM is that the latter treats the properties of rationality as variable, whereas the former treats them as constant.

Unlike Becker, I do not believe the social sciences have no option but to choose between the EUM and causal models explaining behaviour with the help of conjectural cultural, biological or psychological forces.

REFERENCES

Allais, M. (1953), 'Le comportement de l'homme rationnel devant le risque: critique des postulats et axiomes de l'école américaine', *Econometrica*, **21** (4), 503–46.
Allais, M. and Hagen, O. (eds) (1979), *Expected Utility Hypotheses and the Allais Paradox: Contemporary Discussions of Decisions under Uncertainty with Allais' Rejoinder*, Dordrecht: Reidel.
Becker, G. (1996), *Accounting for Tastes*, Cambridge: Harvard University Press.

Boudon, R. ([1979] 2001), *La Logique du Social*, Paris: Hachette, 'Pluriel', in English, (1981), *The Logic of Social Action*, London and Boston: Routledge & Kegan Paul.

Boudon, R. (1998–2000), *Études sur les Sociologues Classiques*, I et II, Paris: PUF.

Boudon, R. (1999), 'Explaining the feelings of justice' (with Emmanuelle Betton), *Ethical Theory and Moral Practice. An International Forum*, **2** (4): 365–98. Also in R. Boudon and M. Cherkaoui (eds) (2000), *Central Currents in Social Theory*, London: Russell Sage Foundation, **6**, 453–84.

Boudon, R. (2001), *The Origin of Values*, New Brunswick (USA), London: Transaction.

Boudon, R. (2003a), 'Beyond rational choice theory', *Annual Review of Sociology*, **29**.

Boudon, R. (2003b), *Raison, Bonnes Raisons*, Paris: PUF.

Coleman, J. (1986), *Individual Interests and Collective Action: Selected Essays*, Cambridge: Cambridge University Press.

Ferejohn, F.J. and Fiorina, M. (1974), 'The paradox of not voting: a decision theoretic analysis', *The American Political Science Review*, **68** (2), 525–36.

Frey, B.S. (1997), *Not Just for the Money: An Economic Theory of Personal Motivation*, Cheltenham: Edward Elgar.

Hagen, O. (1995), 'Risk in utility theory, in business and in the world of fear and hope', in J. Götschl (ed.), *Revolutionary Changes in Understanding Man and Society, Scopes and Limits*, Dordrecht/ London: Kluwer, pp. 191–210.

Hardin, R. (1995), *One for All: The Logic of Group Conflict*, Princeton: Princeton University Press.

Hoffman, E. and Spitzer, M.L. (1985), 'Entitlements, rights and fairness: an experimental examination of subjects' concepts of distributive justice', *Journal of Legal Studies*, **14**, 259–97.

Hollis, M. (1977), *Models of Man: Philosophical Thoughts on Social Action*, Cambridge: Cambridge University Press.

Inglehart, R., Basañez, M. and Moreno, A. (1998), *Human Values and Beliefs: A Cross-Cultural Sourcebook: Political, Religious, Sexual, and Economic Norms in 43 Societies: Findings from the 1990–1993 World Values Survey*, Ann Arbor: The University of Michigan Press.

Kahneman, D. and Tversky, A. (1973), 'Availability: a heuristic for judging frequency and probability', *Cognitive Psychology*, **5**, 207–32.

Kahneman, D., Knetsch, J.L. and Thaler, R. (1986), 'Fairness as a constraint on profit seeking', *The American Economic Review*, **76** (4) September, 728–41.

Kuran, T. (1995), *Private Truths, Public Lies. The Social Consequences of Preference Falsification*, Cambridge: Harvard University Press.

Mills, C.W. (1956), *White Collar: The American Middle Classes*, New York: Oxford University Press.

Oberschall, A. (1973), *Social Conflict and Social Movements*, Englewood Cliffs: Prentice-Hall.

Oberschall, A. (1994), 'Règles, normes, morales: émergence et sanction', *L'Année Sociologique, 44: Argumentation et Sciences Sociales*, 357–84.

Overbye, E. (1995), 'Making a case for the rational, self-regarding, "ethical" voter ... and solving the "paradox of not voting" in the process', *European Journal of Political Research*, **27**, 369–96.

Quattrone, G.A. and Tversky, A. (1987), Self-deception and the voter's illusion', in J. Elster (ed.), *The Multiple Self*, Cambridge: Cambridge University Press, pp. 35–58.

Radnitzky, G. (1987), 'La perspective économique sur le progrès scientifique: application en philosophie de la science de l'analyse coût-bénéfice', *Archives de Philosophie*, **50**, Avril–Juin: 177–98.

Rescher, N. (1995), *Satisfying Reason. Studies in the Theory of Knowledge*, Dordrecht: Kluwer.

Root, H.L. (1994), *The Fountain of Privilege: Political Foundations of Economic Markets in Old Regime France and England*, Berkeley: University of California Press.

Ruse, M. (1993), 'Une défense de l'éthique évolutionniste', in J.P. Changeux (ed.), *Fondements naturels de l'éthique*, Paris: Odile Jacob, pp. 35–64.

Smith, A. ([1776] 1976), *An Inquiry into the Nature and Causes of the Wealth of Nations*, Oxford: Clarendon Press.

Walzer, M. (1983), *Spheres of Justice. A Defence of Pluralism and Equality*, Oxford: Martin Robertson.

Weber, M. ([1920–21] 1999), *Gesammelte Aufsätze zur Religionssoziologie*, Tübingen: Mohr.

Wilson, J.Q. (1993), *The Moral Sense*, New York: The Free Press.

PART IV

Knowledge, Beliefs and Cognitive Economics

9. The cognitive turning point in economics: social beliefs and conventions

André Orléan

9.1 INTRODUCTION

The concept of belief is not commonly used in economics. The reason is simple: by definition, *homo œconomicus* does not believe in anything. He is a fundamentally opportunistic being, always acting in pursuit of his own interests. In all circumstances, his conduct conforms strictly to the dictates of rationality. In this kind of framework, beliefs are considered in an essentially negative way, i.e. as an obstacle to the free reign of rational opportunism, which can lead an individual to take ill-considered decisions. This conception, which defines *homo œconomicus* by abstracting him from all particular beliefs, away from the norms and conventions that structure social life, has played and continues to play a fundamental role in the establishment of economics as an autonomous science, standing separate from all the other social sciences. It has allowed the creation of what has been called a 'pure economics', devoted entirely to the principle of rationality. Here, the 'disembeddedness of economics', a concept used by sociologists and anthropologists to refer to the increasing autonomy of economic relations from any type of social logic, finds its most complete formal expression. Free from the burden of beliefs, economic individuals act without the restraints of community bonds and moral traditions, recognizing only the authority of instrumental rationality. It is only when we consider the importance of individual or collective representations in other social sciences that we can really appreciate the extreme singularity of economics.

We propose the word 'fundamentalist' to characterize this paradigmatic conception which orients, nourishes and structures most of contemporary research in economics. In this approach, because the economy is considered as an efficient and opportunist adaptation to objective constraints of scarcity, as determined *ex ante* by the fundamental variables (i.e.

individual preferences, techniques of production and available resources), individual cognition is reduced to simple rational calculation. It follows that this paradigm leaves no space for beliefs or representations, apart from those required for the pursuit of rational calculation itself. In such a framework, economic evolution can ultimately be explained purely in terms of the fundamental variables. This is the central thesis that defines the fundamentalist paradigm in economics. The Arrow–Debreu general equilibrium model presents us with the most refined expression of this approach, in that it provides a complete analysis of market economies without ever referring to beliefs. We can imagine the astonishment and fascination produced by such a result, which also partly explains its status as a reference model. This brings to mind Laplace's famous reply when Napoleon asked him about the role of God in his system: 'Sire, I had no need for that hypothesis.'

This chapter makes the case for a paradigmatic revolution, that economics must break away from this fundamentalist conception by integrating individual and collective representations into its analytic framework. To put it differently, we argue that economics must take into account what we call a 'cognitive turning point'. The thesis underlying our case is that economic reality cannot be understood in terms of fundamentals alone, for it also depends on beliefs. We should point out that this thesis, in itself, is not particularly original. If we consider the literature of the last couple of decades in the field of economics, we find it present in a number of works, including some which in other respects are deemed to be perfectly 'orthodox'. For example, we can mention 'signalling equilibria' (Spence 1973), 'rational bubbles' (Blanchard and Watson 1982), 'sunspot equilibria' (Azariadis 1981), 'bank runs' (Diamond and Dybvig 1984) and other 'self-fulfilling prophecies' (Farmer 1999). All this research makes the role played by the beliefs of agents in the determination of economic variables clear at the outset. Despite this, it appears that economic theory has not taken this result fully into account. For example, we find no empirical studies attempting to account for these representations, to specify their nature and their evolution. Similarly, no original theoretical elaboration has explored the manner in which this calls traditional conceptions of value into question. Everything continues as if, in the absence of an adequate analytical framework, this reality remained invisible, relegated to the margins of theory, like a curiosity of no great significance or a pure mathematical artefact of no real content. Because economists continue to rely on a fundamentalist epistemology, they are incapable of seeing what their own results show. This paradoxical situation appears to us to be damaging. Economic theory has everything to gain from this conceptual expansion.

In order to convince the reader, we will proceed in two steps. In the first section, we will consider expectations. Once we situate ourselves within the framework of monetary or sequential economies, expectations are imposed on us as an essential given. For example, in a sequential context, an individual trying to maximize his utility must consider at the outset what future prices will be. His demand for goods at time *t* depends on his expectations on the prices that will prevail in the periods to come. In what sense does taking into account this particular type of belief (i.e. expectations) lead to a questioning of the fundamentalist paradigm? For the majority of economists, expectations are revisable conjectures that have no other purpose than that of allowing optimal adaptation to circumstances. In other words, they are a simple means of calculation, a pure instrument that *in fine* must allow the individual to obtain maximum utility. Even when expectations are required to conform to reality (as they often are), the objective of truth is never perceived as an autonomous objective requiring the mobilization of specific resources, but always as a means at the service of individual interests. With regard to this first conception, we must consider expectations as a form of belief which is entirely subject to the jurisdiction of instrumental rationality and as such does not contradict fundamentalist analysis in any way. It is precisely in this way that we should interpret the concept of 'rational expectations' put forward by economists following Muth's article (1961). This notion is the basis of a theory of individual cognition limited strictly to the criteria of instrumental rationality.

Is such a project possible? Are the fundamental constraints sufficiently unambiguous to determine individual expectations in a universe of perfectly rational actors? The fundamentalist position, which has found its most perfect and rigorous formalization in the modern concept of rational expectations, has been criticized time and again by many economists, and by quite important ones at that, well before Muth's work was published. In particular we can think of Keynes, who insisted extensively, in both the *General Theory* and in the 1937 *Quarterly Journal of Economics* article, on the fact that rational calculation is inadequate in situations of uncertainty. He considered this statement to be the cardinal thesis that distinguished his approach from that of his contemporaries: given that probability is powerless when we consider the distant future, as required by any reflection on the accumulation of wealth, the 'methods of classical economics' are no longer applicable (Keynes 1937, p. 213). This critical position towards the possibility of constructing a pertinent analysis of expectations on the sole basis of instrumental rationality is shared by a number of theorists and is not only limited to Keynes. This position lies at the heart of the 'cognitive turning point' in that it considers the predictive activity of economic actors to be a specific kind of activity that cannot be reduced to instrumental rationality, an activity requiring a different set of principles in order to be conceptualized. Although many authors share this critical conception, they differ as to the precise definition of these alternative principles. We shall use the generic term 'cognitive rationality' to describe the set of principles whose objective is to study individual expectations.[1] The assertion that there exists a cognitive rationality, quite distinct from instrumental rationality, is the very foundation of the 'cognitive turning point' in economics.

In our first section, we adopt the same critical view, highlighting the incompleteness of instrumental rationality. However, the reasoning by which we arrive at this position is quite different from that proposed by Keynes. Our point of departure is not a reflection on individual choice in situations of uncertainty where probability cannot be calculated, but the notion of rational expectation. We highlight a point that we believe to have been neglected – the fact that models that make use of rational expectations tend to present multiple equilibria. In other words, these models show that there are a great number of expectations and representations that, when shared by the mass of agents involved in the process of exchange, are self-fulfilling. If one takes this result seriously, it is tantamount to admitting that the criterion put forward by instrumental rationality, in practice the *ex post* conformity of observed variables to their expected level, is insufficient to determine individual expectations in practice. Contrary to an often defended point of view, the criterion of instrumental rationality applied to representations is neither too strong nor too demanding; it is in fact too weak – what we have called the incompleteness of instrumental rationality (Orléan 1994). Other, more specific criteria are therefore required if we want to obtain a true analysis of individual cognition. This is what is studied in the second section.

In this second section, we abandon the critical stance and focus on co-ordination games and their multiple equilibria. These situations are interesting for the project we are pursuing given that, since Thomas Schelling ([1960] 1977), we know that economic actors are able to co-ordinate themselves much more efficiently than standard theory would predict. Reflecting on the way in which these results come about (by focusing on certain specific equilibria) will allow us to expose certain fundamental cognitive mechanisms in the selection of equilibria. In order to highlight them we will put forward the concept of 'social belief'. This concept, which lies at the heart of the second section, is our specific contribution to cognitive economics. By this term we refer to those individual beliefs that take the following particular form: individual *i* believes that 'the group believes that proposition P is true', in other words beliefs about the beliefs of the group itself. We show that these beliefs play a strategic role in situations of co-ordination. The study of social beliefs highlights two interesting properties. On the one hand, social beliefs are strongly dependent on the specific contexts in which they were created. We will also say that they are the product of a 'situated' rationality, in other words, a cognitive rationality based on the explicit elements of the actor's environment, beyond what the fundamentalist analysis would have justified. On the other hand, we will show that social beliefs are partially disconnected from individual beliefs. This autonomy of social beliefs is our strongest result, because it is the most enigmatic, in that it undermines the intuitive idea that the opinion of a group is simply the 'sum total' of individual opinions, and because it produces the notion of the independence of the group in relation to individual data. We have come to this hypothesis by analysing a number of configurations in which all individuals believe P, usually on the basis of a fundamentalist analysis of the context, and in which, simultaneously, all individuals believe that the group believes Q. These situations prove to be perfectly stable. There is no mechanical restoring force to make the social belief converge towards individual beliefs. If this is the case, we must recognize that the level of social representations possesses its own logic, a logic that is partially disconnected from private opinions, which calls into question the individualist, bottom-up model in which collective opinion is seen as the sum of individual opinions. This has considerable theoretical and empirical consequences. On the one hand, the analysis of social beliefs as we have defined them leads to a strong conception of the collective which cannot be reduced to its constituent elements. In our approach, the collective must first and foremost explain itself by the collective and not by the individual. On the other hand, to say that social beliefs are autonomous is to attribute to them the status of a third mediator, overhanging individual interactions. In this sense, the 'cognitive turning point' leads to the need for a renewed dialogue between economics and the other social sciences.

9.2 THE INDETERMINACY OF RATIONAL EXPECTATIONS

From the moment we abandon the Arrow–Debreu general equilibrium model and its restrictive assumptions in order to deal with monetary or sequential economies, the manner in which economic actors interpret their environment and project themselves into the future is imposed on theorists as a decisive question which can no longer be avoided. However, taking expectations into account is not without danger for the fundamentalist paradigm because it confronts economic discourse with a new object, individual cognition. We must, therefore, ask ourselves whether traditional economic tools are capable of proposing a meaningful and complete analysis or whether a deep transformation of fundamentalist discourse must take place in order to open it up to new principles. Is instrumental rationality still pertinent or should we admit the existence of a specific rationality that we shall call 'cognitive'?

In order to face these serious challenges, fundamentalist thought has elaborated a strong response that hinges on the notions of informational efficiency of prices and rational expectations. The central idea consists in proving that although the economic actor certainly acts on the basis of a particular representation of the economy, this representation is unique, in this case the 'true model', and that, on the basis of this unique model, knowledge of the prices is sufficient to determine individual action perfectly. We find a typical illustration of these theses in Hayek (1945), who emphasizes the ability of prices to incorporate all useful information and thus to enable co-ordination of the actions of the many different separate economic agents. This analysis gives credit to the idea of a spontaneous order which, starting from private interests, produces social outcomes, in this specific case equilibrium prices, without the need to postulate any common area of representation other than that of prices. We refer to this as a type of *bottom-up* logic, where equilibrium values result from the mechanical aggregation of private evaluations.

Hayek takes as an example the way in which an economy that is unexpectedly faced with a sudden shortage of tin evolves and adapts. According to his analysis, efficient adjustment to the new situation does not mobilize any global representation of the phenomenon, but a series of local adaptations as a function of private interests in their respective spheres of competence. In this respect, the process considered is of a fundamentally decentralized nature, at the opposite end of what a planned response would involve. The model thus constructed presents us with a set of individual neighbourhoods interconnected by prices and leading to a global adaptation of the economy, despite the fact that no agent has global knowledge of the process itself. Hayek writes: '[t]he whole acts as one market, not because any of its members survey the whole field, but because their limited individual fields of vision sufficiently overlap so that through many intermediaries the relevant information is communicated to all' (1945, p. 526). The simple observation of prices allows each agent to make the right decision. Thus, prices enable fantastic savings to be made in knowledge and intelligence. It is thanks to this property that they derive their essential regulatory quality. Prices are responsible for the miracle by which strictly local knowledge is aggregated into a global price, leading, what is more, to the efficient management of resources.

This vision of market adaptation through the play of informationally efficient prices stumbles on a central difficulty that seems to have totally escaped Hayek in the context of his 1945 article: the difference between relative prices and monetary prices. Given that individuals observe an increase in the price of tin, they must ask themselves whether this observed increase is or is not the consequence of a general increase in prices. Depending on the answer they give to this question they will act differently. It is for this reason that in a monetary economy prices cease to be, strictly speaking, informationally efficient: they do not, in themselves, enable economic agents to make the right decision. This depends on their representations of the behaviour of the Central Bank. We thus recognize the fundamental fact that agents cannot determine the efficient action on the basis of prices alone; they also need to interpret the way in which the economy is operating.

As we know, this consideration has played a central role in the emergence of the new macroeconomics. Indeed, it is to the credit of the school of rational expectations to have fully understood that no serious analysis was possible without considering the way in which agents perceive government policy and the workings of the economy. This is a considerable transformation in that it fully recognizes the importance of individual cognitive activity, which we can no longer simply limit to the mere observation of prices. Rational expectations theorists can no longer be placed in the framework of objectified mediations, leading to a kind of parametric rationality, as in the Arrow–Debreu model. On the contrary, they fully recognize the central role of 'the principle of strategic interdependence, which holds that one person's pattern of behaviour depends on the behaviour patterns of those forming his environment' (Sargent 1986, p. x). Thus, the analysis that each protagonist makes of others becomes an important element in the interaction dynamics, and of the model that describes it.

Initially, this conceptual revolution was not fully perceived, because the new classical economists reasoned within a fundamentalist framework, leading them to believe that there was only one economic model. Thus the question of the economic model was already solved the moment it was raised: the model to take into account was the 'true' economic model, in other words the one put forward by the new classical economists themselves. In this perspective, rational expectations have been defined as 'the application of the principle of rational behaviour to the acquisition and processing of information and to the formation of expectations' (Maddock and Carter 1982, p. 41). The theory of rational expectations presented itself as an economic theory that took individual cognitive activity into account, but which maintained that the criteria of instrumental rationality alone were sufficient in order to reach complete intelligibility. Thus, there was no need to appeal to an autonomous concept of cognitive rationality.

This position was criticized shortly after it was put forward by those who, taking the idea of agents interpreting their economic environment

seriously, emphasized the absurdity of the unique model postulate and the identification of the unique model with the very same model used by the new classical economists. This was the case of David Laidler (1986) analysing an empirical study that Robert Barro had dedicated to the influence of money on unemployment, production and prices in the USA during the period 1945–76. David Laidler noted that 'agents inhabiting the economy at that time are treated by Barro as believing in the equilibrium competitive model of the new-classical economics, and as using this model for forming their expectations. However, if, in the 1945–76 period agents really had held new-classical beliefs, there would have been no need for a new-classical revolution' during the 1980s. He added that during the 1970s, private economic actors, such as those in charge of economic policy, believed firmly in the principles of Keynesian economics, in particular in the existence of an inverse relationship between inflation and unemployment. In these conditions 'logical consistency requires new-classical economics to model the economic history of the period in question by postulating that agents operating within the US economy used an erroneous Keynesian model to form their expectations'.
In other words, once one begins to examine the way in which agents consider their environment and analyse it, one must leave the sphere of pure instrumental rationality – because it then becomes necessary to take the historical context into account and, in particular, the exact states of knowledge prevailing at the moment under consideration. Although Laidler's argument appears perfectly convincing, the decisive critique against the hypothesis of a unique model came from different quarters, namely from the rational expectation models themselves, once they proved the possibility of the self-realization of a multiplicity of expectations. In order to understand their logic, one needs to return to the primary idea on which the notion of rational expectation is based, namely a strictly instrumental approach to cognition.

Indeed, the simple application of instrumental rationality to individual representation leads to an analysis that maintains no other evaluation criterion than the consequentialist performance criterion, namely, the quality of the forecasts these representations allow. Every other type of consideration, such as the search for 'justice' and 'truth' (Boudon, this volume, Chapter 8) is excluded by definition. We want to emphasize that the term 'representation' is used here in a broad sense that includes three types of content: (1) a unique variable, for example, when individuals anticipate a return (Weil 1989) or a future price; (2) a complete economic model where relations between variables are taken into account, for example the sunspot model (Azariadis 1981); (3) the behaviour of another agent, as for example in the Cournot or Bertrand type conjectures. Moreover, a representation is rational when the *ex post* observed result validates the initial belief: (1) the return or the price is equal to the anticipated return or price; (2) the observed relations conform to the ones postulated by the hypothetical model; (3) the agent has acted in line with the conjecture. Although this is not always stated explicitly, the fact that we generally assume a situation in which all agents share the same representation is equally understood to be a consequence of rationality. The surprising result of rational expectation models consists in the fact that large numbers of representations are self-fulfilling. Moreover, we also obtain a great number of possible equilibria. This is a troubling result for the fundamentalist approach because it means that beliefs have a real impact, in line with the arguments developed by the American sociologist Robert Merton ([1949] 1968) who wrote that 'collective beliefs engender their own realization'. In other words, the constraints of scarcity alone are not sufficient to model the economy, because this also depends on the way in which agents interpret it. The idea of a unique model has to be abandoned: many models are possible, far more than we could imagine *a priori*. As Chiappori (1994, p. 75) writes: 'the hypothesis of the rationality of expectations is perfectly compatible with the indetermination of equilibrium'.

This essential role played by the *a priori* representations of agents leads rational expectations models away from the initial ideas defended by the new classical economists towards Keynesian results (Bryant 1983). Philippe Weil's model (1989) is a typical example of this apparent paradox. In a two-period model, he showed that there are multiple rational expectations equilibria, by introducing the assumption that returns on savings are positively correlated to total savings. Confronted with this result, Weil had to appeal to Keynesian 'animal spirits', which gave the title to his paper, in order to 'determine' the equilibrium that would effectively prevail: whether economic actors form optimistic or pessimistic expectations on the expected return on capital, we will observe a high or low equilibrium. As in Keynes, the psychological attitudes of individuals become an independent variable on which the entire system depends. Weil wrote: 'the equilibria are dependent on the optimism or the pessimism of the consumers' (p. 889).

We believe that this massive indeterminacy of rational expectations is the most striking expression of the inadequacy of instrumental rationality as a tool for considering individual and collective representations. If we want to take economic discourse out of this crisis situation where anything or nearly anything is possible,[2] we need to move towards a better understanding of cognitive activity. This becomes an essential task for the economist and is the goal of the 'cognitive turning point'. Economists have spontaneously mostly turned towards psychology. This was the case for Keynes as it is for the contemporary stream of thought called 'behavioural finance' (Thaler

1993). For our part, we have assigned a primal place to the analysis of collective cognitive activity.

9.3   TOWARDS A THEORY OF SOCIAL COGNITION

To begin with, it is useful to give a precise definition of what we mean by 'collective belief'. Economic theory suggests two definitions, 'shared belief' and 'common belief'. In order to clarify this central point, we will introduce the notation C_iQ that reads: 'individual i believes that proposition Q is true'. We then say that Q is a shared belief of group G if we have C_iQ for all individuals i belonging to group G. We say that Q is a common belief for group G when the following set of propositions is true: C_iQ; C_jC_iQ; $C_kC_jC_iQ$ ... to an infinity of crossed beliefs, for all is, for all js, for all ks in the group. The notion of common belief is much more restrictive than that of a shared belief, as it implies not only that everyone believes Q, as in the case of the shared belief, but also that everyone believes that everyone believes Q, and so on to an infinite order of crossed beliefs.

As we can see, these two notions of collective belief refer strictly to individual beliefs. They are only collective in the sense that *all* individuals, one way or another, have adopted them. Thus, these concepts are quite distinct from another concept, which can be written in the form C_GQ: 'group G believes that proposition Q is true'. In this case, we attribute the beliefs to an abstract entity, namely, the group itself. On the face of it, this notation is absurd, because, properly speaking, the group as such has no belief, as it is not a human being. However, empirical analysis reveals that in many co-ordination contexts individuals are led to make use of this kind of enigmatic cognitive object, for example when they say: 'the market believes that this currency is undervalued'. How can we explain this strange fact? The object of this section is to provide an answer to this question. More broadly, we will show that social beliefs play a central role in co-ordination situations. Let us start by clarifying the meaning that individual i gives to the proposition C_GQ.

9.3.1   Definition of Social Belief

A priori, we can conceive of two definitions. According to the first interpretation, denoted (i1), individual i believes that the group believes that proposition Q is true if he believes that a large part[3] of the group believes proposition Q to be true. We are close to the notion of shared belief, but only in the eyes of individual i. According to (i1), a 'group belief' is just a way of saying that a large number of individuals of a group believe a particular proposition. According to the second interpretation, denoted (i2), individual *i* believes that the group believes in Q, to the extent that he believes that a large part of the group also believes that the group believes in Q. This definition is essentially self-referential in that in the end it leaves indeterminate what the meaning of 'believes' in the expression 'the group believes that proposition Q is true' is. It simply assumes that all the individuals of the group attribute to other individuals the ability to accept or refuse the proposition according to which 'the group believes that proposition Q is true'. It follows that proposition Q is the object of a group belief for the individual if he believes that a great number of individuals accept this proposition as the answer to the question: 'what does the group believe?' Put another way, we have $C_i C_G Q$ if and only if $C_i C_j C_G Q$ for approximately all the individuals *j* of the group. It follows that $C_G Q$ is close to the notion of common belief in the eyes of individual *i*.

The difference between these two interpretations is very important. According to the first interpretation, in the eyes of *i*, it is the proposition Q itself that is put forward as shared belief; in the second case, in the eyes of *i*, it is the 'belief' $C_G Q$, rather than Q, that is put forward as a common belief. In this latter case, the precise nature of what it means that a group 'believes in something' remains indeterminate, whereas for (i1) group belief is defined easily as the belief of a large number of individuals of this group. If we go back to our example of an individual *i* who believes that the market believes that a given currency is undervalued, these two hypotheses correspond to the following two interpretations: (i1) the individual in question believes that almost all the other agents operating in the market, taken one by one, believe the currency to be undervalued; (i2) the individual believes that almost all of the other agents operating, taken one by one, believe that 'the market believes that the currency is undervalued'.

The two interpretations (i1) and (i2) appear to us *a priori* to be equally interesting, in that both bring to the fore a particular cognitive task which aims to grasp the group as a group and attribute a belief to it. We believe this to be a fundamental property. It seems to us that it is very precisely through the indirect medium of this cognitive capacity, which attributes beliefs to the group *as such,* that the collective acquires an effective *de facto* existence. It is through the social beliefs to which it gives rise that it proves capable of shaping individual behaviours, and thus establishes itself as an autonomous force that must be taken into account. Put in another way, in accordance with an analytical perspective developed by Mary Douglas (1986) following Émile Durkheim, cognition is for us a privileged place of social expression (Orléan 1996). We shall see in the series of examples presented in what follows that interpretation (i2) should be considered the proper way of defining what a 'social belief' is, in particular with respect to the idea of autonomy in relation to individual beliefs. This assertion will be confirmed from an analysis of pure co-ordination games, a particularly appropriate configuration for those attempting to think about situations with multiple equilibria (Orléan 1994). We will begin by proving that what is called the 'Schelling salience' constitutes a prime example of social belief in the sense of (i2).

9.3.2　An Example of Social Belief: Schelling Salience

Thomas Schelling ([1960] 1977) dedicated a large part of his book to the analysis of two-player pure co-ordination games. If every player has to choose his strategy in a set $\{1,2,...,i,...,n\}$, the pay-off for both players is equal to 1 if they both choose the same strategy and 0 if they do not. Each player, therefore, tries to copy his partner in order to maximize his pay-off. Schelling noted that individuals co-ordinated themselves a lot more efficiently than standard theory would have predicted. According to the latter, if there are n possible strategies, the probability of co-ordination is equal to $1/n$ because each strategy is perfectly indistinguishable from every other.

In all the experiments Schelling realized, he noted that the players co-ordinated a lot more efficiently than $1/n$. This occurred for a very simple reason: because the players used the wording of the choices available to them. In this way they were able to recognize 'salient' equilibria. We are thus faced with a double peculiarity. On the one hand, in the classic situations considered by game theorists, the way in which strategies are named is of no pertinence. It is not a part of what we could call the 'fundamentalist' description of the game, which is generally constituted by the matrix of pay-offs and the assumption of player rationality, in the sense of common knowledge. It is solely on this basis that the researcher seeks to characterize the equilibria. From the point of view of fundamentalist rationality, the labelling of the strategies is not to be used. We suggest the term 'situated rationality' (Orléan 1994) to designate the form of rationality that draws on contexts that go beyond what would be justified by fundamentalist analysis. On the other hand, individuals actually prove to be able, on the basis of the wording, to select certain equilibria. Let us examine this form of doubly enigmatic rationality starting from the empirical work carried out by Mehta et al. (1994).

These authors considered a particular pure co-ordination game consisting in choosing a natural number $n \geq 1$. More precisely, a group G of individuals was first put together and individuals were paired randomly, in such a way that each individual knew nothing about their partner except that they were drawn at random from group G. In order to better interpret the results obtained, Mehta et al. began by selecting a first group, denoted P. P was then asked to choose a natural integer equal or greater to 1, in the absence of any co-ordination task. The authors thus obtained information on the distribution of the 'personal opinions' of the population tested. In the second group, denoted C, the co-ordination game was played according to the rules outlined above. What were the results?

In control group P, answers 7 (11.4%), 2 (10.2%), 10 (5.7%) and 1 (4.5%) came top. In group C, on the other hand, number 1 received most votes, and by a large margin: 1 was preferred in 40 per cent of cases, followed by the number 7, which took 14.4 per cent. According to the authors, the choice of the number 1 constitutes an example of what they call a 'Schelling salience', namely the ability to determine a single, prominent equilibrium capable of obtaining a large number of votes.

They noted that the choice of the number 1 by group C was the result of a very specific and enigmatic cognitive elaboration, in that it did not consider the 'personal' preferences of the players with regard to numbers, which would have led to the choice of numbers like 7 and 2, but, instead, sought directly to determine the number that could plausibly be the result of a unanimous choice by the group *when each individual analysed the problem from the same angle.*

This appears clearly in the fact that 1, the final choice, was only in the fourth position of the primary choices for control group P. It was not because it was the players' preferred number that it was chosen by group C. The reasoning was completely different. If the individuals utilized the rule of 'choosing the first number', it was by virtue of the following property: when all the players follow this rule, it allows the unambiguous design of a unique response and leads to a successful co-ordination. This is exactly what Schelling had revealed. He spoke in this case of a 'focal principle', a principle which, when employed by all, allows the determination of a unique strategy. This is a case of the principle 'select the first number' and not of the principle 'choose a number that you like'. In the co-ordination situation experienced by group C, individuals do not start from their individual beliefs, nor by asking themselves what the personal beliefs of the others are (which would have led to the selection of number 7), but by placing themselves in a more general level of abstraction in such a way as to determine a principle which is able to produce, in the eyes of all, a unique equilibrium. Cognitive activity is thus turned towards the group as a separate entity in the attempt to produce a common ground on a non-cooperative basis.

We find here a first example of a 'social belief' in the sense of (i2). Let us remember that, by definition, Q is a social belief in the sense of (i2) for an individual *i*, if he thinks that it is a social belief for (nearly) all the individuals in the group. Such is the very nature of the cognitive activity that leads certain individuals to select the number 1: the players of group C choose 1, because they see in it the choice capable of attracting the choice of the others, when the others consider the problem from the same perspective. The cognitive activity that this mobilizes is turned fully towards the group as such and not towards the individual preferences of the players.

Indeed, if the latter were the case, we would obtain what we have called a social belief in the sense (i1), which leads to choosing the number 7 when all the players are well informed of the personal opinions of the group members such as the ones revealed by control group P. The strength of definition (i2) depends on the fact that it totally abstracts from the variability of the intrinsic preferences of individuals to devote itself to the definition of a belief proper to group C *as a group*. This is a strength because, in a large number of situations, social belief in the sense (i1) is very uncertain due to the very fact that the nature of individual tastes is variable and, as such, is ineffective. When individual i asks himself about the belief shared by others, a large number of plausible answers come to his mind. In interpretation (i2) this fact is of no significance because, by definition, each individual tries to determine what is capable of being the social belief for (nearly) all the others. Nevertheless, in those particular cases where a choice is clearly a majority choice, the definition (i1) of the social belief effectively allows scope for good co-ordination. In this case, we would say that we are dealing with a 'stereotype'. Nevertheless, note that the stereotypical preference is equally a social belief in the sense (i2) and is of such a nature that this particular case does not weaken the generality of the hypothesis according to which we must retain definition (i2) in order to think of a 'Schelling salience'.

9.3.3 Situated Rationality and the Role of Contexts

In his analysis, Schelling insists on the role that contexts play in the elaboration of focal principles. The preceding example does not allow one to go too far in this direction, to the extent that the context is strictly limited to the wording of the choices and nothing else is specified about group C. The following example that we owe to David Kreps (1990, p. 120) allows us to go a bit further in showing that the equilibrium selected depends directly on the manner in which the players analyse the identity of the participants in the game. Depending on the way in which the definition of group C varies, the social belief is modified.

Kreps considered the co-ordination game[4] consisting in dividing the 10 letters *A, B, C, D, H, L, M, N, P, S* into two sub-groups that should not intersect, or should do so as little as possible, given that the first team [denoted 1] must necessarily choose the letter B and the opposing team, [2], the letter S. Amongst the 256 possible partitions of the 8 remaining letters, which form as many equilibria in this game, the focal point equilibrium, when nothing specific is said about the group of players,[5] is, according to Kreps, the one which gives team [1] the first five letters, i.e. *A, B, C, D* and *H* and team [2] the last five, i.e. *L, M, N, P* and *S*. This is a new illustration of a Schelling salience. Kreps nevertheless added: 'Note that the rule applied here is entirely dependent on the context.' In order to demonstrate this, he considered a variation of the game in which team [1] is made up of Harvard students and team [2] is made up of Stanford students and where this fact is brought to the attention of the players. Ten towns are proposed to them: Atlanta, Boston, Chicago, Dallas, Houston, Los Angeles, Miami, New York, Philadelphia and San Francisco. Team [1] must necessarily choose Boston and team [2] San Francisco. From the perspective of fundamentalist rationality, the two game situations are strictly equivalent. Yet, in approximately 75 per cent of the cases, Kreps noted (p. 121), the Harvard students chose Atlanta, Boston, Chicago, Miami, New York and Philadelphia while those of Stanford retained the rest, i.e. Dallas, Houston, Los Angeles and San Francisco. The focal point here was a geographical division of the USA according to what lies east or west of the Mississippi. This case is different from the focal equilibrium in which players are not capable of dividing player group G in groups of distinct geographical origin.

We see here, in full, the effect of context in the determination of a social belief. This depends strictly on the group under consideration, on what we know about it, and not only on the intrinsic content of the question as such. Thus, if this list of towns was given to players that were not American, who were ignorant of the geography of the USA but who knew the Latin alphabet, they would go back to the first solution – for they would not be able to assume that each player knew American geography. In these conditions, taking into account the first letter may emerge as the 'focal principle'. Even more paradoxically, this could also be the case when all the players are American but do not know it. In this case, each player can no longer assume that the geographical partition on the basis of the Mississippi is a social belief of the group. We can see here that the way in which the players conceive 'the collective identity of the group' is an essential element in the problem, playing a determining role in the formation of social beliefs in the sense (i2). Whatever belongs to the common past of the group, be it historical precedents or cultural values, is utilized. The example considered by Kreps allows us to see the effect of a cultural context, but the same result could be obtained with a historical 'precedent'.

Financial markets provide a good example of the role played by historical precedents in the determination of social beliefs. More precisely, we can refer to the work that Shiller (1991) has devoted to the crash of 19 October

1987, the day in which the New York stock exchange suffered its sharpest ever slump, with a dizzying plunge of 508 points, representing a 22.6 per cent fall. How can we explain a fall of such magnitude? Analysts agree that no fundamental information can provide the explanation. One has to look elsewhere, in the inter-subjective and self-referential dynamic on which the stock markets are based. Shiller had the idea of sending out a questionnaire to individual and institutional investors to discover their motivations. The results he obtained highlighted the role that the 1929 crisis played in these events, serving as a reference model for investors attempting to decipher events and adapt to them.

He noted, in fact, that the 1929 crisis was strongly present in the minds of investors when the October 1987 crash began. Thirty-five per cent of individual investors and 53 per cent of institutional ones answered 'yes' to the question 'Do you remember having thought or spoken of the events of 1929 in the course of the few days which preceded 19 October 1987?' For Shiller, the 1929 crisis imposed itself on all minds as the relevant salience; in other words as the model that allowed them to understand how a stock market crash unfolds. Let us remember that on the Wednesday, Thursday and Friday that preceded the crash the stock market had already experienced three significant price drops. Moreover, investors were nervous during the weekend and on Monday morning. The substantial 200-point drop that took place on Monday 10 October 1987 when the stock market opened bewildered investors, who found themselves faced with events of a most unusual nature. How were the market and the other investors going to react? In these circumstances, what could one expect of the market? Investors interpreted the events of 1987 in the light of those of 1929. Clearly, the comparison did nothing to reassure them. It provoked an anticipation of further drops and contributed to the climate of panic that the stock exchange experienced during 19 and 20 October 1987. According to Shiller, we cannot understand the overreaction of the market without taking into account the role played by the salience '1929 crash' as the prototype of a stock market crisis. It is the adoption of this reference model during that period that explains the excessive character of the sales and the price drops. This analysis forcefully illustrates the role played by historical precedents in the determination of the collective expectations of the market.

9.3.4   The Autonomy of Social Beliefs

The analysis of the role of contexts, whether historical or cultural, in the production of social belief allows us to see the strange absence of any connection to individual beliefs. It seems that individuals are somehow powerless because the legitimate interpretations that determine the co-ordination equilibrium are imposed upon them regardless of their own opinions.

The origin of these social beliefs lies in the multiplicity of common historical and cultural reference points that define the group's identity. Because the past imparts habits, narratives and legitimacies, individuals, whatever their opinions may be, are not free to propose legitimate collective representations. Moreover, equilibria that they may well not have wished for will impose themselves upon economic actors, as we saw in the example of the 1987 crisis.

This autonomy of social beliefs reveals itself forcefully in the fact that situations may exist in which all the individuals believe in proposition P and, simultaneously, all individuals believe that the group believes proposition Q, which is different to proposition P and where neither of the beliefs is wrong. As they are not based on any error, these situations can, therefore, persist without any need being felt to modify beliefs, on one level or another. In other words, this means that we can have C_iP for all individuals i of the group and at the same time C_iC_GQ for all individuals i of the group, without the appearance of restoring forces to reduce the divergence between personal and social beliefs. Let us note that it is an entirely different case when we consider social beliefs according to definition (i1).

In this case, there is no autonomy of the social belief, in the sense that the divergence between individual beliefs and social beliefs cannot exist, except in the hypothesis of false beliefs. Once again it is confirmed that definition (i2) provides the most innovative and rich conception. Thanks to the property of autonomy that characterizes it, the way in which we understand interactions in the economic sphere is profoundly modified. It highlights a logic of a new type, which breaks away from the classical individualist model that views collective representation as the sum total of individual opinions. Hereafter, two levels and two logics coexist whose articulation we have to analyse.

The analysis of co-ordination games allows us to fully understand why things are so. Effectively, it has shown that we must carefully distinguish between what the individual really thinks and his collective choice. This holds for the very nature of the interaction under consideration, which rewards, not those who are 'right' and who answer the question posed 'correctly', but those who are more successful in predicting the movements of the majority opinion. This distinction, when applied to financial markets, allows one to avoid premature judgements of irrationality which are frequently attributed to financial investors, for example when we see a significant discrepancy between a quoted price and what the community of economists considers the valuation based on fundamentals to be.

Let us take the case of a currency that is already undervalued, but which nevertheless continues to be sold heavily in the currency market, leading to a further fall in value. We would reproach traders for being irrational, in the sense of having poorly evaluated the fundamental value of the currency in question. Such a hypothesis does not stand to reason and, in any case, is not even necessary. Traders, like everybody else, may know very well that the currency is undervalued and nonetheless continue to sell. Effectively, what matters for them when they intervene on the market is not what they think the real value of the currency is, to the extent that they can estimate it correctly, but what they anticipate the market will do. In a market, agents make a profit when they succeed in correctly predicting the evolution of the opinion of the group. This is the rule of the game. We do not require the agents involved to be right and to estimate the fundamental values correctly. From this point of view, the quote reproduced below, which comes from a trader interviewed during the major fall of the euro in September 2000, is revealing of the dichotomy between fundamentalist personal evaluation and investment choices. We witness an individual thoroughly convinced of the undervalued character of the euro, who nonetheless explains that he must sell it if he is not to lose money:

> The financial operator in me can well believe in a particular evaluation of the euro, but this has no weight when one sees all the others who intervene on the currency market selling the euro. Even if I estimate that the euro deserves to be priced higher than the dollar, I will still hesitate to buy the European currency. Practically speaking, if I am the only buyer of euros facing 50 sellers, I am dead. I do not necessarily do what I really believe, but rather what I believe the market will do, as this is what will prevail in the end. The job of the financial operator is to attempt to evaluate as precisely as possible the sentiments of the currency market.[6]

Despite his personal conviction that the euro is undervalued, this trader plays along with the selling, and his behaviour is perfectly rational: if he bought euros he would do so at a loss! A first way of considering this situation consists in following the interpretation proposed to us by the trader himself. He contrasts two assessments, the fundamentalist evaluation and the belief of the market as defined by (i1), i.e. as being the belief of the largest number of traders. Against this background, the individual questioned justified his uncritical following of the crowd by the fact that a large number of investors were selling, to be precise there were '50 sellers' and they determined the belief of the market. According to this analysis, these '50 sellers' sold because they thought that the euro was overvalued. From a fundamentalist viewpoint, it is this mistaken conception that led them to sell. Faced with this situation, our trader had no choice. He had to bow before the dictates of the majority opinion.

If we stick to this interpretation, we will not observe what we have called the 'autonomy of social beliefs', in other words a situation where, for all the players, there is a divergence between their personal opinions and their social beliefs. In fact, according to the interpretation offered by the trader, the personal and social beliefs of all the '50 sellers' converged perfectly when predicting a future drop in the price of the euro. Only our trader stated that there was a divergence between his fundamentalist evaluation and the belief of the market. There is nothing surprising about this lack of autonomy. It is a consequence of the fact that we have considered that the interpretation of the trader is based on an interpretation (i1) of the belief of the market.

This interpretation is not necessarily wrong. It may well be that in some or other financial situation there are investors who are naïve, poorly informed or irrational. This is a fact. If so, the bearish euro bubble is easily interpreted by the fact that there are a large number of ignorant investors. Nonetheless, we must clearly see that this interpretation leaves a central point unanswered: why are the '50 sellers' making this mistake? What mechanism can explain how the same error is propagated throughout the market? Moreover, it is interesting to explore an alternative analysis that abandons the suspect asymmetry between our perfectly rational trader and a market consisting of obtuse operators. According to this new interpretation, the '50 sellers' operated exactly like our trader: they acted in a self-referential manner, starting from their own social belief with respect to the functioning of the market. However, in line with our previous analysis, the social belief that we must consider corresponds to definition (i2) and not (i1): 'each seller believed that the market believed in a drop in the price of the euro'. From this perspective, each seller was equally rational, acting on the basis of the same belief with regard to the behaviour of the others. What we have is not 50 fanatical sellers, but 50 traders who, after reflecting on what the other traders were going to do (including the trader interviewed by *Libération*), anticipated that they were going to sell. If we had asked them, they would have commented that it is of no use to go against a market that is so determined in its short sightedness – and they would be right. The true belief here does not concern the value of the euro, but the fact that 'each trader believes that the market is on a downward trend'.

Then we see a divergence between private beliefs on the undervalued nature of the euro and the social belief in the (i2) sense that the market expects the euro to drop further. We have C_iP for all individuals i of the group, where P is the proposition 'the euro is undervalued' and at the same time C_iC_GQ for all individuals i of the group, where Q is the proposition 'the euro is overvalued'. If they all believe that 'everyone believes in a fall', then they will all be sellers and the market will plummet, effectively validating the initial belief *ex post*.

Once again, we encounter the phenomenon of the self-fulfilling prophecy. Thus, a bubble emerges without us having to assume the presence of irrational actors. Each actor is perfectly rational in his private evaluations and in his evaluation of the market. Indeed, there is no need to assume any incorrect evaluations. It is enough to have all actors assuming a certain market model in making their choices, conceived of as expressing a distinct logic. Investors who believe they are simply reacting to this market model confirm their idea of a market autonomy, because despite their generalized belief in an overvalued euro it continues to fall. This autonomy appears to them all the more undeniable since the evolution observed cannot be coherently explained through a fundamentalist analysis. Also, far from producing an adjustment of the social belief to the private opinions, this situation leads to the further reinforcement of the social belief that imposes itself as the only plausible explanation. The experience of the market confirms the hypothesis of the autonomy of the collective evaluation.[7]

At all levels then, beliefs are confirmed: the fundamental evaluation of the euro suggests it is undervalued; the market believes it will fall further; the market acts autonomously, in other words it is disconnected from fundamentalist evaluations.

9.4   CONCLUSION

The concept of cognitive rationality is now prompting a great deal of research, as is amply demonstrated in this volume. This can only be welcome. The field is vast and has been neglected for too long by traditional economic theory. For our part, we have sought to demonstrate why the concept of social belief is an indispensable element in the economic analysis of many important situations. This kind of research can serve two convergent purposes: on the one hand, it can give a new balance to cognitive approaches that have traditionally been centred on individual cognition to the detriment of social cognition; on the other hand, it opens up a channel of dialogue between economics and the other social sciences, such as sociology, anthropology and history, which have a lot to teach us on these subjects.

NOTES

1. At least two authors contributing to the present volume refer explicitly to the notion of 'cognitive rationality' and suggest precise definitions: Raymond Boudon (Chapter 8) and Bernard Walliser (Chapter 5).
2. The idea that 'the hypothesis of rationality is in itself weak' is defended by Kenneth Arrow (1987, p. 206). Sonnenschein's theorem provides him with an exemplary illustration of this

point. However, there are plenty of other examples. We can think of the article by Boldrin and Montrucchio (1986), where it is shown that intertemporal dynamic optimization is compatible with all types of dynamic paths for the economy, without exception, including chaos. In other words, assuming that individuals are rational in no way limits the total number of possible economic paths!

3. The fact of using a term as vague as 'a large part of the group', or even 'approximately the whole group' or 'approximately all the members of the group', will have to be rendered more precise in later work. In the context of this chapter, we will deliberately remain imprecise on this point. The rest of the chapter can be read replacing 'a large part of the group' by 'all the group members'.

4. The game effectively proposed by Kreps is slightly different and significantly more complicated. In what follows, I present a simplified version that leads to the same conclusions but avoids an unnecessarily long presentation.

5. In fact, in most situations, each individual knows or assumes a certain number of common characteristics, such as speaking the same language as that in which the experiment takes place.

6. *Libération*, 8 September 2000, p. 24.

7. This enigmatic configuration in which private information does not succeed in modifying the collective choice is not without an equivalent in the theoretical literature. In situations such as the one exemplified in the '*electronic mail game*' (Rubinstein 1989), we observe similar hindrances in the sense that the exchange of messages between two individuals, regardless of the number of players, does not manage to engender the common knowledge necessary for the two players to take a particular course of action. Information cascades also share this characteristic.

REFERENCES

Arrow, K.J. (1987), 'Rationality of self and others in an economic system', in M. Hogarth Robin and W. Reder Melvin (eds), *Rational Choice*, Chicago: University of Chicago Press, pp. 201–16.

Azariadis, C. (1981), 'Self-fulfilling prophecies', *Journal of Economic Theory*, **25** (3), 380–96.

Blanchard, O. and Watson, M. (1982), 'Bubbles, rational expectations and financial markets', in P. Wachtel (ed.), *Crises in the Economic and Financial Structure*, Lexington, MA: Lexington Books, pp. 295–315.

Boldrin, M. and Montrucchio, L. (1986), 'On the indeterminacy of capital accumulation paths', *Journal of Economic Theory*, **40** (1), October, 26–39.

Bryant, J. (1983), 'A simple rational-expectations Keynes-type model', *Quarterly Journal of Economics*, **98**, August, 525–8.

Chiappori, P.-A. (1994), 'Anticipations rationnelles et conventions', in André Orléan (ed.), *Analyse Économique des Conventions*, Paris: PUF, Chapter 2, pp. 61–77.

Diamond, D. and Dybvig, P.H. (1983), 'Bank runs, deposit insurance, and liquidity', *Journal of Political Economy*, **91** (3), 401–19.

Douglas, M. (1986), *How Institutions Think*, Syracuse: Syracuse University Press.

Farmer, R.E. (1999), *Macroeconomics of Self-Fulfilling Prophecies*, Cambridge, MA and London: The MIT Press.

Hayek, F.A. (1945), 'The use of knowledge in society', *American Economic Review*, **35** (4), September, 519–30.

Keynes, J.M. (1937), 'The general theory of employment', *Quarterly Journal of Economics*, **51**, February, 209–23.

Kreps, D. (1990), 'Corporate culture and economic theory' in Alt James and Shepsle James (eds), *Perspectives on Positive Political Economy*, Cambridge: Cambridge University Press, pp. 90–141.

Laidler, D. (1986), 'The new-classical contribution to macroeconomics', *Banca Nazionale Del Lavoro Quarterly Review*, March, 27–55.

Maddock, R. and Carter, M. (1982), 'A child's guide to rational expectations', *Journal of Economic Literature*, **20** (1), March, 39–51.

Mehta, J., Starner, C. and Sugden, R. (1994), 'The nature of salience: an experimental investigation of pure coordination games', *American Economic Review*, **84** (2), June, 658–73.

Merton, R.K. ([1949] 1968), 'The self-fulfilling prophecy', in *Social Theory and Social Structure*, New York: The Free Press, Chapter XIII.

Muth, J.F. (1961), 'Rational expectations and the Theory of Price Movements', *Econometrica*, **29** (3), July, 315–35.

Orléan, A. (1994), 'Vers un modèle général de la coordination économique par les conventions', in A. Orléan (éd.), *Analyse Economique des Conventions*, Paris: Presses Universitaires de France, pp. 9–40.

Orléan, A. (1996), 'Réflexions sur la notion de la légitimité monétaire: l'apport de Georg Simmel', in J.M. Baldner and L. Gillard (eds), *Simmel et les Normes Sociales*, Paris: L'Harmattan, pp. 19–34.

Rubinstein, A. (1989), 'The electronic mail game: strategic behavior under "almost common knowledge"', *American Economic Review*, **79** (3), June, 385–91.

Sargent, T. (1986), *Rational Expectations and Inflation*, New York: Harper & Row Publishers.

Schelling, T. ([1960] 1977), *The Strategy of Conflict*, Oxford: Oxford University Press.

Shiller, R. (1991), *Market Volatility*, Cambridge, USA and London, UK: The MIT Press.

Spence, M. (1973), 'Job market signalling', *Quarterly Journal of Economics*, **87** (3), August, 355–74.

Thaler, R. (1993), *Advances in Behavioral Finance*, New York: Russell Sage Foundation.

Weil, P. (1989), 'Increasing returns and animal spirits', *American Economic Review*, **79** (4), 889–94.

10. A cognitive approach to individual learning: some experimental results*

Marco Novarese and Salvatore Rizzello

10.1 INTRODUCTION

The economic analysis of social phenomena does not deal with omniscient and perfectly rational agents. Understanding the role of individual learning in decision making is, therefore, considered increasingly important in explaining the ways in which people make choices. Economists have tended to use analytical concepts like learning, which traditionally have pertained to other disciplines such as psychology, in a very superficial way. Though this still applies to most traditional economists,[1] it should be noted that the multifarious panorama of contemporary economics currently features a number of exceptions to this rule.

A substantial group of economists has recently put forward an interdisciplinary approach to the study of human behaviour that stands at the crossroads between the heterodox tradition in economics and the cognitive sciences, giving birth to a new branch of economics now known as cognitive economics.[2]

Although there is no doubt that the analytical novelties proposed by this new approach are relevant to, and concern, all aspects of economic analysis and method, we will be focusing our attention exclusively on the role of human learning in problem solving, the core theme of this chapter. The literature makes a distinction between two different kinds of learning: learning from direct experience (learning by doing, learning by using) and vicarious learning (learning through the observation of others).[3] In what follows, we will be dealing exclusively with the former category. In particular, we will be concentrating on experimental economics, an area of research located within the broader domain of cognitive economics, whose interest in learning is on the increase. Even more specifically, our interest is in the area of experimental economics devoted to experiments on individual and organizational learning (Novarese and Rizzello 1999; Novarese 2003).

Our starting point is an attempt to provide an answer as to what happens when individuals are faced with a problematic situation under bounded information, one of the most widespread conditions in economics. In such circumstances, people are forced to act without making use of routines they have relied upon in similar conditions.

When such conditions are recurrent, many psycho-neurobiological processes that have been more extensively analysed elsewhere (Rizzello 1999) are spontaneously activated to help individuals make a decision. First of all, a process of representation and framing of the problematic situation is activated. This depends on both subjective mental structures and on the individual's previous experience. However, psychological evidence shows that this process of framing is incomplete. This is mainly due to the economic nature of the brain's cognitive activity and its use of shortcuts to reduce complexity. It is reasonable to think that these mechanisms of human reasoning and learning differ[4] from one individual to another, just like the perception of external data on which they strongly depend.[5]

Generally speaking, learning can be defined as the human capacity to modify behaviour in a more or less permanent way, whenever new experience is acquired. Cognitive psychology further specifies that this ability depends on a subjective cognition of the environment (it is linked to perception and the process of mental imagination) and on the way in which this cognition affects behaviour (Droz 1977). These characteristics of human cognition and the link between previous experience and perception set the stage for a further hypothesis, namely, that learning happens in a path-dependent way (Rizzello 1997 and 2000a; Egidi and Narduzzo 1997).

Based on these two simple hypotheses about human learning (differentiation and path-dependence), we designed an experiment with which to observe individuals in laboratory conditions in order to describe their behaviour in a decision-making context. We were also interested in explaining how rules and regularities in behaviour are produced and why individuals tend to confirm them when they appear to be incorrect.

Typically, experimental economics tends to test strong theories by building simple contexts in which to investigate them. This was not our goal here. Instead, our attention was devoted to the comprehension of the nature and functioning of learning. In this sense and unlike most of the experimental literature on learning,[6] we did not simply focus on the outcomes of the learning process but on the process itself.

This chapter is structured in the following manner: Section 10.2 illustrates the characteristics of the experiment, Section 10.3 presents the detailed results and section 10.4 offers some concluding remarks.

10.2   THE EXPERIMENT

Subjects were given the following instructions:

- They were to take a series of exams.
- Each of these exams would be evaluated according to the following scale: 'very good', 'good', 'average', 'bad' and 'very bad'.
- If they scored 'very good' or 'good', they would pass the exam. If, on the other hand, they scored 'bad' or 'very bad' they would fail.
- If the score was 'average' the exam would have to be repeated.

Each exam was evaluated on the basis of the following scoring system, which included a colour (black, blue, white or yellow), a shape (heart, circle, square or rectangle) and a size (large or small). Therefore, for example, an exam could be evaluated as 'blue – heart – small'. The connection between shapes, colours and sizes and the final result of the exam was not known.

The game worked in the following way. Subjects were presented with the first shape-colour-size combination and were asked to choose one of the possible scores. They were then told whether their answer was correct and were given the right solution. Following this, they were presented with a further combination for a total of 231 rounds.

A specific piece of software was realized to perform the experiment. Figure 10.1 shows the main screen presented to the players. The subjects were given points according to their answers, knowing that these would be converted into exam credits. Therefore, the students were strongly motivated to do their best. We will discuss these points more extensively at a later stage.

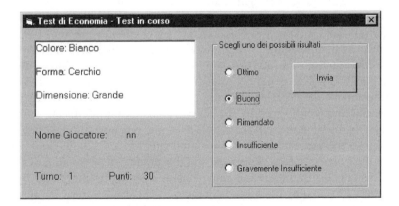

Figure 10.1   The screen presented to the players

A logical relation existed between the combinations of information and the correct answers. This was stable for all rounds and is described in Table 10.1.[7]

Table 10.1   Logical relation between combinations and results

Score	Colour	Shape	Size
Very good	Bright (white and yellow)	Not angular shapes (circle and heart)	Large
Good	Bright (white and yellow)	Not angular shapes (circle and heart)	Small
Average	Dark (black and blue)	Not angular shapes (circle and heart)	Small or large
	Bright (white and yellow)	Angular shapes (square and rectangle)	
Bad	Dark (black and blue)	Angular shapes (square and rectangle)	Small
Very bad	Dark (black and blue)	Angular shapes (square and rectangle)	Large

The data gathered through this experiment enabled us to link choices to available information and to observe changes in the behaviour of the players during the game. Such changes were obviously the consequences of learning processes.

At the beginning of the game, the players did not know the relationship between information and results. It was up to them to identify and learn it. Given that the game was based on a relatively small number of different sequences of information (there were $4 \times 4 \times 2 = 32$ different shape-colour-size combinations and the same combination appeared repeatedly during the game), subjects could try to memorize them. Had this been the case, the results of the experiment would probably be less interesting (i.e. more artificial and conditioned by the experimental setting). Subjects were not explicitly told that the sequences were fixed and repeated (though they were aware of the logical relation between information and results) and, given that their mathematical skills were low, it is unlikely they would have come to this conclusion before the game began. This fact is supported by the answers provided by the subjects in the post-experimental survey. Besides, remembering 32 sequences is not an easy task. Subjects were, therefore, reasonably expected to try to understand the game instead of learning single answers by heart.

10.3   RESULTS

The experiments were realized in Alessandria (Italy) in October 2000 and involved the participation of 64 subjects (all law students with no economics background).[8] The length of the experiments varied between 30 minutes and 1 hour. Subjects were arranged in different rooms and were unable to communicate with each other during the experiment. The main results are presented in the following sections.

10.3.1   Tendency to Develop Rules

As previously mentioned, a single shape-colour-size combination appeared repeatedly during the game (though never in two consecutive rounds). By taking into account all the answers a subject provides when presented with a given combination during the course of a game, we can count the number of wrong answers s/he gives and the number of times s/he confirms wrong choices.

Table 10.2   Answers given by Player 1 to some combinations

Round	Colour	Shape	Size	Correct result	Subject's results
9	Yellow	Rectangle	Large	Average	Average
16	**Yellow**	**Square**	**Small**	**Average**	**Good**
33	**Yellow**	**Square**	**Small**	**Average**	**Good**
43	Yellow	Rectangle	Large	Average	Very good
50	**Yellow**	**Square**	**Small**	**Average**	**Good**
60	Yellow	Rectangle	Large	Average	Very good
67	**Yellow**	**Square**	**Small**	**Average**	**Good**

For example, the sequence yellow–square–small (bold type in Table 10.2) appears four times in the part of the game reported in Table 10.2. This means that this particular participant in the experiment (let us call him/her Player 1) confirmed the same wrong answer after 3 mistakes, as can be seen from the table. We can therefore say that s/he confirmed 3 mistakes following 3 wrong choices (100 per cent confirmation). By proceeding along these lines, it is possible to determine a similar rate per player for all possible combinations (and for the whole game) in order to build a mean value. The distribution of these values for all players is shown in Table 10.3.

Thus the tendency to confirm wrong choices is quite generalized among subjects. In many cases they understand the right choice after confirming the wrong one. Sometimes they never understand it, and confirm the wrong answer till the end of the game. We might explain this event through the subjects' bad memory, thus wrong choices would be the result of a random process. This hypothesis has been verified and rejected with a statistical test (99 per cent of significance) for most of the subjects (47 out of 64).[9]

Table 10.3   Distribution of the mean ratio of wrong answers confirmed by players

Confirmed answers (%)	Players
0–25	13
25–50	38
50–75	13
75–100	0
Total	**64**

Table 10.2 also shows the sequence yellow–rectangle–large. At its first appearance, Player 1 gives a right answer (round 9) but at the following one he gives a wrong one. Then we can say that (at round 43) he does not confirm a right solution. Many other players show a similar behaviour. There are players who give a right answer to the same sequence for a number of rounds (at least two in the data shown in Table 10.4)[10] and then change it till the end of the game.

Table 10.4   Distribution of the number of right answers given at least two times and then no longer confirmed

Unconfirmed answers	Players
0	21
1	10
2	9
3	11
4	5
5	5
6	0
7	2
8	0
9	1
Total	**64**

The results shown above refer to the whole game, starting from the very beginning. However, it is also necessary to concentrate on the last part of the game, in order to see whether players tend to develop behavioural regularities and whether they understand the rationale of the game.

As a first step, it is necessary to define some rules (specific for this experiment). Let us consider the third part of the game (the last 77 rounds), where many sequences appeared 3 or 4 times. We can count how many times a subject gives the same (right or wrong) answer for a particular sequence:

- 'rule 75' means that the subject provides the same answer 75 per cent of the time; and
- 'rule 100' means that the subject provides the same answer 100 per cent of the time.

The idea is that if a player always or almost always provides the same answer when faced with the same sequence, s/he has probably developed a kind of routine.[11]

Table 10.5 reports the distribution of the percentage of 'rule 75' developed by the players for all sequences appearing at least four times during the course of the game (we shall turn to a more detailed analysis of some of the sequences that appeared only a few times later on). The table shows that, although there was considerable heterogeneity among the players, most of them appear to have developed very routinized behaviour.

Table 10.5   Distribution of percentage of rules developed by players

%	Rule 75	Rule 100
0	0	0
0–25	1	4
25–50	9	10
50–75	12	22
75–100	31	18
100	11	10

It is also important to note that, while only 22 subjects developed exclusively correct rules (Table 10.6), there were also many players who developed a significant percentage (15 per cent or 16 per cent) of incorrect rules. Therefore, routinization does not imply that subjects have in any way understood the correct rules. In other words, not all the rules developed by the subjects were correct.

Table 10.6   Percentage of rules (total and wrong) developed by players, mean values[†]

	Rule 75	Rule 100
Total percentage of rules developed	75	70
Percentage of wrong rules developed	16	15

Note: [†] Values were computed only for the sequences that appear at least four times during the game.

It is useful to focus our attention on the behaviour of Player 1. We have seen that s/he confirmed the wrong answer (i.e. 'good') for the sequence yellow–square–small several times, while at the same time s/he failed to confirm the right answer to the sequence yellow–rectangle–large. Table 10.7 helps us understand the reason for this apparently strange behaviour and to link it to the rules developed by the same subject in a previous period. This table shows results for the first 77 rounds (period I) and for the last 77 rounds (period III), in terms of the answers given to each sequence. For example, in the first period, the subject answered 'very good' to the sequence yellow–circle–large in all cases (100 per cent), which appeared three times (Freq.=3). Shaded cells indicate correct answers.

This table suggests the reason underlying this particular player's mistakes. The answer 'good' (which was confirmed despite being wrong) to the sequence yellow–square–small is consistent, given the routines developed by the player from the very beginning of the experiment in relation to the sequences yellow–circle/heart–small. On the other hand, the correct answer, 'average', (which was not confirmed) for the yellow–rectangle–large sequence is inconsistent both with the other answers provided by the player and with the system of rules that emerged in the final part of the game in which 'square' and 'rectangle' were compared to 'circle' and 'heart'. Therefore, although the system of rules developed in the course of the game (including the part which is not presented here) was wrong, the answer appears to be coherent. Similar results were obtained for other players (see also, for example, Table 10.11 below).

10.3.2   Answers to the New Sequences

It is interesting to understand the features of the rules developed by the subjects and the ways in which they are built. Do subjects build broader categories starting from the information available to them? A different way of stating the problem is: do subjects extend the domain of validity of rules

Table 10.7   Detailed analysis of the behaviour of Player 1

Period	Colour	Shape	Size	Very bad	Bad	Average	Good	Very good	Freq.
I	Yellow	Circle	Large					100%	3
			Small				100%		5
		Heart	Large					100%	2
			Small				80%	20%	5
		Square	Large						0
			Small				100%		4
		Rectangle	**Large**			50%		50%	4
			Small						0
III	Yellow	Circle	Large					100%	3
			Small				100%		4
		Heart	Large					100%	1
			Small				100%		3
		Square	Large					100%	1
			Small				100%		4
		Rectangle	Large					100%	3
			Small				100%		1

Note: Shaded cells indicate correct answers.

beyond the field in which they were developed and tested? The extension of the validity of a rule is obviously dependent on a process of abstraction.

As already mentioned, eight new unseen sequences were given to the players in the last rounds of the game. In this case, players were clearly unable to remember the correct solutions. A right answer to (most or all of) these sequences can, therefore, be taken as evidence that the players understood the rationale of the game and that they had created categories.[12] Table 10.8 shows the distribution of right answers to the new sequences.

Twenty-five players gave the right answer to all the new sequences and several others responded to many of the new sequences correctly. The average time used to give an answer in the cases under examination amounted to about 5.8 seconds. This was a very short time compared to the amount required to respond to new sequences at the beginning of the game, which was equal to 12.8 seconds.

The players were therefore not simply relying on memory, but were clearly able to extend the domain of the validity of rules correctly. Yet, some results presented in the previous section seem to suggest that sometimes rules were also applied in a less appropriate fashion and that wrong categories were built. Another example can also be used to illustrate this point.

Table 10.8 Distribution of right answers to the new sequences in the last part of the game

Number of right answers	Frequency
0	0
1	4
2	7
3	7
4	5
5	5
6	7
7	4
8	25

The new sequences presented in the last part of the game were: white–heart–small, white–square–small, blue–circle–large, blue–heart–small, yellow–square–large, yellow–rectangle–small, black–circle–large, black–heart–small. For each of these cases, let us consider sequences featuring the same size and shape but a different colour: yellow instead of white (and vice versa) and blue instead of black (and vice versa). The sequences then become respectively: yellow–heart–small, yellow–square–small, black–circle–large, black–heart–small, white–square–large, white–rectangle–small, blue–circle–large and blue–heart–small.[13]

Now, let us restrict our attention to these sequences and consider the cases in which subjects have developed a wrong 'rule 75' (i.e. they have provided the same wrong answer in at least 75 per cent of cases). Table 10.9 shows the distribution of wrong answers to the new sequences that are identical to those given to the similar sequences (for which subjects have developed a 'rule 75'). So, for example, 10 players developed wrong 'rule 75' for the sequence white–square–large.[14] Let us say that they answered 'very good' (instead of 'average') in at least 75 per cent of the cases in which they came across this sequence. Three of them answered 'very good' even when faced with the yellow–square–large sequence. It is possible to carry out similar tests for all the sequences and count the number of identical answers.

There are common elements between groups of the so-called 'new sequences' and those we have called 'similar sequences' (blue–circle–large being the sequence 'similar' to black–circle–large and vice versa, and blue–heart–small being 'similar' to black–heart–small). These are therefore considered only once (so that the total number of new sequences becomes six).

Table 10.9   Number of wrong answers identical to those of the similar sequence

Number of wrong answers identical to those of the similar sequence	Number of players
0	38
1	15
2	7
3	2
4	1
5	1
6	0

One player seems to have 'transferred' five wrong rules to the new sequences; another one (henceforth Player 2) appears to have transferred four of them, and so on. Before continuing, it is important to stress that this test is only a way of demonstrating (from a different point of view and for more players) a fact that has already been established elsewhere.

Table 10.9 shows that some players provided the same answer for many different but similar sequences. Although relatively few players 'transferred' a large number of wrong rules, it should be noted that we are only analysing one of a number of possible similar rules. The fact that some players provided the same answer does not constitute definite proof of the transfer of rules (or of the building of higher-level categories). These could just be random results, though, in all probability, this was not the case for some of the players. The reason is that the probability of a random similarity between four or five answers is very low. Moreover, a detailed analysis of the players' behaviour supports the idea that these are not random results.

Table 10.10 shows the last part of Player 2's game. As we can see, s/he had developed a 'rule 75' that stated: white–square–small = very good. S/he also replied 'very good' to the sequence yellow–square–small. This may have happened by chance, but the answer is coherent with his/her overall system of rules. In fact s/he compared 'square' to 'circle' and 'heart' for all colours.

Similar analyses could be carried out for all sequences (not only for the new ones) and using other 'similar rules' (in fact subjects could build other kinds of categories), in which case other examples of rule transfer would probably emerge.

Table 10.10 A more detailed analysis of the behaviour of Player 2

Period				Very bad	Bad	Average	Good	Very good	Freq.
III	White	Circle	Large					100%	4
			Small				100%		3
		Heart	Large					100%	4
			Small				100%		1
		Square	Large					100%	3
			Small				100%		1
		Rectangle	Large			100%			1
			Small			100%			3
	Blue	Circle	Large	100%					1
			Small		100%				2
		Heart	Large	33%		67%			3
			Small		100%				1
		Square	Large	75%		25%			4
			Small		100%				1
		Rectangle	Large	100%					1
			Small		100%				4
	Yellow	Circle	Large					100%	3
			Small				100%		4
		Heart	Large					100%	1
			Small				100%		3
		Square	Large					100%	1
			Small				100%		4
		Rectangle	Large			100%			3
			Small			100%			1
	Black	Circle	Large	100%					1
			Small		100%				2
		Heart	Large	100%					2
			Small		100%				1
		Square	Large	100%					3
			Small		50%	50%			4
		Rectangle	Large	100%					3
			Small		100%				4

10.3.3 The Effect of Compensation Systems

Points were given to subjects according to two different systems (Table 10.11) The first tended to reward correct answers highly, while penalizing very wrong answers. Decent answers received an almost null reward. In the second system, the variance of the points given to right and wrong answers was low.

Table 10.11 Systems of compensation[‡]

Distance from the correct solution[*]	Points gained – Case 1	Points gained – Case 2
0 – right answer	+10	+6
1	+2	+3
2	0	+1
3	–2	0
4	–10	–1

Note: ‡ For example if the right answer is 'very good' and the answer given is 'very bad', the difference is 4; if the right answer is 'very good' and the answer is 'good', the difference is 1.

The two systems seem to have had a strong influence on the players' learning processes, leading to some surprising results. Players in Group 1 tended to develop a lower number of rules overall and a higher ratio of wrong rules (Table 10.12).

Table 10.12 Mean values of many indicators by system of compensation

	Group 1	Group 2
Right answer by subject	137	158
Percentage of 'rule 75's	0.74	0.81
Percentage of 'rule 100's	0.65	0.76
Percentage of wrong rules on rule 100	0.18	0.10
Percentage of wrong rules on rule 75	0.19	0.12

A single chapter does not provide scope for a full discussion of these results in detail. However, it seems necessary to stress that these results, once again, highlight the fact that individual learning is not a process that necessarily converges towards a predefined path (i.e. leading necessarily to the 'best rule'). Environment and context (in this case the system of compensation) seems to exercise a strong effect on actions and can therefore influence the direction of the process significantly.

10.4 CONCLUDING REMARKS

Though the emergence of routines and regularities in human decision-making and the role played by learning are widely acknowledged in the literature, some relevant problems remain open in economics. Among these, we decided to focus our attention on the crucial question: how are rules consolidated after they emerge? We are aware that finding a satisfactory answer to this question is a very hard task, as any answer should include both an individual and a social level of analysis (applicable to individual and vicarious learning). There is also no doubt that, apart from the area of decision making, this open question is particularly relevant to a sizeable part of the economic tradition, including Austrian economics, evolutionary economics, the economics of innovation and new institutional economics.

Following a number of theoretical and methodological investigations (see in particular Novarese 2003; Rizzello 1999; Novarese and Rizzello 1999), we are now convinced that only the experimental domain, with its observation and description of human learning, can help us move towards an answer to our open question. As accurate observations can only be made in successive stages, the experiment we have just described can only be considered as a very first step in a long process. We intend to continue with the production of new experiments, which will also tackle vicarious learning and co-ordination, in order to accumulate results and build a more complete picture.

The results achieved to date are encouraging so we are continuing our research in this specific branch of cognitive and experimental economics. In fact, our results appear to provide a few answers to the question of rule consolidation outlined above. If, on the one hand, results appear to confirm what is already largely known in the literature (i.e. that individuals tend to generate new decision-making rules spontaneously when they cannot use pre-existing routines), on the other hand and much more interestingly, it has also emerged that individuals manifest a tendency to consolidate such regularities even when they are aware that these rules are wrong (see also Novarese 2006, forthcoming). However, the very same individuals also appear to exhibit the opposite predisposition and fail to confirm correct rules. We believe this to be an important result and, though we are not yet in a position to generalize it, a more detailed analysis (a kind of case study) of some of the players' results seems to confirm that:

> the strategy's rules have to be memorized and represented with some degree of abstraction, to allow one drastically to reduce their number. Raising the level of abstraction with which a strategy's rule is represented, means to extend the domain of validity of the rule beyond the field in which the rule has been experimented,

and it may therefore induce one to include inadvertently domains in which the rule is inefficient. (Egidi 2002)

Besides, as we have seen, the rules developed by the players under exam conditions appear to be coherent. Though not entirely correct, they can be deemed to be satisfying in many ways; for example, they are easy to remember and apply.

Finally, it could be argued that these results cannot be read in a general and comprehensive way and that this is an insurmountable limit preventing the development of a robust model. In this case, we would have to conclude that the only way forward is to abandon this kind of research. However, this is not the case. When the starting point is 'observation and description' and not the confutation or validation of some model, it is acceptable to consider behaviour which *prima facie* appears to be a niche performance in the hope that in the not too distant future it could become the foundation of a new theory.[15]

NOTES

* The experiment presented here was realized at the Centre for Cognitive Economics at the Università del Piemonte Orientale in Alessandria, Italy. The authors are grateful to the staff of the Centre and in particular to Chiara Antonello, Simona Mazzarello, Elena Passalacqua and Cesare Tibaldeschi. Earlier versions of this chapter were presented as a paper at the Workshop on Cognitive Economics (November 2000) held in Alessandria and Turin, at the workshop on Simulation in Economics with Artificial and Real Agents (June 2001) organized in Turin by Silvia Occelli (Ires-Piemonte) and at a seminar at the Creuset, University of St. Etienne (July 2001). We wish to thank all the participants in the discussions during the workshops and seminar and in particular Michel Bellet, Massimo Egidi, Pierre Garrouste and Pietro Terna for their comments. The authors are very grateful to the Società per l'insediamento universitario per Alessandria–Asti which has partially supported this research.

1. As Börgers wrote (1996, p. 1384) the reason for this might be that 'economists naturally do not welcome research which calls into question the foundations of their work'. In support of the idea that psychological concepts are often used superficially we refer readers to Piaget who thought it very unfortunate for psychology that everyone believed him to be a psychologist.
2. On the foundations and historical evolution of the cognitive approach to economics see Egidi and Rizzello (2003) and on the characteristics of cognitive economics see Rizzello (1999).
3. The theory of social cognitive learning based on vicarious learning has been elaborated by the Canadian psychologist Albert Bandura, but is still not widespread among economists. A few exceptions are: Witt (2000) and Rizzello and Turvani (2002).
4. Rizzello (2000a and 2000b).
5. Hayek (1952) illustrated these mechanisms, later confirmed by psychology and neurobiology (see Rizzello 1999).
6. In 'diagnostical task experiments' (see for example Kelley and Friedman 1999; Kitzis et al. 1998 and the related theoretical work of Marcet and Sargent 1989), which present some similarities with the experiment described here, the authors' attention is focused on the subjects' ability to correctly estimate the parameters of a known model.

7. The categories of colour and shape are not explicitly used in the description of the game given to players.
8. Similar results were obtained in a pilot experiment realized in March 2000 in Alessandria, with a smaller group of subjects remunerated with money.
9. The probability of confirming by chance n wrong answers on m confirmations is equal to the probability of n successes in m independent repetitions in a binomial casual variable with probability equal to 1/5.
10. As the same right answer is given in at least two following appearances of the same sequence, it is unlikely that they are given just by chance.
11. Given that the game is very long and repetitive, it seems reasonable to think that a subject who has developed a rule can make a mistake and give a different answer in some cases. Moreover, the rule could be evolving and not perfectly defined at the beginning of what we call period III. This is why we also make use of definitions like 'rule 75'.
12. This hypothesis could be tested in other ways with the data of this experiment. Table 10.6 is also proof that at least a few players are not just memorizing the answers.
13. It seems reasonable to think that a player can spot a similarity between these kinds of sequences as similarities are suggested by the game itself. There are other possible and reasonable similarities (for example sequences with the same colour and size and with similar shape, or sequences with the same colour and shape and a different size). The test presented here is necessarily very partial and only hopes to provide an idea of the process of extension of rules.
14. It is not possible to give a detailed account of the complete distribution of these values here.
15. Herbert Simon's (1992, p. 20) following methodological remark on the analysis of the firm seems to apply here as well: 'If you are trying to understand what firms are and how they operate, you will learn a lot from this kind of very detailed study of the processes of decision ... Of course, we should not stop with five firms. Biologists have described millions of species of plants and animals in the world, and they think they've hardly started the job. Now, I'm not suggesting that we should go out and describe decision making in a million firms; but we might at least get on with the task and see if we can describe the first thousand. That doesn't immediately solve the aggregation problem, but surely, and in spite of the question of sampling, it is better to form an aggregate from detailed empirical knowledge of a thousand firms, or five, than from direct knowledge of none. But the latter is what we have been doing in economics for too many years.'

REFERENCES

Börgers, T. (1996), 'On the relevance of evolution and learning to economic theory', *Economic Journal*, **106**, 1274–1385.

Droz, R. (1977), *Apprendimento in Enciclopedia*, vol. I, Torino: Einaudi.

Egidi, M. (2002), 'Biases in organizational behavior', in M. Augier and J. March (eds), *The Economics of Choice, Change and Organization: Essays in Memory of Richard M. Cyert*, Aldershot: Edward Elgar, pp. 190–242.

Egidi, M. and Narduzzo, A. (1997), 'The emergence of path-dependent behaviours in cooperative contexts', *International Journal of Industrial Organization*, **5**, 677–709.

Egidi, M. and Rizzello, S. (eds) (2003), *Cognitive Economics*, two volumes for the series, The International Library of Critical Writings in Economics, Cheltenham: Edward Elgar.

Friedman, D. (1998), 'Evolutionary economics goes mainstream: a review of the theory of learning in games', *Journal of Evolutionary Economics*, **8**, 423–32.

Fundenberg, D. and Levine, D.L. (1988), *The Theory of Learning in Games*, Cambridge, MA: MIT Press.

Hayek, F.A. (1952), *The Sensory Order. An Inquiry into the Foundations of Theoretical Psychology*, London: Routledge & Kegan Paul.

Kelly, H. and Friedman, D. (1999), *Learning to Forecast Price*, University of California Santa Cruz, Economics Department working papers.

Kitzis, S.N., Kelley, H., Berg, E., Massaro, D.W. and Friedman, D. (1998), 'Broadening the tests of learning models', *Journal of Mathematical Psychology*, **42**, 327–55

Marcet, A. and Sargent, T. (1989), 'Convergence of least squares learning mechanisms in self referential linear stochastic models', *Journal of Economic Theory*, **48**, 337–68.

Novarese, M. (2003), 'Toward a cognitive experimental economics', in S. Rizzello (ed.), *Cognitive Paradigms in Economics*, London: Routledge

Novarese, M. (2006, forthcoming), 'Learning in different social contexts', *Journal of Socio-Economics*.

Novarese, M. and Rizzello, S. (1999), 'Origin and recent development of experimental economics', *Storia del Pensiero Economico*, 37.

Rizzello, S. (1997), 'The microfoundations of path-dependency', in L. Magnusson and J. Ottosson (eds), *Evolutionary Economics and Path-dependence*, Cheltenham: Edward Elgar, pp. 98–118.

Rizzello, S. (1999), *The Economics of the Mind*, Aldershot: Edward Elgar.

Rizzello, S. (2000a), 'Economic change, subjective perception, and institutional evolution', *Metroeconomica*, **51** (2), 127–50.

Rizzello, S. (2000b), 'Hayek e la conoscenza come processo path-dependent' in S. Rizzello and G. Clerico (eds), *Organizzazione, Informazione e Conoscenza. Saggi su Hayek*, vol. I, Torino: UTET.

Rizzello, S. and Turvani, M. (2002), 'Subjective diversity and social learning: a cognitive perspective for understanding institutional behaviour', *Constitutional Political Economy*, **13**, 201–14.

Simon, H. (1992), 'Colloquium with H.A. Simon', in M. Egidi and R. Marris (eds), *Economics, Bounded Rationality and the Cognitive Revolution*, Aldershot: Edward Elgar.

Witt, U. (2000), *Social Cognitive Learning and Group Selection – A Game-theoretic Version of Hayek's Societal Evolution*, paper presented at the INEM–ASSA Session 'Austrian Economics and Game Theory', Boston, 8 January.

PART IV

Agents, Communities and Collective Beliefs

11. Consumer communities, self-organization and beliefs

Stéphane Ngo-Maï and Alain Raybaut

11.1 INTRODUCTION

The diffusion of Information and Communication Technology (ICT) in our economies has led to a vast increase in the number of electronic social and information good exchanges. The economic consequences of this phenomenon remain unclear.[1] Electronic markets could lead to an increase in competition thanks to a decrease in search and transaction costs, a reduction in informational asymmetries and an improved understanding of economic fundamentals. In this sense, one could reasonably expect the market mechanism to perform better overall.

However, a closer look at electronic technologies, goods and behaviour reveals a strong departure from the standard competitive hypothesis. Non-rival goods, for instance, can lead to zero or very low marginal cost production, which, in turn, leads to very specific types of economic behaviour. This gives rise to complex market structures in which imperfect competition could be understood not as a sign of inefficiency but instead as a compromise between co-ordination and market power.[2]

Although some researchers have focused on the economic consequences of the emergence of electronic markets, it is generally true that their attention has been restricted to price and quantity interactions and, in particular, to the study of the supply side of the market. In this chapter, we argue that the increased social interaction that has followed the development of ICT (and particularly the internet) has given rise to strong positive feedback effects on the demand side, where collective beliefs and imitative behaviour play a major role in the constitution of communities. Such communities are of economic interest because they are self-organized groups of potentially identical consumers. Low marginal cost producers are interested in such communities and in determining their size. In what follows, we will present a model of self-organization that sheds some light on the determinants of the emergence of such communities and on some of their statistical properties. More precisely, we will focus on the role of individual and collective beliefs of consumers confronted with information and experience goods on electronic markets.

11.2   SOCIAL INTERACTIONS AND SELF-ORGANIZED COMMUNITIES

As we briefly mentioned in the introduction, our understanding of the dynamic economic properties of complex social interactions remains limited. Recently, Alan Kirman put forward the hypothesis that in such a context:

> information is not transmitted fully through prices and bubbles may occur. This inferring of information is but one example of the direct interaction that takes place between agents. Yet we cannot exclude considerations of such interaction on the grounds that it constitutes a mere imperfection of the standard model. Such interaction is a fundamental and not a marginal feature of economic behaviour. Taking such interaction into account should lead us to less demanding and less introspective assumptions about individual behaviour.[3]

'Herd behaviour' is a type of economic phenomenon that can arise in this context and one which requires an understanding of influence and imitation as key economic variables rather than a simple focus on a maximizing individual agent.

When attempting to deal with such phenomena as the self-organized communities we find on the web, we can rely on three different areas of research. First, there are the recent developments in cognitive economics, engaged in the study of the beliefs and reasoning underlying agent adaptation to mutual dynamic interactions.[4] An interesting approach that moves away from the strategic behaviour model is the idea of 'self-referential' mimesis put forward by Orléan (2001), which modifies the agents' utility functions in order to capture some of the effects of social interaction. Club and network effects are simple examples of the use of this approach.

Another way of tackling the problem is through 'informational mimesis' or 'informational cascades'.[5] Unlike in the previous case, the influence agents exercise on each other is not considered to be a direct argument of individual utility functions. Beliefs constitute the central variable, in the sense that it is sufficient for agents to believe that the actions of others reflect a better quality of information than their own for them to adopt an imitative behaviour that leads to informational cascades. Individual beliefs on the information sets of other agents arising from the observation of their actions can give rise to imitative behaviour featuring strong feedback effects and leading to the formation of collective beliefs.

Our chapter is based on this idea and our model focuses on the self-organization properties of a population which we assume to be composed of imitative and non-imitative agents, according to the kind of beliefs they hold. This type of analysis, which is based on population modelling, is a convenient tool with which to study global social interactivity. It also provides an interesting link between the micro elements and macro properties of social systems, though some precision in terms of microfoundations is lost in the process.

Another set of interesting contributions for our purposes are the recent advances in the area of random networks applied to the web. Evidence of the existence of power laws has been discovered in such evolutive networks.[6] The probability $P(k)$ that a randomly chosen node has k bonds is $P(k) = k^{-\lambda}$, where λ is a positive real number. This kind of very skewed distribution with scale-free properties has been discovered and studied in many large networks such as electric or telecom networks and, more interestingly, on the internet and web. For instance, the distribution of visitors for all categories of websites or by category of website is a power law. More precisely, 10 per cent of sites receive 80 per cent of total web visitors. We have the following characteristic plot:

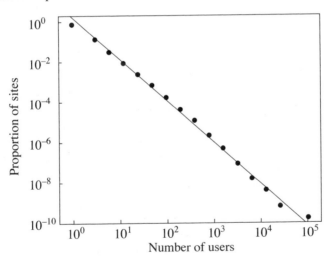

Source: Adamic and Huberman (2000).

Figure 11.1

It is worth noticing that the first explanations of the properties of the results stemming from random network theory are related to the preferential attachment hypothesis. This states that the probability a node has of receiving new bonds is positively related to the number of bonds already connected to it.[7] From an economic standpoint, the phenomenon can be explained by making use of the idea of imitative behaviour stemming from beliefs such as the ones described above.

The third type of research we would like to mention is the literature on electronic markets. Most authors now believe that these markets have certain features that set them aside from traditional ones. One convenient and abstract way of understanding the peculiarities of these markets is based on the large number of positive feedbacks they display. These feedbacks counterbalance the effects arising from lower search and transaction costs and lead to new forms of co-ordination. The lower elasticity of demand observed on the web could, for instance, be explained through the complex interactions the web itself requires, which cannot be reduced to price comparisons. Many researches have, in fact, established that agents do not rely on ICT as much for price and quality comparisons as they do for the exchange of a whole host of types of information including the characteristics of the goods, trust etc. It has also been shown that this type of communication can have a positive feedback effect on consumer behaviour, which eventually leads to the constitution of self-organized communities (Gensollen 2001).

Communities, defined here as groups of agents engaged in non-commercial exchanges of information, are an important stylized fact in internet economics. A first attempt at constructing a typology of such communities could, for example, include the following categories: communities of transaction, facilitating the matching of supply and demand; communities of interest, organizing communications around objects and subjects; and communities of practice, attempting to improve specific objects or knowledge. From an economic point of view, such communities have been identified as core entities in co-ordination mechanisms,[8] be they organizations or markets. In final markets, which are of particular interest in this case, this kind of enhanced social interaction can lead to homogeneous self-organized communities. These differ from traditional segmentations in a number of ways.

First, these communities are not statistically defined through behavioural analysis but correspond to a spontaneous partition of potential consumers. Secondly, they lead to finer segmentations than those produced by standard statistical analysis. Finally, a process of preference convergence means they display homogeneous tastes and usage. Such a process relies heavily on an assumption of agent preference instability caused by influences on beliefs (such as fashion, opinion leaders, etc.). Relationships between communities allow for a fine and spontaneous partition of demand. Clearly, the information made available to potential consumers can itself be subject to business mechanisms due to the kind of demand such a high degree of segmentation allows. This also means that supply side economic strategies become possible, such as bundling and then targeting information to specific communities. In this perspective and against a background of near zero marginal production costs, the size of the community becomes a key variable. It is precisely to an analysis of the emergence of such communities that we shall now turn.

11.3   BELIEFS AND SELF-ORGANIZATION OF COMMUNITIES

We consider a population of N consumers distributed in M communities G_i, $i = 1, 2,...M$, with $M \le N$, where each agent belongs to only one community.[9] We suppose that a unique set of demand characteristics corresponds to each community. This means that consumers belonging to a particular community have homogeneous preferences for a given type of good.[10] Since we are dealing with information or experience goods, agents do not have an *a priori* objective knowledge of the utility provided by such goods (see, for example, Curien et al. 2001). Moreover, since the characteristics of such goods change rapidly, consumers are assumed to change communities stochastically according to individual and collective beliefs.

Given this framework, we are interested in determining the size and mean number of communities. Our model relies on mean field analysis as used in statistical mechanics or random networks (Weinsbuch 2001; Barabasi et al. 1999). Models describing stochastic interactions between heterogeneous groups of agents do not commonly give rise to analytical solutions, and are generally limited to numerical simulations.[11] The mean field technique is, therefore, of some interest because it can give rise to purely analytical solutions (Solé et al. 2002). In what follows, we shall be making use of this technique in order to study the self-organization properties of communities. More specifically, we are interested in the stationary distribution of the size and mean number of non-empty communities.

This dynamical process of the constitution of communities allows us to examine two distinct cognitive aspects: one with an individual dimension, the other with a more collective one.

1. A first process relies on individual beliefs. A consumer, randomly chosen in the population, leaves a community to become a member of another,

while a different consumer joins the first community. This behaviour is directly linked to individual beliefs and is independent of the existing interactions between communities. Since, in this context, we are more interested in population dynamics, the precise individual programme remains implicit. In what follows, we suppose that this process is running with a weight p, $0 < p < 1$.

2. A second process is related to collective beliefs. We suppose that two consumers belonging to two different but interacting communities i and j meet and enter into a process of influence. Interactions between communities are modelled by an $M \times M$ matrix Ω. This matrix is initially randomly chosen and composed of real numbers ω_{ij}, $i \neq j$, which stand for the direction of the influence between i and j. Therefore, Ω is an anti-symmetric matrix with a zero diagonal. The connectivity of Ω, i.e. the relative number of non-zero elements of Ω, is labelled c, $c \in [0,1]$ and, once determined, is assumed to be fixed. If ω_{ij} is positive, then i influences j and the number of agents in community i increases by one (or diminishes by one if ω_{ij} is negative). This process can either refer to an individual calculation relying on the belief that other agents are better informed (such as in cascades) or refer directly to some collective or social belief (cf. Orléan in this volume, Chapter 9). In what follows, we assume that such a process is running with a weight $1 - p$.

In a mean field framework, let us consider a representative community of size n among the M. In this case, the two processes described above can be formalized as follows (Solé et al. 2002):

- With probability (weight) p, a randomly chosen consumer with probability n/N in this representative community leaves and another one belonging to another group, chosen with probability $1 - 1/M$, becomes a member of the representative community. Then, the probability of a random individually based process of change of communities is given by:

$$R_p = p \frac{n}{N}\left(1 - \frac{1}{M}\right). \tag{11.1}$$

It is worth noticing that for all n, N, M, this probability R_p only depends on p and is independent of social or collective interactions symbolized by Ω. It therefore represents an individually based process of change of communities.

- With a probability (weight) $1 - p$, two agents, one member of the representative community of size n, the other a member of a different community, get into a process of influence. Since the connectivity of Ω is c, the probability that these two agents will interact is $C^* = 1 - (1 - c)^2$. This happens with a probability n/N on a proportion $(N - n)/(N - 1)$ of agents. Then, the probability of a collectively based process of change of communities is given by:

$$R_\Omega = (1 - p)C^* \frac{n}{N}\left(\frac{N - n}{N - 1}\right). \tag{11.2}$$

The sum of (11.1) and (11.2) gives the probability r_n that in each period the size of the representative community will diminish by one unit:

$$r_n = C^*(1 - p)\frac{n}{N}\left(\frac{N - n}{N - 1}\right) + \frac{p}{M}(M - 1)\frac{n}{N}. \tag{11.3}$$

Applying the same reasoning, we obtain the probability g_n that the size of the community will increase by one unit in each period of time:

$$g_n = C^*(1 - p)\frac{n}{N}\left(\frac{N - n}{N - 1}\right) + \frac{p}{M}\left(1 - \frac{n}{N}\right). \tag{11.4}$$

For simplicity reasons it is convenient to write:

$$p^* = \frac{p}{(1 - p)MC^*}$$
$$\lambda^* = p^*(N - 1) \tag{11.5}$$
$$v^* = N + p^*(N - 1)(M - 1).$$

We then obtain:

$$g_n = \frac{C^*(1 - p)}{N(N - 1)}(N - n)(\lambda^* + n) \tag{11.6}$$

and:

$$r_n = \frac{C^*(1 - p)}{N(N - 1)}n(v^* - n). \tag{11.7}$$

It is therefore possible to build the *master equation* associated with the dynamics described previously. Define as $P(n,t)$ the probability that the representative community includes n members in period t. Then the master equation becomes:

$$\frac{dP(n,t)}{dt} = r_{n+1}P(n+1,t) + g_{n-1}P(n-1,t) - (r_n + g_n)P(n,t). \quad (11.8)$$

Let us consider the stationary value $P_S(n)$ of the difference equation (11.8), solution of

$$\frac{dP(n,t)}{dt} = 0$$

for all n.[12] It can be shown for $p \neq 0$ that a unique and stable stationary value $P_S(n)$ exists,[13] where (see Appendix 11.1):

$$P_S(n) = \binom{N}{n}\frac{\beta(n + \lambda^*, v^* - n)}{\beta(\lambda^*, v^* - N)}. \quad (11.9)$$

This relation (11.9) gives the stationary probability distribution that a mean field community of consumers includes n members. This distribution takes the shape of a ratio of Beta functions[14] characterized by the extent of the total population N, the initial number of communities M, the connectivity c of the communities network and the probability p.

As shown on Figure 11.2 below, the properties and shape of this distribution are modified as the probabilities p and $1-p$, which respectively capture the weight of individual and collective beliefs of consumers in the dynamics, change. By contrast, it appears that these properties are robust with respect to changes in the total population N, the initial number of communities M, and, more surprisingly, the connectivity c.

As the weight of collective beliefs increases (p decreases), the stationary distribution progressively loses its single peak shape. That is to say, the initial Log-Normal distribution gradually turns into a power law distribution. It should, however, be emphasized that the latter is obtained only for very small values of p, which means that in that case social beliefs and mimetic behaviour are dominant (in this example with $N = 5000$, $M = 300$, $c = 0.5$, when p changes from 0.75 to 0.05).

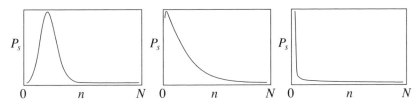

Figure 11.2   Modifications of Ps(n) as the weight of collective beliefs increases (p decreases)

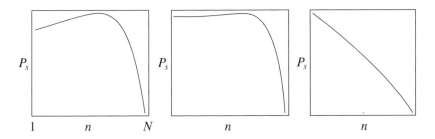

Figure 11.3   Modifications of Ps(n) LogLog scale

These findings are synthesized in the following diagram:

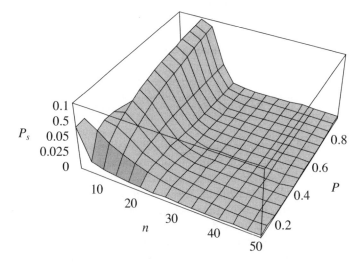

Figure 11.4   Ps(n) as function of n and p

Finally, it is possible to complete the model by computing the stationary average number $\bar{M}$ of non-empty communities. One can easily check that (see Appendix 11.2) this number is equal to:

$$\bar{M} = \left(1 - P_S(0)\right)M \tag{11.10}$$

where

$$P_S(0) = 1 - \sum_{n>0}^{N} P_S(n).$$

Using (11.9) with $n = 0$, we obtain:

$$P_S(0) = \frac{\Gamma\left(v^*\right)}{\Gamma\left(v^* + \lambda^*\right)} \frac{\Gamma\left([v^* - N] + \lambda^*\right)}{\Gamma\left(v^* - N\right)}.$$

Notice that this average number, which depends on the initial maximum number of communities M, is also not very sensitive to the connectivity c, but increases with the probability p (see Figures 11.5 and 11.6):

It appears that when the weight of individual beliefs is greatest (i.e. p is close to unity) the distribution of the size of communities n, is Log-Normal and admits a most probable size equal to

$$\frac{N}{M} = \frac{Total\ Population}{Potential\ Number\ of\ Communities}.$$

Conversely, when herd behaviour and collective beliefs prevail (p is close to zero), the distribution of the size of communities is a power law. In this case N/M is no longer the most probable size, because the distribution displays a strong bias in favour of small communities. On a logarithmic scale, the distribution linearly decreases with the size of n. Since the whole population is distributed among the communities and the average number of non-empty communities decreases, one can expect a configuration with a small number of large communities. In other words, a pattern characterized by both diversity and strong polarization obtains.

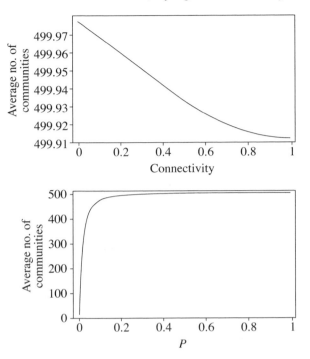

Figure 11.5   Average number of communities as a function of c *and as a function of* p

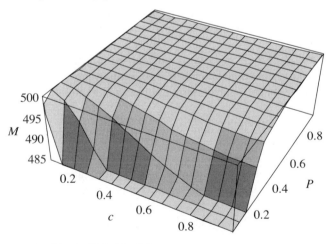

Note: Example with *N* = 5000, *M* = 500.

Figure 11.6   Average number of communities as a function of c *and* p
(example with N = 5000, M = 500)

11.4   CONCLUSION

The increasing weights of both social interactions and information goods in our economies should lead us to discard traditional individual rationality for a more thorough analysis of the nature and role of beliefs. In this chapter, we have attempted to study the ways and the extent to which self-organized communities of homogeneous agents can emerge in a market as a result of two forms of beliefs. The theoretical interest of such an analysis is straightforward.

First, communities constitute an intermediate level of analysis between the individual and the collective. Secondly, communities make an important difference to the analysis of market co-ordination modes. What we have put forward is a self-organization model of consumer communities in a final market which relies on a combination of individual and collective beliefs. We were able to determine the stationary distribution of the size of communities and their mean number. These variables depend strongly on the weight given to individual and collective beliefs.

While the diversity of communities depends on the weight of individual beliefs, polarization effects emerge when collective beliefs are at play. It is worth noting that this mix of polarization and diversity follows a power law distribution, which is a strong stylized fact of the Internet economy. In other words, we witness the simultaneous presence of small numbers of large communities and large numbers of small communities. This very skewed distribution is obtained in the presence of mimetic dynamics. This imitative behaviour can either be the result of individual beliefs concerning the relative quality of their own informational sets or the result of pure social beliefs.

These first analytical results on the self-organization of consumer communities may contribute to a better understanding of the peculiar co-ordination patterns that characterize electronic markets.

APPENDIX 11.1

Appendix 11.1 examines the characterization of the stationary value $P_S(n)$ and gives an outline of the proof (see Solé et al. (2002) for details).

Assume first that $p \neq 0$. Then, the stationary distribution $P_S(n)$ of the master equation (11.8) verifies for all n:

$$r_{n+1}P_S(n+1) - g_n P_S(n) = r_n P_S(n) - g_{n-1}P_S(n-1). \quad (11.11)$$

Since (11.11) holds for all n, we have $r_n P_S(n) - g_{n-1} P_S(n-1) = K$, where K is a constant. Applying the boundary condition for $n = 0$, we get $K = 0$. Hence, we have:

$$r_n P_S(n) = g_{n-1} P_S(n-1); n = 1, ..., N.$$

(11.12)

If $p \neq 0$, then $r_n \neq 0$ for all n such that $0 < n \leq N$. Consequently, we obtain:

$$P_S(n) = \frac{g_{n-1} g_{n-2} \cdots g_0}{r_n r_{n-1} \cdots r_1} P_S(0); n = 1, ..., N$$

(11.13)

where $P_S(0)$ is determined by the following normalization condition:

$$\sum_{n=0}^{N} P_S(n) = P_S(0) + \sum_{n>0} P_S(n) = 1.$$

(11.14)

Thus, one can deduce that:

$$\left(P_S(0)\right)^{-1} = 1 + \sum_{n=1}^{N} \frac{g_{n-1} g_{n-2} \cdots g_0}{r_n r_{n-1} \cdots r_1}.$$

(11.15)

Substituting the respective values g_n and r_n given by (11.6) and (11.7) into (11.15) we obtain:

$$\left(P_S(0)\right)^{-1} = \sum_{n=0}^{N} \binom{N}{n} \frac{\Gamma(n + \lambda^*)\Gamma(v^* - n)}{\Gamma(\lambda^*)\Gamma(v^*)}$$

$$= \sum_{n=0}^{N} \binom{N}{n}(-1)^n \frac{\Gamma(n + \lambda^*)\Gamma(1 - v^*)}{\Gamma(\lambda^*)\Gamma(n + 1 - v^*)}.$$

(11.16)

This summation has the form of a polynomial $P_N^{(\alpha,\beta)}(x)$ with $\alpha = -v^*$, $\beta = \lambda^* + v^* - (N + 1)$ and $x = -1$. Hence, $P_S(n)$ using (11.13) we get:

$$P_S(n) = \binom{N}{n} \frac{\Gamma(n + \lambda^*)\Gamma(v^* - n)\Gamma(\lambda^* + v^* - N)}{\Gamma(\lambda^*)\Gamma(v^* - N)\Gamma(\lambda^* + v^*)}.$$

(11.17)

Finally, let us write

$$\beta(p,q) = \frac{\Gamma(p)\Gamma(q)}{\Gamma(p+q)},$$

then the stationary distribution becomes :

$$P_S(n) = \binom{N}{n} \frac{\beta(n+\lambda^*, v^* - n)}{\beta(\lambda^*, v^* - N)}. \tag{11.18}$$

Secondly, let us consider the case $p = 0$. If $p = 0$, then $r_N = 0$. Consequently relation (11.13) holds only for $n \neq N$. In this limited case, knowing that $g_0 = 0$, we have $P_S(n) = 0$ for $n = 1, 2...N - 1$. By normalization, we can write $P_S(0) = \zeta$ and $P_S(N) = 1 - \zeta$ where ζ is a constant. As a result, we have for $p = 0$:

$$P_S(0) = \frac{1}{M}; P_S(N) = 1 - \frac{1}{M}; P_S(n) = 0 \text{ for } 0 < n < N \tag{11.19}$$

which completes the proof on the characterization of $P_S(n)$.

APPENDIX 11.2

Appendix 11.2 examines the average number of non-empty communities.

Let us denote by $P_i(n)$ the probability that community i has n members. Then the probability that this community i has at least one member is $1 - P_i(0)$. Thus, the average number of communities is

$$\sum_i (1 - P_i(0)).$$

In a mean field approach, $P_i(0)$ is approximated by $P_S(0)$. Consequently, we obtain:

$$\bar{M} = \sum_{i=1}^{M} (1 - P_S(0)) = (1 - P_S(0))M,$$

where $\bar{M}$ refers to the average number of non-empty communities.

NOTES

1. In all probability the economic impact of the phenomenon is to be found at the microeconomic level, because from a macroeconomic point of view composition effects could leave the global dynamics unchanged.
2. See, for example, Gaudeul and Jullien 2001.
3. Kirman 2001.
4. See, for example, Walliser in this volume (Chapter 5).
5. See, for example, Banerjee 1992, and Bikhchandani et al. 1998.
6. See, for example, Albert and Barabasi 2001.
7. See, for example, Albert and Barabasi 2001 or Medina et al. 2000.
8. See, for example, Brousseau and Curien 2001.
9. It is therefore *a priori* possible that the number of communities is the same as the number of consumers.
10. Communities of interest correspond only to subsets of consumption.
11. For a general presentation in economics see, for example, Lesourne et al. 2002.
12. Relation (0.8) generally holds for $n \neq 0$ and $n \neq N$, since no transition can occur outside the interval $[0,N]$. Thus, for these limit values we have $g_N = 0$ and $r_0 = 0$. If we assume that $r_{N+1} = 0$ and g_{0-1}, then (0.8) holds for all $n = 0,1,2,...,N$.
13. With stationary transitory probabilities, these properties result from the ergodic theorem.
14. With

$$\beta(a,b) = \frac{\Gamma(a)\Gamma(b)}{\Gamma(a+b)}$$

and where function $\Gamma(x)$ is defined by

$$\Gamma(x) = \int_0^\infty t^{x-1} Exp(-t) dt.$$

REFERENCES

Adamic, L. and Huberman, B. (1999), 'Growth dynamics of the World Wide Web', *Nature*, September.

Adamic, L. and Huberman, B. (2000), 'The nature of markets in the WWW', *Quarterly Journal of Electronic Commerce*, **1**, 5–12.

Albert, R. and Barabasi, A.-L. (2001), 'Statistical mechanics of complex networks', arXiv:cond-mat/0106096.

Banerjee, A. (1992), 'A simple model of herd behaviour', *Quarterly Journal of Economics*, **108**.

Barabasi, A.L., Albert, R. and Jeong, H. (1999), 'Mean-field theory for scale-free random networks', *Physica*, **A 272**, 137–87.

Bikhchandani, S., Hirshleifer, D. and Welch, I. (1998), 'Learning from the behavior of others: conformity, fads and informational cascades', *The Journal of Economic Perspectives*, **12**, (3), 151–70.

Brousseau, E. and Curien, N. (eds) (2001), 'Economie de l'internet', *Revue Economique*.

Curien, N., Fauchart, E., Laffond, G., Laine, J., Lesourne, J. and Moreau, F. (2001), 'Forum de consommation sur internet; un modèle évolutionniste', *Revue Economique*, Economie de l'internet, Brousseau, Curien (eds).

Gaudeul, A. and Jullien, B. (2001), 'E-commerce: quelques éléments d'économie industrielle', *Revue Economique*, Economie de l'internet, N° hors série, **52**.

Gensollen, M. (2001), 'Marché électronique ou réseaux commerciaux ?', *Revue Economique*, Economie de l'internet.

Kirman, A. (2001), 'Some problems and perspectives in economic theory', Ecole d'Economie Cognitive, CNRS, Porquerolles, September.

Lesourne, J. and Orléan, A. (1998), *Advances in Self-organization and Evolutionary Economics*, Paris: Economica.

Lesourne, J., Orléan, A. and Walliser, B. (eds) (2002), *Leçons de microéconomie évolutionniste*, Paris: Odile Jacob.

Ngomai, S. and Raybaut, A. (1996), 'Microdiversity and macro-order: toward a self organization approach', *Revue Internationale de Systémique*, **10** (3).

Orléan, A. (2001), 'Comprendre les foules spéculatives: mimétismes informationnel, autoréférentiel et normatif,' in J. Gravereau and J. Trauman (eds), *Crises Financières*, Paris: Economica.

Orléan, A., 'The cognitive turning point in economics: social beliefs and conventions', (this volume, Chapter 9).

Smith, S., Bailey, J. and Brynjolfsson, E. (1999), 'Understanding digital markets: review and assessment', in E. Brynjolfsson and B. Kahin (eds), *Understanding the Digital Economy*, Cambridge, MA: MIT Press.

Solé, R.V., Alonso, D. and Mckane, A. (2002), 'Self-organized instability in complex ecosystems', *Philos. Trans. Royal Society*, **B 357**, pp. 667–81.

Walliser, B., 'Justifications of game theoretic equilibrium notions', (this volume, Chapter 5).

Weinsbuch, G. (2001), 'What can we learn from the complex systems approach to improve our understanding of markets, firms and institutions?', contribution to l'Ecole CNRS d'Economie Cognitive de Porquerolles, Chapter 4, September.

12. Informal communication, collective beliefs and corporate culture: a conception of the organization as a 'community of communities'

Patrick Cohendet and Morad Diani

12.1 INTRODUCTION

This chapter puts forward an interpretation of the firm based on the division of knowledge rather than the division of labour. This kind of perspective gives central importance to collective beliefs and corporate culture, two features of the firm whose importance has greatly increased in the knowledge-based economy. The idea of the firm as a bundle of interacting communities allows us to focus on voluntary cooperative exchange and informal communication as sources of collective beliefs and corporate culture. Given that community-level analysis allows scope for the examination of the creation, validation and diffusion of knowledge, in what follows, it will be considered as complementary to traditional modes of co-ordination of the firm.

Many recent works (e.g. Brousseau 2001; Gensollen 2001; Cowan and Jonard 2001) emphasize that in an economy that is increasingly based on knowledge, a growing part of the process of knowledge generation and diffusion relies on the workings of *knowledge-intensive communities*. These communities consist of frequently interacting agents in a non-hierarchical communication architecture. An important observation emerging from the analysis of such systems of voluntary cooperative exchange is the importance of behavioural norms in guiding the actions of community members and the intensity of the trust relations that underlie them.

Most of the current economic literature on communities focuses on the workings of virtual communities by looking at the development of the Internet (Lerner and Tirole 2001) or at scientific communities (Knorr-Cetina

1998). The objective of this contribution is to show that the methods used in the study of communities can usefully be extended to the theory of the firm. As the knowledge-based economy develops, firms increasingly appear as clusters of interconnected communities interacting within a common cultural framework. Indeed, as the knowledge-base of society expands and progressively becomes more complex, traditional hierarchical structures face difficulties in integrating and consolidating dispersed parcels of knowledge. These parcels are increasingly generated by and consolidated into informal collective contexts or *communities* that are well suited to dealing with some of the irreversible *sunk costs* associated with the processes of creation and maintenance of knowledge.

Thus, communities appear to be genuinely active units of competencies, which are useful to the organization as a whole since they are involved in a significant part of the processes of production, accumulation and validation of knowledge. These communities can be formed within traditional hierarchical settings (such as functional departments or project teams), but can also cut across the hierarchical structures of the firm by bringing together members interested in a particular field of knowledge.

Given that the production and diffusion of knowledge generally appear to be embedded in informal contexts and structures, one of the major roles of the firm is to give some coherence to the interactions between these various communities. As underlined by Brown and Duguid (1991, p. 54), in this representation, the firm is perceived:

> as a collective of communities, not simply of individuals, in which enacting experiments are legitimate, separate community perspectives can be amplified by inter-changes among communities. Out of this friction of competing ideas can come the sort of improvisational sparks necessary for igniting organizational innovation. Thus large organizations, reflectively structured, are perhaps well positioned to be highly innovative and to deal with discontinuities. If their internal communities have a reasonable degree of autonomy and independence from the dominant worldview, large organizations might actually accelerate innovation.

This *interactional* analysis, in terms of communities, raises the essential questions of co-ordination and cooperation and the role of representations and collective beliefs in creating a context for the production and diffusion of knowledge.

Given that communities interact and learn in strongly heterogeneous ways, coherence requires a firm to provide a common direction and vision that can guide heterogeneous actors and reconcile their conflicting interests. In this contribution, we support the hypothesis that this common reference system, or this common vision, will be produced through intra- and inter-community interaction in these specific contexts, an idea that corresponds to the concept of 'corporate culture'.

In this kind of analytical framework, corporate culture is essential to the co-ordination of actions and the creation of resources. This genuinely 'collective grammar' connects the various communities in the organization and underlies the homogenization of their objectives. It is also important to note that in some contexts of creation, which we will be discussing in more detail later on, co-ordination by communities is not only efficient but also appears to be less expensive than other modes of co-ordination within the firm. This contribution on the concept of community is, therefore, close to the idea put forward by Crémer (1998, p. 16), arguing for an advanced theoretical analysis of the networks of non-hierarchical communication within the firm:

> A considerable amount of work is yet to be done on non-hierarchical communities in firms. In contrast with the theory of hierarchies, the research in this perspective should aim at a better understanding of the advantages and drawbacks of the different networks of communication. It should also aim at exploring their organizational consequences.

This final chapter is structured in the following way. In the first section, we briefly review the limitations that key theories of the firm (primarily the transactional and evolutionary theories) display, once we take into account some of the main characteristics of resource creation. In the second section, we examine the properties of communities and, more precisely, what they can *add* to the analysis provided by other approaches to the theory of the firm. We highlight the main types of knowledge-intensive communities (epistemic communities and communities of practice) and discuss the advantages and limitations of this mode of co-ordination. The third section is devoted to an analysis of the firm considered as a cluster of interacting heterogeneous communities, underpinned by the idea that a firm's coherence is given by its corporate culture. In the final section, we discuss the extent to which co-ordination by communities is complementary to other forms of co-ordination (hierarchy and market).

12.2   LIMITATIONS OF TRADITIONAL AND NEW THEORIES OF THE FIRM WHEN CONFRONTED WITH THE PROBLEM OF KNOWLEDGE CREATION

12.2.1   Limitations of the Transactional Approach

As emphasized by many authors (e.g. Milgrom and Roberts 1988; Langlois and Foss 1996), the transactional approach, which is the dominant form of representation of the firm, has great difficulties in accounting for the process of creation and diffusion of 'new' knowledge. Transactional theory assumes that resource allocation takes place in a context in which productive capabilities are *given*. The firm is an institutional device allowing the establishment of incentives that correct informational biases and prevent the unproductive search for opportunistic rents, which can arise thanks to the imperfect nature of the information. This is a theory of the firm based on the problems of exchange, where the aspect of production or creation of resources is either neglected or considered of secondary importance.

In a context in which resources are actually being created, the contractual devices put forward by transaction cost economics are not best placed to explain the alignment of agent behaviour to a hierarchy's desires. Indeed, the cognitive dynamics of knowledge creation require a review of the logical relation between the existence of informational asymmetries and the risk of opportunism. When a firm is focused on a process of creation and diffusion of knowledge, the divergence of preferences, intentions or capabilities can give rise to effects that differ from those generated by informational asymmetries. Cohen (1984) has shown that diversity of preferences and objectives of agents located in a disturbed environment, where learning and the creation of competences are the principal factors of success, can be a source of improved performance. He suggests that when agents pursue objectives that are specific to their units, even when these conflict with those of other units, they can still outperform situations in which the whole set of organization members are focused on the same objective. This superiority can be explained, for example, by cross-fertilization effects in problem solving.

Another difficulty in dealing with the processes of learning and creation of knowledge is that the transactional approach supposes that the cognitive capabilities of agents are either given or assumed to change in a similar manner according to the information accumulated by the agents. The theory therefore allows virtually no place for genuine learning, understood as a transformation of the agents' cognitive capabilities or a change in the cognitive distances between agents.[1]

The limitations of the transactional approach in accounting for the process of creation of resources becomes very clear when we consider the concrete 'organizational forms' to which Williamson refers: though horizontal and vertical co-ordination can explain how organizations set up efficient routine tasks for the integration of existing knowledge, they encounter insurmountable difficulties in accounting for the co-ordination of innovating tasks aiming at the production of new knowledge. As Marengo (1994) has shown, the specialization inherent in horizontal co-ordination hinders hierarchical efforts to promote a creative collaboration between separate functional divisions. Similarly, though vertical co-ordination facilitates communication with the knowledge base, it is ineffective when attempting to co-ordinate non-routine tasks because, as underlined by Adler (2001), 'lower levels lack both the knowledge to create new knowledge and the incentives to transmit new ideas upwards'.

12.2.2 Limitations of the 'New Theories of the Firm'

According to Fransman (1994), transactional theory, like the other contractual theories of the firm, fails to take into account the phenomenon of knowledge creation because the firm is designated as a simple 'processor of information'. The firm becomes an alternative to the market only when the market proves incapable of processing information. Instead of treating the firm as a 'processor of information', where the cognitive dimension of the agents, their ability to treat knowledge or their learning capabilities are of secondary importance, Fransman puts forward the idea of the firm as a 'processor of knowledge' in a new framework that has recently emerged from the combination of a variety of approaches (strategy, evolutionary theory, industrial history, science of organizations). Drawing on the writings of Chandler (1962, 1992), Alchian (1950), Penrose (1959) and Richardson (1960, 1972), recent works at the forefront of current research – starting with the seminal work of Nelson and Winter (1982) and including contributions by Dosi (1988), Teece (1988), Prahalad and Hamel (1990) and March and Simon (1993) – have put forward a common hypothesis: the essential attribute of the firm is grounded in its 'competences', which correspond to a set of routines and know-how expressing the efficiency of a firm's resolution procedures. The firm is then primarily designated as a locus of arrangement, construction, selection and maintenance of competences. It is a 'processor of knowledge' favouring the acquisition, production and distribution of the knowledge indispensable for the maintenance of its competences. As underlined by Nonaka and Takeuchi (1995, p. 56):

> when organizations innovate, they do not simply process information from outside in, in order to solve existing problems and adapt to a changing environment. They actually create new knowledge and information, from the inside out, in order to redefine both problems and solutions and in the process, to re-create their environment.

Although the approaches that see the firm as a processor of knowledge offer a better explanation of knowledge creation within firms compared to the transaction cost approach, they also have difficulties in capturing some of the essential features of this process, where we believe the concept of community is better placed to succeed.

To better illustrate this point, a distinction among the competence-based approaches is necessary. Although all the competence-based theories rely on the principles we refer to above, the various approaches can be broadly divided into two main categories. The first, which draws its inspiration from the strategic approach (Prahalad and Hamel 1990), considers competence primarily as the result of an *a priori* vision of the management, which seeks to create a 'field' of virtuous learning in the organization in order to support the learning processes that move towards its vision. The second approach, which is based on the evolutionary approach (Teece 1988), considers competence as an *ex-post* construction (*a posteriori sense-making*), resulting from a process of general selection of diversified routines:

1. The strategic vision of competences, which is broadly inspired by the managerial literature, sees competences as the result of the long-term cognitive construction of comparative advantages (assuming an irreversible engagement of firms and 'sunk costs'). Such comparative advantages result from the hierarchy's selection of a set of privileged activities (the 'core-competences'), which focus a firm's cognitive resources. The choice of a selective perimeter of high cognitive intensity activities reflects a phenomenon of attention allocation, attention being the genuinely rare resource in the March and Simon (1993) sense of the firm. For Prahalad and Hamel (1990), the delimitation of this cognitive core lies at the strategic centre of the firm and results in a long-term 'vision' intended to structure the collective beliefs of the whole of the organization and to direct the processes of learning within the firm. However, as Stalk et al. (1992) observe, the main limit of this approach is that it only explains the cognitive process of managers: because capabilities are cross-functional, the change process cannot be left to middle managers; it requires the hands-on guidance of the Chief Executive Officer (CEO) and the active involvement of top line managers. An in-depth analysis of the process of knowledge construction within the organization is, therefore, not even broached.

2. The evolutionary vision considers that competences are gradually formed over time, through the selection (primarily by the market) of the most effective routines. As Paoli and Principe (2001) underlined, routines embody the successful solutions to problems solved by the organization in the past. They are retrieved and executed whenever the organization faces a problem resembling one already solved. Organizational memory is stored in routines, so that Nelson and Winter (1982) see the firm as a 'repertoire of routines'.[2]

The evolutionary approach is undoubtedly the theoretical approach that best accounts for firms' resources creation. However, it lets knowledge creation slip because it proceeds as if the firm *possessed* (hence the concept of a 'repertoire') the knowledge incorporated into routines and suggests that competence results from the selection of the best routines stored within the repertoire. However, many recent works (see, for example, Cook and Brown 1999) show that most of this knowledge is not accessible through a 'given' repertoire, but is instead rooted in the practices of small active groups or 'communities' which form the firm. The very nature of a routine (its capacity for replication, degree of inertia and potential for evolution) depends heavily on the group which implements it. Although evolutionary analysis offers a rich context of interpretation of the relations between the individual and collective efforts in the creation of resources through the concept of routine, it still lacks an analysis of the 'intermediate links' which are the genuine catalysts of the process of creation in the organization, where the creative ideas emerge or are tested and where the first validation of any innovation is carried out. It is precisely this failure that justifies taking the concept of community seriously into account.

12.3 THE ORGANIZATION CONCEIVED AS A COMMUNITY OF COMMUNITIES

In order to think of the firm dynamically as a myriad of overlapping communities we first need to identify and characterize the various communities which form the firm and then we have to illustrate their role in the collective process of knowledge creation by understanding their advantages and limitations. These premises are necessary in order to interpret the interaction of the various communities (necessary to understand how the coherence of a firm is established), the intensity of their structuring, their mutual transformation and the ways in which they contribute to important organizational changes.

Before analysing the various types of communities and their properties, it is important to distinguish them from traditional hierarchical groupings (functional groups and project teams in particular), where group membership is controlled by the hierarchy. Such hierarchical groups need to provide constant incentives in order to maintain adhesion. Functional groups are relatively homogeneous and consist of agents sharing the same disciplinary specialization (finance, mechanical engineering, etc.) under the hierarchical responsibility of a department manager or a functional group manager. Project teams are, by definition, more heterogeneous and are born out of a will to cut across disciplines, but they are also placed under a hierarchical authority (project manager).

In this contribution we will be considering genuinely 'autonomous' communities based upon the principle of voluntary adhesion, due to the sharing of a number of values, norms or common interests. Voluntary adhesion is accompanied by the sharing of a common passion or the mutual respect of a procedural authority. Hence the assumption that these communities (which are places where permanently local models, shared representations and jargons are built) rely upon trust relations that are non-strategically calculated and founded on the same social values. Thus, *a priori*, the risk of opportunism in this form of co-ordination is of secondary importance.

12.3.1 Various Forms of Communities

Two major types of communities can be distinguished among the active and autonomous communities involved in the process of knowledge creation. These are the epistemic communities, which are explicitly geared towards the creation of new knowledge, and communities of practice, which aim to carry out an activity successfully and only create knowledge unintentionally. In terms of knowledge, each community is characterized by a principal learning mechanism: 'best practice' dissemination in the case of communities of practice, and peer-reviewed publications in some of the epistemic communities. The frequent interactions between members of the community naturally reinforce the cohesion of the learning processes.

12.3.1.1 Epistemic communities

According to Cowan et al. (2000, p. 234), epistemic communities are 'small groups of agents working on a commonly acknowledged subset of knowledge issues and who at the very least accept a commonly understood procedural authority as essential to the success of their knowledge activities'. The members of an epistemic community have a common objective of deliberate knowledge creation. To this end, they gradually construct a common structure that allows them to share understanding. These communities are, for example, groups of researchers, a 'task-force' or a group of designers within a firm, a 'school' in painting or music. What binds each community is the existence of a procedural authority, i.e., a set of rules or codes of conduct defining its objectives and the means required to attain them. Epistemic communities are thus structured around an objective 'to be reached' and a procedural authority established by themselves (or by virtue of which they were founded) in order to attain this objective. This form of organization generates knowledge creation by supporting the synergy of individual varieties. Because of the heterogeneity of the representatives involved, one of the first tasks of epistemic communities is to create a 'codebook', in the sense of setting out a dictionary and a grammar to allow the cognitive work to take place. The cognitive activity of a representative of this community is validated according to the criteria fixed by the procedural authority. What is evaluated each time is the individual contribution to the collective objective to be reached.

12.3.1.2   Communities of practice

Communities of practice (Lave and Wenger 1991) represent groups of people engaged in the same practice communicating regularly between themselves about their activities. The members of a community of practice primarily seek to develop their competences in the practice in question, while incessantly spreading and comparing the 'best practices' tested by other members. Communities of practice can be seen as a means for the development of individual competences through the continuous improvement of the common practice. This objective is reached through the construction, exchange and sharing of a common, though not necessarily formally clarified, repertoire of resources. Self-organization is, thus, an essential characteristic of communities of practice. More precisely, the autonomy and identity of communities (the two key characteristics of self-organization) authorize the collective acquisition and treatment of the stimuli provided by the environment (Wenger 1998; Dibiaggio 1998). Thus, it is the mutual commitment of its members that ensures a community's cohesion and it is this same commitment that governs the recruitment of new members. The evaluation of an individual by a community of practice depends both on the values adopted by the individual and on the progress vis-à-vis its practice.

Clearly then, knowledge in communities of practice is primarily 'know-how' (Brown and Duguid 1991), which is both tacit and socially localized. This collective know-how is constantly enriched by individual practices, so that the collective device generates a process of continuous knowledge creation, which is useful to the organization, but, contrary to the epistemic communities, remains *unintentional*.

12.3.2   Advantages and Limitations of Co-ordination by Communities

12.3.2.1   Advantages of co-ordination by communities

In a knowledge-based economy, co-ordination by communities has some distinct advantages compared to the market or hierarchical mechanisms. One of the major advantages is that, insofar as the implementation of knowledge rests on the existence of a common language and representations, the accumulation and treatment of knowledge is carried out 'naturally' within a given community, without a pressing need to resort to powerful incentive mechanisms. The community constitutes a place of trust, in the strong sense, for each of its members. Thus, when unforeseen circumstances arise, commitments will not be guided by the spirit of any existing contracts, but by the respect of the social norms specific to the community.

One of the main characteristics of communities is that they 'freely' absorb the *sunk costs* associated with building the infrastructure needed to produce or accumulate knowledge, either in a completely non-deliberate manner (embedded in their daily practices) or in a more deliberate (but still 'free') way corresponding to their willingness to contribute to the cognitive building of knowledge. Viewed from the perspective of a hierarchical organization, the building (or reproduction) of an infrastructure to accumulate knowledge (definition of a common language, definition of dominant learning processes, etc.) would entail significant sunk costs, comparable to the sunk costs required by any process of codification. Members of communities can take charge (through passion and commitment to a common objective or practice) of the sunk costs of the process of generation or accumulation of specialized parcels of knowledge.

Communities are developers and repositories of useful knowledge embedded in their daily practices and habits. The local daily interactions constitute an infrastructure that supports an organizationally instituted learning process that drives the generation and accumulation of knowledge by the community. Most of the time the accumulation of knowledge by a given community is shaped by a dominant mode of learning adopted by the community itself (such as by circulation of best practices) and knowledge therefore circulates thanks to the existence of a local language understandable only by its members. Another related characteristic of communities is that, once knowledge has been assimilated in the practices of a given community, the degree of inertia of routines and their power of replication become much stronger than the power to replicate routines encapsulated in a given hierarchical organization. Routines 'stick' easily in a given community, while organizations must deploy considerable effort to deliberately replicate the knowledge contained in an organizational routine (Cohen et al. 1996).

Co-ordination by communities does not require the implementation of heavy (and costly) extrinsic incentives. A key characteristic of communities is the absence of a visible hierarchy and the fact that, unlike other institutions, communities do not need 'alternative bundles of contracts understood as mechanisms for creating and realigning incentives' (Langlois and Foss 1996).

As informal groups, communities exhibit specific characteristics that distinguish them from the traditional organized entities usually analysed in economics or business science. Communities usually have no clear boundaries, and there is often no visible or explicit central authority controlling the quality of work or enforcing compliance to any standard procedure. The notion of a contract is meaningless to members of the community and, in particular, there is no *a priori* reason to establish any financial or contractual incentive to align the behaviour of a community's members. It has been repeatedly argued that what holds the community together is the passion and commitment of each of its members to a common objective or practice. Members of a given community share common values and the interactions between them are governed by a type of trust grounded in the respect of the community's common social norms.

The workings of trust within a community can be observed when the behaviour of participants exposed to an unexpected event is not guided by any form of contractual scheme, but by the respect of the social norms of the group. An effective community monitors the behaviour of its members by rendering them accountable for their actions. In contrast with hierarchical co-ordination modes, communities foster and utilize more effectively the social incentives that collectives have traditionally deployed to regulate their common activity: trust, solidarity, reciprocity, reputation, personal pride, respect, vengeance and retribution, among others.

The development of various communities corresponds to a progressive division of the tasks of knowledge creation where each community specializes in a parcel of new knowledge. Such communities, which are situated at intermediate levels of organizational structure, can efficiently set out heuristic and exploratory routines in order to deal with specific problem-solving activities (Cohendet and Llerena 2001).

Moreover, communities allow the stabilization of individual commitments in an uncertain universe. Individuals remain attentive to the specificities of particular situations and can consequently update the forms of their cooperative commitment. Sense construction in a community is essentially a procedural step as the 'community provides the interpretative support necessary for making sense of its heritage' (Lave and Wenger 1991). Communities are thus 'suppliers' of sense and collective beliefs for agents and play a central co-ordination role in the organization. The community framework provides the context within which the collective beliefs and reference systems that structure individual choice are built. Adopting the idea that knowledge creation is primarily realized in contexts of action and that action is always collective, consideration of the intermediate level represented by communities is thus necessary in order to focus on *learning from action* (Dupouët and Laguecir 2001).

12.3.2.2 Limitations of co-ordination by communities

In certain circumstances, autonomous communities can pose problems as a knowledge governance mechanism. They can give rise to many risks and failures. One of the major causes of failure is the risk of parochialism, discrimination or vengeance on other communities and autism towards or incompatibility with the hierarchical imperatives of organizations. A second associated problem is a weakness inherent in communities themselves, described by Bowles and Gintis (2001, pp. 11–12) in the following terms:

> Where group membership is the result of individual choices rather than group decisions, the composition of groups is likely to be more culturally and demographically homogeneous than any of the members would like, thereby depriving people of valued forms of diversity. To see this imagine that the populations of a large number of residential communities are made up of just two types of people easily identified by appearance or speech, and that everyone strongly prefers to be in an integrated group but not to be in a minority. If individuals sort themselves among the communities there will be a strong tendency for all of the communities to end up perfectly segregated for reasons that Thomas Schelling (1978) pointed out in his analysis of neighbourhood tipping. Integrated communities would make everyone better off, but they will prove unsustainable if individuals are free to move.

A third limitation is the risk of lack of *input* variety. Here perhaps lies the main potential disadvantage of communities as compared to deliberate governance.

> The personal and durable contacts that characterize communities require them to be of relatively small scale, and a preference for dealing with fellow members often limits their capacity to exploit gains from trade on a wider basis.
> Moreover, the tendency for communities to be relatively homogeneous may make it impossible to reap the benefits of economic diversity associated with strong complementarities among differing skills and other inputs. (Bowles and Gintis 2001, p. 11)

Most of the time, the attention of members of a given community is focused on a specialized topic and the emergence of diversity generally requires the creative interaction of different communities. Working by community (which by definition means working around a practice or particular cognitive objective) can stifle the organizational knowledge fit (e.g. the integration of several heterogeneous professional bodies, cross-fertilization, etc.). The problem becomes particularly acute when different communities find it difficult to communicate with each other (we will come back to this point in the next section). Organized schemes, by offering the possibility of a voluntary bridging of disciplines or groups, such as team projects or interdisciplinary groups, can offer significant advantages in such cases.

In some respects moreover, the hypothesis that incentives and hierarchy are weak within communities should not be taken at face value. Although the economic foundations of communities deviate from the characteristics of standard institutions, this does not imply the total absence of hierarchy or the disappearance of economic motivation. Recent work, in particular on virtual communities, has shown how communities develop specific organizational structures (such as the community 'kernel', community 'developers' and 'browsers'), a fact that implicitly signals the existence of an 'invisible' hierarchy in the division of work. Some communities progressively build a 'procedural authority', such as professional codes of conduct, that help resolve potential disputes as well as providing a reference point that helps members recognize the completion of various stages in the knowledge generation process. Similarly, recent literature (Lerner and Tirole 2001) has emphasized that some of the motives underlying the behaviour of community members can be of an economic nature, the main one being the search for reputation. Thus, although some characteristics of communities deviate substantially from the classic ways of understanding organizations in terms of principles of hierarchical order and incentive devices, others can be reinterpreted through an economic lens.

In what sense can we say that this myriad of heterogeneous groups interacting with one another constitute a community, underpinned by certain global norms and a unique organizational culture? Communities are disparate and dispersed, so that the alignment of different types of community within the firm is yet another management challenge. Nothing guarantees the systematic alignment of interests and objectives of the different communities *a priori*. An organization's constituent communities are not necessarily homogeneous nor do they converge towards a common objective. There are latent risks of inter-communal conflicts, autism or parochial partitioning. A global vision of the organization conceived as a coherent assembly of communities is therefore necessary. This implies thinking in terms of combining soft and hard structures of learning within a given organization.

Understanding the ways in which trade-offs between alternative co-ordination mechanisms work and defining appropriate types of governance presupposes a thorough analysis of the interactions between communities.

12.4   THE INTERACTION OF COMMUNITIES AND THE EMERGENCE OF COLLECTIVE BELIEFS WITHIN THE ORGANIZATION

The representation of the firm as a set of overlapping heterogeneous communities poses the crucial problem of analysing the spontaneous or intentional emergence of the reference systems that structure individual and collective beliefs.[3] In this context, we believe that there are two fundamental mechanisms through which existing communities can interact: the 'degree of repetition of interactions' between communities and the 'nature of communication' between communities.

- Some communities may meet frequently (e.g. workers and managers using the same canteen), a fact that can have beneficial effects on the firm (e.g. the formation of common knowledge or the circulation of news that 'something is not going well'). However, the quality of such communication can be poor (e.g. minimal common language or grammar to improve the circulation of knowledge between the communities).
- Conversely, some communities can be joined together through a rich texture of communication even if the 'degree of repetition' of interaction is weak. Mintzberg (1982), for example, quotes the well-known example of operations in hospitals where members of the different communities involved (surgeons, anaesthetists, nurses) meet infrequently. However, when they do so, they know exactly what to do and how to work together thanks to communication tools provided by their respective training.

The two phenomena share common features but a distinction between them helps us understand the nature of the coherence of a firm conceived as a community of communities.

12.4.1 The Degree of Repetition of the Interactions between Communities

The degree of repetition of interactions stimulates processes of learning and common knowledge. It creates favourable conditions for the resolution of conflicts and encourages the realization of economies of scale. As underlined by Patry (2002), it is in the dynamic interaction in which people are involved that one should look for the source of this 'interested interiorization'. One important insight of game theory is that cooperation is a rational option when an individual contemplates the losses that might follow from sanctions resulting from non-cooperation. In this case, co-ordination is achieved through a process of reciprocal adjustment. Kreps (1990) described the mechanism underlying the emergence of beliefs by ascribing a sense to events: if two players are confronted with a situation of pure co-ordination that they have already encountered and, for unspecified reasons, solved, they will *spontaneously* reproduce the previous equilibrium. The last choice thus becomes the focal point of the new situation. The logic of the focal point is closely related to the question of Simon's 'limits to rationality': in the absence of external landmarks because of the multiplicity of equilibriums, players do not succeed in co-ordinating their expectations. The logic of the focal point is then analysed as the spontaneous production, from contextual data common to the organization, of a collectively recognized collective landmark that allows agents to avoid the specular logic arising from crossed expectations and fill the undefined vacuum that would have otherwise prevailed (Schelling 1960).

The degree of repetition of interactions within an organization is captured by the notion of 'routine'. In fact, the constitution of routines and their evolution can be based on the development of a collective basis of knowledge, the definition of a set of rules, codes and common languages. Therefore, devices, such as group projects or frequent meetings encouraging the socialization of experiences, are regularly introduced by the management to offset the lack of spontaneous interaction between heterogeneous communities, in other words, to compensate for the inadequacies of the common co-ordination mechanism. This enables us to better understand the importance given to the construction of privileged learning platforms by firms ('ba' in the sense of Nonaka and Konno (1998)).

Thus, the frequency of interactions between communities promotes the construction of the collective rules which Hayek described as abstract, due both to their spontaneous emergence and to their persistence by virtue of their adaptation to 'situations' as these arise. This gradual construction, in turn, allows a central mechanism of intercommunity 'mimesis' to come into being (Orléan 2001). For Orléan, a context of uncertainty induces mimetic behaviours, which in time become effective strategies and improve all-round performance. Mimesis in this context becomes a central simplifying rule guiding choice and action in situations of uncertainty. It is based on 'trust', which acts as the cementing element at the heart of this kind of cooperation. Mimesis is not always conscious: it often results from the replication of tried and tested solutions that are known to be effective. Given that general adhesion in itself validates the conventional landmarks that are built into interactions, they effectively become essential elements in situations of co-ordination.

12.4.2   The Quality of Communication between Communities

The quality of the communication between different communities in an organization cannot be reduced to that of the 'systems of information' prevailing within the firm. Such communication is no longer a simple matter of information flow within and beyond a firm as it is in the classical contract-based model designed to minimize transaction costs and other frictions impeding information processing.

In a knowledge-based economy, the cognitive efforts made by each community to transmit mobilized knowledge and particularly the type of knowledge embodied in its routines are also important. For example, a significant obstacle confronting organizations is the restitution of the knowledge and routines acquired by the members of a project team once they return to their original functional group. Another example is the impulse to form routines between agents not belonging to the same communities. The circulation of knowledge in an innovating enterprise rests essentially on the sharing of codes and languages allowing the various communities to interact. It therefore depends crucially on relational or cognitive proximity (Nooteboom 1999) between distributed units and requires linguistic and semantic communication, shared tacit knowledge, the flow and common interpretation of information and trust or other collaboration conventions.

The communication established between communities is partly transcribed and therefore somehow materializes by permanent efforts to *codify* knowledge within the firm.[4] The construction of a cognitive setting allowing the various communities to communicate can be understood by making use of the concept of *translation* suggested by Callon and Latour (1990), which allows 'the understanding between universes that were initially strangers to each other ... universes that are progressively reconfigured as they are connected' (Callon 1999, pp. 42–3). The cognitive efforts made by a community to interest one (or several) other(s) in its knowledge production activities (which, in turn, underlie the search for a common commitment, voluntary adhesion and a common language and beliefs) correspond to the mechanism of interest/enrolment/ alliance (intéressement/enrôlement/alliance) advanced by Callon (1999) that sees the construction of an *intermediary* supporting the translation itself and the alignment of interests. The community has procedural features that are established gradually and are constantly reconfigured. The validation and collective dissemination of new knowledge can thus be interpreted as a process of diffusion and progressive contagion of the communities themselves. Within this framework, collective decision-making procedures can be regarded as processes of construction of sense, formation and revision of collective beliefs. The behaviour of choice is thus affected by the various social and cognitive structures in which the actors are 'embedded' (March and Olsen 1976).

In the context of knowledge creation, two extreme situations can be considered:

1. The first situation is a situation of 'emerging relations' corresponding to the cases where the process of creation is at an embryonic stage, such as when only one community (generally the epistemic one) has experienced and validated a creative idea. The problem in this case becomes the construction of the translation/sharing process of other communities within the firm. The degree of uncertainty in this case is so high that agents cannot anticipate the behaviour of others. In fact, the agents' behaviour remains largely opportunist and calculative. It is also deliberately procedural: the community will start a procedural process of convergence and formation of collective beliefs through a series of negotiation processes and continuous feedback until it stabilizes. The period of convergence (elimination of uncertainty) is generally a fertile period in the process of formation of collective beliefs. However, collective beliefs are more likely to converge rapidly when a 'metacode' between communities already exists. As underlined by a recent OECD report (2000), every process of knowledge codification is 'ambivalent': whereas the production and use of highly specialized jargons harm knowledge circulation, an insufficiency of codification efforts also creates an obvious obstacle to the diffusion of creative ideas. As the report states: 'This ambivalence indicates the importance of designing and implementing metacodes or semicodes as mechanisms for developing compromises between the need to make knowledge more explicit and the need to avoid excessive technicalities and local jargons' (ibid., p. 27).

2. The second situation is a situation of 'stabilized relations', where the existence of shared codes and common languages allows the various communities to share their respective knowledge on a specific domain of creation and to interact by means of ceaseless feedback in order to improve the creative principles. The degree of uncertainty is very much reduced in this case. The actions of agents will be informed by their earlier experiences. In fact, when the interactions between communities are stable, agent behaviour is conditioned by history and past experiments and therefore becomes increasingly substantive. The reason is that the environment becomes stable thanks to the set of tacit or abstract elements expressing the simplified schemes developed to interpret our experiments (such as routines, conventions and heuristics). It is, therefore, no longer necessary to know all the possible states of the world, as our ignorance is compensated by our knowledge of history. This also means that the stabilization of the interactions between communities plays a significant role in the stabilization of the agents' collective beliefs and the construction of sense. In a stabilized community or organization (conceived as a community of communities), the 'crystallization' and

'encoding' of history into routines, conventions and a corporate culture allows agents to diminish their uncertainty and focus their attention on a single objective, thereby effectively adopting substantive behaviour.

In summary, the degree of repetition of interactions and the similarity of representations due to the communication that takes place between communities are essential to fixing a future knowledge state, the convergence of expectations and the adaptation to common norms. This leads us to the key concept of 'corporate culture'.

12.4.3 Corporate Culture

Corporate culture is a complex and elusive concept, which we could summarize as a *common grammar* allowing agents to make sense of the world, codify history and past experiences and develop their actions. It corresponds to a process of co-construction of sense between communities, a co-construction of a 'common vision' (Weick 1995).

The culture of an organization comes down to its global vision, its objectives and its everyday, and therefore typical, mode of behaviour. It also depends on the role representations, collective beliefs and common enactments play in strategy and objective sharing (convergence mechanisms). Co-ordination in this context can be either devised or negotiated and is featured in routines, conventions, focal points and corporate culture. This mode of co-ordination should be distinguished from the two others, insofar as it is generally spontaneous and involves an element of trust. It can also remedy the cognitive deficiencies of agents and act as an attention-saving device. The passage from an explicit relation to a spontaneous one allows scope for cognitive economy because a conventional agreement requires very limited information synthesized by the convention itself. From this perspective, the organization can be defined as the place where rules and conventions are established and where a corporate culture emerges. This is the corporate culture required for decision making and functional efficacy (Orléan 1994; Gomez 1998).

The two levels of co-ordination (structuring beliefs and representations) can be linked. On the one hand, the existence of a common knowledge basis is essential to the establishment of informal interaction structures: 'common knowledge not only helps a group co-ordinate, but also to some extent can create groups, collective identities' (Chwe 2001, p. 11). On the other hand, the emergence of small groups or communities is a prerequisite for sharing representations and mental models: 'sharing common mental models requires that individuals form communicating groups' (Cohendet and Llerena 2001, p. 18). This system of cross-co-ordination through communities is therefore evolutionary, since the agents, while referring to a given system of beliefs, foreshadow its evolution. So, the system corresponds to a continuous learning process.

In a framework of co-ordination oriented towards organizational learning based on the explicit mobilization of corporate culture, we must consider corporate culture or the referential system as cognitive devices (corporate culture in its own right, of course, is never purely cognitive). This is a setting of situated rationality in which agents' behaviours depend on past experiences and networks of interaction. Despite remaining firmly within the domain of methodological individualism (in the sense that the self of each individual remains intact), the unit of analysis in this context becomes the group, the community or the interaction. Therefore, an individual's interest must be defined as 'seeing a certain rule implemented in a social community within which he operates' (Vanberg 1994, p. 21). Situated rationality refers to tacit knowledge specific to particular agents and contexts. So, the construction of sense and collective beliefs becomes a procedural process: individuals and communities construct sense through a process of translation. This sense remains intimately bound to action and is not fixed at any one time (Marmuse 1999).

In this sense, corporate culture can be regarded as a weakly formalized and codified entity, and one in which the experiences and history of the organization resulting from the three different co-ordination modes (market, hierarchy and communities) come pouring in. Whereas co-ordination *ex ante* by leadership is necessarily conscious and purposeful, co-ordination *ex post* by communities is essentially spontaneous. Thanks to its procedural construction (as the non-intentional and tacit result of repeated interactions), corporate culture essentially originates from an organization's communal and inter-communal dimensions.

The fact that all three co-ordination modes are considered gives rise to the question of their consistency and complementarity. This means that clarifying the governance mechanisms also becomes a delicate issue, a problem underlined by Foss (1998, p. 28):

> there are both cognitive and incentive aspects to these coordination problems. For example, the problem of adapting to an unexpected event has the cognitive dimension of categorizing and interpreting the event, and it may also have the incentive dimension of avoiding that one of the parties to a contractual relation utilizes the unexpected contingency to effect a hold-up.

It is therefore vital for an organization to establish governance mechanisms that strive to achieve complementarity between the three different co-ordination modes. A whole spectrum of different corporate cultures can be distinguished along the lines we have used to define corporate culture depending on the degrees of interaction and repetition and the quality of communication between communities.

12.5   CORPORATE CULTURE AND GOVERNANCE: MARKET, HIERARCHY AND COMMUNITIES

In order to clarify the problem of governance, we suggest a typology of the contexts of firms corresponding to different platforms of knowledge division within an organization. The concept of corporate culture set out above allows us to outline a spectrum of different corporate cultures depending on (1) the intensity of the repetition of interactions and (2) the quality of the communication between communities. This typology leads to the idea that the nature of corporate governance must depend on the nature of the corporate culture of a firm.

Table 12.1   Different forms of corporate cultures corresponding to different platforms of knowledge division within the organization

	Weak repetitiveness of interactions between communities	Strong repetitiveness of interactions between communities
Poor quality of communication between communities (lack of common codes and languages)	Case 1: 'weak' communicative culture	Case 2: strong 'tacit' culture
High quality of communication between communities (existence of common codes and languages)	Case 3: strong 'codified' culture	Case 4: 'strong' communicative culture

Different forms of corporate cultures also correspond to different contexts of knowledge creation:

In *Case 1*, the communities do not interact frequently and cannot rely on a rich cognitive architecture (common jargons, codes, etc.) in order to communicate. This situation can arise in highly unstable contexts or in activities that are distant from an organization's core competences (Amesse and Cohendet 2001). Where the communication culture is 'weak', hierarchical rules can help the achievement of coherence by prescribing procedures and methods and imposing a common unified language. Classic incentive and co-ordination mechanisms such as Taylorist time and motion management principles drive decision making. Management by design clearly dominates management by communities in this case, although local mechanisms of learning in communities (e.g. at shop floor level) can still transmit learning-by-doing effects at the global level. In such a context, as Foss (1998, pp. 27–8) suggests, a 'weak' corporate culture may also emerge and fulfil a classical role:

> The firm may have an implicit contract (or corporate culture) that solves incentives co-ordination problems by signalling to employees that management will not opportunistically take advantage of them in case of unforeseen events, although nothing specific is said (or can be said) about the event. Likewise, we can have shared interpretative schemes that solve other types of co-ordination problems by allowing employees to categorize unexpected events as being the same overall type and therefore reacting in a co-ordinated manner. Here, there is the creation of a 'convergence of expectations' that Malmgren (1961) saw as a primary benefit of firm organization, but only convergence of expectations with respect to typical features.

In *Case 2*, the weak quality of the communication between communities, which is especially noticeable in emergent relations, can lead to an expensive search for cognitive alignment between communities. Co-ordination by leadership (which is necessarily conscious and intentional) appears to be the ideal solution in instances where communication or compatibility costs are onerous or where the resolution of co-ordination problems is urgent. Therefore, a leadership script emerges, charged with co-ordinating intricate actions or beliefs while producing sense. Foss (1999) has shown that, in some circumstances, leadership can offer less expensive solutions than complex mental processes or the formation of conventions. In particular, it can facilitate the co-ordination of beliefs:

> Leadership [is] designed to co-ordinate the interlocking actions of many people through the creation of ... '*common knowledge*' ... [It is] *the ability to resolve social dilemmas, by influencing beliefs* ... Leaders may create a common knowledge when none exists previously. They also may solve co-ordination problems that persist even in the presence of common knowledge. (Foss 1999, pp. 1–2)

This type of situation also requires a specific coupling between management by design and management by communities. Part of the solution might reside in the hands of 'middle management', who play, for authors such as Nonaka and Takeuchi, a decisive role in the innovative quality of the business. Middle managers can be seen as mediators who know the norms and habits of the communities sufficiently well to translate the hierarchy's messages into a jargon that is intelligible to different communities, but also, conversely, to translate the messages coming from the communities for the hierarchy. As Schelling (1960, p. 144) noted:

> a mediator can do more than simply constrain communications – putting limits on the order of offers, counter-offers, and so forth – since he can invent contextual material of his own and make potent suggestions. That is he can influence ... expectations of his own initiative. When there is no apparent point for agreement, he can create one by his power to make a dramatic suggestion.

Case 3, which is marked by a strong 'codified' culture, involves the existence of a common cognitive architecture linking different communities (e.g. different work communities in a hospital, such as nurses, surgeons, anaesthetists). The existence of such an infrastructure of knowledge (common grammar, common codes, common languages) may be due to very different historical factors (a type of education that has anticipated the cognitive forms of relationships between heterogeneous communities, shared experience that has lasted long enough to allow a common grammar to be built, a decision taken by the hierarchy to build a modular platform of knowledge, etc.).

Whatever its origin, the common infrastructure of knowledge always takes time and sunk costs to be built. This means that it does not only define what the communities have in common, but also, implicitly, what they do not.[5] Standardized interfaces between each community and the common platform of knowledge allow each community to work independently from the others. This *modus operandi* has specific advantages, in particular the fact that, provided that the platform holds, the need for co-ordination by the hierarchy is significantly reduced. In this case, management by communities temporarily dominates management by design. However, if the interface constraints are not respected, then the efficacy of the common platform becomes questionable. This can happen, for example, when an innovation made by a particular community requires a reformulation of the whole cognitive platform. In such a context, 'sense-making' interventions by the hierarchy can occur in order to decide whether the novelty produced should lead to a reformulation. Should this turn out to be the case, a new cognitive process to define a common grammar, codes and languages has to be initiated. In summary, the role of the hierarchy is to intervene at critical times, when the need to reformulate a common platform of knowledge is deemed to be essential.

In *Case 4*, which is characterized by a strong communicative culture based on the interaction between communities, memory and the rapid co-ordination of divergent interests, an organization can generally operate in a self-organized manner (including the determination of its core interests, which can take place without excessive market or hierarchical intervention) in both consolidated and emergent contexts. It is probable that in such cases the unceasing bubbling of communities allows an organization to innovate constantly, because innovation here does not disrupt corporate integrity in any way (an idea that is related to the creative spiral put forward by Nonaka and Takeuchi 1995). Where management by communities clearly dominates management by design, the main role of the hierarchy is simply to endorse the innovative results produced by the constant interactions of the communities.

12.6 CONCLUSION

Our understanding of the role of communities within organizations falls under the broad research area studying the nature and evolution of the direct interactions between economic agents. In this way, the emergence of bonds between individuals can be explained by the use of simple rules of behaviour, without resorting to explanations based on optimizing or strategic behaviour which presuppose a very 'thick' rationality.

Our suggested framework leads to an idea of collective rationality which differs from individual rationality. In Kirman's (2000) words, 'aggregation produces rationality, and cannot be reduced to the simple sum of individual actions'. As repeated exchanges occur, the norms and conventions constructed during the process can influence the anticipations of different individuals. Some individuals can discount their own information in favour of the information emerging as a result of the actions of third parties. This kind of behaviour corresponds to the forms of normative mimesis suggested by Orléan (2001).

In this kind of framework, collective beliefs emerge from the complex interactions between individuals, and, though clearly informed by market signals and hierarchical prescriptions, are typified by their respect for the community's social norms. What leads this analysis to the idea of a 'community' is that the aggregate result is in fact based on the interaction between 'intermediate' categories that lie between the individual level and the level of the organization as a whole.

In particular, we have tried to show that the coherence of an organization rests on the nature of its corporate culture. The various categories of corporate cultures put forward in this contribution allow us to establish the appropriate forms of governance for a firm aiming to identify the complementarities of the market, hierarchy and community mechanisms. We have seen that the intensity of relations and the nature of the codification process existing between communities play an essential role in this trade-off.

This work leaves a number of questions unanswered. One of the major limitations of this study comes from the fact that communities within the organization are assumed to be given. A study of the ways in which existing communities change and new communities are created would give a genuinely dynamic vision to the analysis. Moreover, we have assumed throughout this contribution that the communities not only reside within an organization, but also remain 'faithful' to it over time. The development of virtual communities located far from the heart of traditional organizations shows that communities are by no means necessarily contained within the framework of any particular organization.

Despite these limitations, we maintain that the concept of community is useful in clarifying important aspects of the workings of co-ordination and knowledge creation within organizations. Following Bowles and Gintis (2000, p. 3), we also suggest that the community is a better way of expressing the nebulous concept of 'social capital':

> Community better captures the aspects of good governance that explain social capital's popularity, as it focuses on what groups do rather than on what people own ... This idea, old hat in sociology, long predates recent interest in social capital even among economists. A generation ago, Kenneth Arrow and Gerard Debreu provided the first complete proof of Adam Smith's conjecture two centuries earlier on the efficiency of invisible hand allocations. But the axioms required by the *Fundamental Theorem of Welfare* economics were so stringent that Arrow stressed the importance of what would be now called social capital in coping with its failure: 'In the absence of trust ... opportunities for mutually beneficial co-operation would have to be foregone ... norms of social behaviour, including ethical and moral codes [may be] ... reactions of society to compensate for market failures (Arrow 1971, p. 22)'. Communities are one of the ways these norms are sustained.

Given that the economy is increasingly knowledge-based, the study of the division of knowledge, following Hayek's original intuitions, will become increasingly important in the near future. Studies of organizational forms allowing the mutual overlap of the division of labour and the division of knowledge should therefore be fostered. By considering the firm as a community of communities, our exploratory work is an attempt to shed some light on the role of collective beliefs and corporate culture in this context. In this sense, our work is closely related to the ideas put forward by Richard Langlois (2002) on cognitive modularity, which appear to us to form its natural extension.

NOTES

1. It is obviously possible to describe certain forms of learning such as 'learning by doing' by using the traditional approach to the firm, but this type of cumulative phenomenon is only a 'by-product' of the resolution of informational problems.
2. In complex and evolutionary contexts, agents need heuristics and routines that simplify the process of decision-making (March and Simon 1993): 'Since agents have to deal with scarce cognitive resources in a complex competitive environment, it proves rational to minimize the cognitive efforts spent on routine decision cases in which singular case-by-case decisions would probably yield very similar results – but to far higher costs' (Budzinski 2001, p. 6). The agents' bounded capabilities lead them to adopt explicit or spontaneous modes of behaviour which require 'compensating institutions'. These institutions cannot be reduced to explicit contracts, as contractual theory would have it, because they are largely based on tacit conventional landmarks or 'corporate culture': agents follow rules without necessarily *understanding* their meaning at all times (Polanyi 1967). 'The adaptive or evolutionary approach is reminiscent of "invisible hand" explanations in that people do not purposefully co-ordinate; co-ordination "just happens" without anyone planning or even thinking about it' (Chwe 2001, p. 92). Though it is not impossible for a hierarchy to construct sense *a posteriori*, in this largely self-organized setting, the collective beliefs guiding and structuring behaviour within the organization and allowing it to articulate routines are formed primarily through the prevailing corporate culture.
3. This kind of representation runs into great difficulties if a dynamic perspective is adopted because communities can change substantially over time: new communities may emerge and existing ones can disappear, change or become institutionalized. In our perspective, in order to simplify the analysis, we will assume that the communities are *given* (their norms, learning process, recruitment mechanisms, and so on will be assumed to be constant). This will allow us to focus on the mechanisms of intra-community coherence. In other words, this assumption means that the evolution of each community is a slow process. It also means that the community becomes the unit of analysis.
4. As stressed by Cohen et al. (1996), the 'technology of replication of best practices' usually implies (i) learning a language within which to code successful routines, (ii) creating cognitive artefacts that can be diffused and (iii) translating the high-level description contained in the cognitive artefact into actual practice, generating a new routine adapted to the new context.
5. This can be related to the well-known idea put forward by Bourdieu that a community's acceptance of what it 'does not want to know' (about what another community is doing) is more important than the notion of common knowledge. A radical reconsideration of the way informational asymmetries are understood in economics would be necessary in order to take this idea into account.

REFERENCES

Adler, P. (2001), 'Market, hierarchy, and trust: the knowledge economy and the future of capitalism', *Organization Science*, **12** (2), 215–34.

Alchian, A. (1950), 'Uncertainty, evolution and economic theory', *Journal of Political Economy*, **58**, 599–603.

Amesse, F. and Cohendet, P. (2001), 'Technology transfer revisited in the perspective of the knowledge based economy', *Research Policy*, **30** (9).

Arrow, K. (1971), 'Political and economic evaluation of social effects and externalities', in M. Intriligator (ed.), *Frontiers of Quantitative Economics*, Amsterdam: North-Holland, pp. 5–25.

Bowles, S. and Gintis, H. (2000), 'Social capital and community governance', Working Paper, Department of Economics, University of Massachusetts.

Bowles, S. and Gintis, H. (2001), 'Social capital and community governance', Working Papers, 01–01–003, Santa Fe Institute.

Brousseau, E. (2001), 'Régulation de l'Internet: l'autorégulation nécessite-t-elle un cadre institutionnel?', *Revue Économique*, **52**, October, 349–78.

Brown, J.S. and Duguid, P. (1991), 'Organizational learning and communities of practice: toward a unified view of working, learning and innovation', *Organization Science*, **2** (1), 40–57.

Brown, J.S. and Duguid, P. (1998), 'Organizing knowledge', *California Management Review*, **40** (3), 90–111.

Budzinski, O. (2001), 'Cognitive rules and institutions: on the interrelation of intrapersonal and interpersonal rules', Discussion Paper, 241, University of Hanover.

Callon, M. (1999), 'Le réseau comme forme émergente et comme modalité de coordination: le cas des interactions stratégiques entre firmes industrielles et laboratoires académiques', in M. Callon et al. (eds), *Réseau et Coordination*, Paris: Economica.

Callon, M. and Latour, B. (1990), *La science telle qu'elle se fait*, Paris: La Découverte.

Chandler, A. (1962), *Strategy and Structure*, Cambridge, MA: MIT Press.

Chandler, A.D. (1992), 'Corporate strategy, structure and control methods in the United States during the 20th century', *Industrial and Corporate Change*, **1** (2), 263–84.

Chwe, M.S.Y. (2001), *Rational Ritual: Culture, Coordination, and Common Knowledge*, Princeton, NJ: Princeton University Press.

Cohen, M.D. (1984), 'Conflict and complexity: goal diversity and organizational search effectiveness', *American Political Science Review*, **78**, 435–51.

Cohen, M.D., Burkhart, R., Dosi, G., Egidi, M., Marengo, L., Warglien, M. and Winter, S. (1996), 'Routines and other recurring action patterns of organizations: contemporary research issues', *Industrial and Corporate Change*, **5** (3), 653–98.

Cohendet, P. and Llerena, P. (2001), 'Routines and the theory of the firm: the role of communities', contribution to the Nelson and Winter Conference, Aalborg, 12–15 June, organized by DRUID.

Cook, S.D.N. and Brown, J.S. (1999), 'Bridging epistemologies: the generative dance between organizational knowledge and organizational knowing', *Organization Science*, **10** (4), 381–400.

Cowan, R. and Jonard, N. (2001), 'The workings of scientific communities', Working Paper, MERIT-Infonomics Research Memoradum series, 2001–031.

Cowan, R., David, P. and Foray, D. (2000), 'The economics of knowledge codification and tacitness', *Industrial and Corporate Change*, **6** (3).

Crémer, J. (1998), 'Information dans la théorie des organisations', Working Paper, Institut d'Economie Industrielle, University of Toulouse.

Dibiaggio, L. (1998), *Information, Connaissance et Organisation*, Doctoral Thesis, University of Nice-Sophia Antipolis.

Dosi, G. (1988), 'The nature of the innovative process', in G. Dosi et al. (eds), *Technical Change and Economic Theory*, London: Pinter Publishers.

Dupouët, O. and Laguecir, A. (2001), 'Elements for a new approach of knowledge codification', paper presented to ETIC (Economics on Technological and Institutional Change) Final Conference, Strasbourg, France, 19–20 October.

Foss, N. (1998), 'Firm and coordination of knowledge: some Austrian insights', Working Paper, DRUID.

Foss, N. (1999), 'Understanding leadership, a coordination theory', Working Paper, DRUID.

Fransman, M. (1994), 'Information, knowledge, vision and theories of the firm', *Industrial and Corporate Change*, **3** (3).

Gensollen, M. (2001), 'Internet: marchés électroniques ou réseaux commerciaux?', *Revue Économique*, **52**, October, 137–64.

Gomez, P.Y. (1998), 'De quoi parle-t-on lorsque l'on parle de conventions?', Séminaires de l'université de Nantes, Nantes, June.

Kirman, A. (2000), 'La rationalité individuelle et la rationalité collective: l'importance des interactions entre des individus, Ecole Thématique, Economie Cognitive', Ile de Berder (Morbihan), 14–19 May.

Knorr-Cetina, K. (1998), *Epistemic Cultures. The Cultures of Knowledge Societies*, Cambridge, MA: Harvard University Press.

Kreps, D. (1990), 'Corporate culture and economic theory', in J. Alt and K. Shepsle (eds), *Perspectives on Positive Political Economy*, New York: Cambridge University Press, pp. 90–143.

Langlois, R. (2002), 'Modularity in technology and organization', *Journal of Economic Behavior and Organization*, **49**, 19–37.

Langlois, R. and Foss, N. (1996), 'Capabilities and governance: the rebirth of production in the theory of economic organization', *Kyklos*, **52** (2), 201–18.

Lave, J. and Wenger, E.C. (1991), *Situated Learning: Legitimate Peripheral Participation*, New York: Cambridge University Press.

Lerner, J. and Tirole, J. (2001), 'The open source movement: key research questions', *European Economic Review Papers and Proceedings*, **35**, 819–26.

Malmgren, H.B. (1961), 'Information, expectations and the theory of the firm', *Quarterly Journal of Economics*, **75**, 399–421.

March, J. and Olsen, J. (1976), *Ambiguity and Choice in Organizations*, Oslo: Universitetsforlaget.

March, J.G. and Simon, H.A. (1993), 'Organizations revisited', *Industrial and Corporate Change*, **2**, 299–316.

Marmuse, C. (1999), 'Le diagnostic stratégique: une démarche de construction de sens', *Actes de la VIIIème Conférence Internationale de Management Stratégique*, Ecole Centrale Paris, 26–8.

Milgrom, P. and Roberts, J. (1988), 'Economic theories of the firm: past, present, future', *Canadian Journal of Economics*, **21**, 444–58.

Mintzberg, H. (1982), *Structure et dynamique des organisations*, Paris: Les Editions d'Organisation.

Nelson, R.R. and Winter, S. (1982), *An Evolutionary Theory of Economic Change*, Cambridge, MA: Harvard University Press.

Nonaka, I. and Konno, N. (1998), 'The concept of Ba: building for knowledge creation', *California Management Review*, **40** (3), Spring.

Nonaka, I. and Takeuchi, H. (1995), *The Knowledge-Creating Company: How the Japanese Companies Create the Dynamic of Innovation*, New York: Oxford University Press.

Nooteboom, B. (1999), *Inter-firm Alliances. Analysis and Design*, London: Routledge.

OECD (2000), *Knowledge Management in the Learning Economy: Education and Skills*, Paris.

Orléan, A. (ed.) (1994), *Analyse Economique des Conventions*, Presses Universitaires de France.

Orléan, A. (2001), 'Psychologie des marchés. Comprendre les foules spéculatives: mimétismes informationnel, autoréférentiel et normatif', in Jacques Gravereau and Jacques Trauman (eds), *Crises financières*, Paris: Economica, pp. 105–28.

Paoli, M. and Principe, A. (2001), 'The relationships between individual and organizational memory: exploring the missing links', mimeo, SPRU.

Patry, M. (2002), 'De la théorie de la firme à l'économie des organisations', *Cahiers de Leçons Inaugurales*, Montréal: HEC.

Penrose, E. (1959), *The Theory of the Growth of the Firm*, Oxford: Oxford University Press.

Polanyi, M. (1967), *The Tacit Dimension*, New York: Doubleday.

Prahalad, C.K. and Hamel, G. (1990), 'The core competence of the corporation', *Harvard Business Review*, **68**, May–June, 79–91.

Richardson, G.B. (1960), *Information and Investment*, Oxford: Clarendon Press.

Richardson, G.B. (1972), 'The organisation of industry', *The Economic Journal*, September, 883–96.

Schelling, T.C. (1960), *The Strategy of Conflict*, Cambridge: Harvard University Press.

Schelling, T.C. (1978), *Micromotives and Macrobehavior*, New York: Norton.

Stalk, G., Evans, P. and Schulman, L.E. (1992), 'Competing on capabilities: the new rules of corporate strategy', *Harvard Business Review*, **70** (2), 57–70.

Teece, D.J. (1988), 'Technological change and the nature of the firm', in G. Dosi et al., *Technical Change and Economic Theory*, London: Pinter Publishers, 256–81.

Vanberg, V.J. (1994), *Rules and Choice in Economics*, London: Routledge.

Weick, K. (1995), *Sensemaking in Organizations*, London: Sage.

Wenger, E. (1998), *Communities of Practice: Learning, Meaning and Identity*, Cambridge, UK: Cambridge University Press.

Index

a priori method of belief fixation 6
abductive reasoning 91
abstract rules 47
Accounting for Tastes (Becker) 155
active experimentation 99
Adler, P. 243
administration, centralized 158–9
agent heterogeneity 2–3
Alchian, A. 243
Allais, M. 66, 160
Allais paradoxes 160
Andrews, P. 26–7, 28, 30
apriorist approach, human action
    36–42
Arena, R. 3, 5
Arrow–Debreu general equilibrium
    model 17, 60–61, 62, 70, 182,
    185, 187, 262; *see also* general
    equilibrium theory; Walrasian
    equilibrium
Arrow, K.J. 1, 17, 62
assets, redundant 69–71
asymmetric games 98
asymmetric information, and
    equilibrium 23
Aumann, R.J. 95, 97, 107–8, 121
Aumann's canonical model 125–7
Austrian tradition 3, 35–56, 216
authority, method of belief fixation 6
autonomous communities 246
axiological rationality 164–6, 171, 175

Bacharach, M.O.L. 128–9
backward induction 94–5
bank runs 182
Barro, R. 188
basic knowledge (referential
    knowledge) 122
Bayes conditioning rule 91
Bayes rule 85
Bayesian decision theory, dynamic
    consistency 141–8

Bayesian rationality 86–7
Bayesian updating rule 139–41
Becker, G. 155, 156, 176
behaviour 36, 156–9
behavioural finance 189
behavioural learning 100
beliefs
    circumstantial 45
    co-ordination 256–7
    collective, *see* collective beliefs
    consistency 4–5
    decision making 122
    diffusion of 53–4
    equilibrium 87
    expectations 183–4
    expected utility model (EUM) 162–4
    factual 4–5, 86
    fixation of 6–7
    framing 162
    game theory 1–2, 86–7, 107–9
    individual, *see* individual beliefs
    logic 84–6, 89–92
    multiple prior 137
    non-additive 137
    probabilistic 5, 12, 87, 137–9
    rationality 4–5
    revision rules 96
    role of 1, 4, 181–2
    social, *see* social beliefs
    social class 50–1, 54–5
    strategic 4–5, 86
    structural 4–5, 45, 86
Bertrand 188
'best practice' dissemination 246, 247
Binmore, K. 95, 117
Birner, J. 46
Böhm-Bawerk, E. von 35
bottom-up logic 186
Boudon, R. 3, 5, 44, 158
Bowles, S. 250, 262
Bowman, D. 73

Brandenburger, A. 108
Brown, J.S. 240

Callon, M. 254
Cambridge, St John's College 13
canonical model (Aumann's) 125–7
capabilities, differentiated 28
cascades 228
Cass, D. 67, 68
causal decision theory 92
causal independence 97
causality, principle of 38
cautious monotony axiom 91
centralized administration 158–9
Chandler, A. 243
chaotic attractors 101
Chiappori, P. 189
Chichilnisky, G. 69
choices 31, 111
Christianity, influence of 13–14, 157
circumstantial beliefs 45
Clark, J.B. 16
Clifford, W.K. 14
co-ordination and equilibrium 64–6,
    74–6
co-ordination and knowledge diffusion
    advantages 247–9
    corporate culture 256–61
    vs hierarchical system 248, 250
    horizontal 242–3
    interactional analysis 240
    limitations 250–251
    vertical 242–3
co-ordination games 120, 184, 192
co-ordination in learning 74–6, 216
co-ordination mechanisms 226
codifying knowledge 254, 255, 262
cognition
    co-ordination and equilibrium 74–6
    equilibrium 64–6
    importance of 19–20, 35, 38–9
    individual 185, 242
    and knowledge 44, 254
    role of 191
    social 190–200
cognitive economics 83–4, 203–4
cognitive frames 160
cognitive modularity 262
cognitive proximity 254
cognitive psychology 204

cognitive rationality 44, 95, 162–3,
    165–6
    vs instrumental rationality 44,
        162–3, 183–4, 186, 187–90
cognitive turning point 182, 183–4,
    185, 189
Cohen, M.D. 242
Cohendet, P. 3
Coleman, J. 156
collective beliefs
    collective rationality 261
    communities, self-organized 227–8,
        232, 234
    communities, within firms 239, 240,
        249, 255
    concept of 184–5
    corporate culture 256, 263
    definition of 190
    and individual beliefs 5–6, 35–6
    social rules 6–7, 47–9
    strategic vision of competences 244
collective intentionality 5
collective knowledge 6
collective rationality 261
collective representations 182, 240
commercial disorganization 24–5
common beliefs 190
common knowledge, of game structure
    4, 96
common man 39–40
common structure, of individuals 46
communication, between communities
    250, 251–6
communication networks 241
communication, quality of 252, 253–6
communities
    autonomous 246
    co-ordination by 247–51
    co-ordination modes 257, 258–61
    communication between 250, 251–6
    concept of 243
    consumer, in electronic markets
        223–36
    corporate culture 240, 256–8, 258–61
    definition of 226
    dynamic 262
    epistemic 246–7
    in firms 239–41, 245–58
    hierarchy in 251
    interaction of 251–8

knowledge 239
  of practice 246, 247
  procedural authority 251
  self-organized 223–36, 247
community values 172–4
compensation, effect of 215
competence-based theories of the firm
  243–5
competences, developing 247
comprehension 164, 167
conditional reasoning 91–4
conditioning rule 91
confrontation principle 98
conjectures 86
consequential principle 93
consequential reasons for public
  opinion 167–70, 171, 172–4
consequentialism 150–151, 164, 167
conservation principle 90
conservative framing 121
consistent alignment of beliefs 5
consolidation in learning 216–17
consumer communities, in electronic
  markets 223–36
consumer theory 17–18
contaminated blood trial, public
  opinion 172–4
context
  group beliefs 194–6
  historical 188, 195
  individual behaviours 45–6, 51
  influence on learning 215
  public opinion, reasons for 167–70,
    172–4
  role of 194–6
continuity, principle of 24
contract-based model 253–4
conventional beliefs 6; *see also*
  collective beliefs
conventions 256
convergence, in knowledge creation
  255, 256
cooperation, diffusion of knowledge
  240
cooperative games 109–10
core-competences 244
corporate culture 239, 240, 256–61,
  263
corporate governance 257–61
correlated equilibrium 88

costs
  short-run 24
  sunk 240, 244, 248, 260
Cournot, A.A. 16, 188
Cowan, R. 246
creativity 22, 53
creators 39–40
Crémer, J. 241
cross-fertilization in problem solving
  242
cultural context 195
cultural evolution, theory of 48–9
culture, corporate 239, 240, 256–61,
  263
cumulative proportional reinforcement
  (CPR) model 100, 102
currency markets, social beliefs in
  198–200
custom, human 20
cyclical attractors 101

Darwin, C. 14, 19, 20, 24, 25
*Das Wesen und der Hauptinhalt der
  theoretischen Nationalökonomie*
  (Donzelli) 50
Davidson, D. 157–8
Debreu, G. 17
decision-making
  beliefs 122
  editing phase 127–30
  evaluation phase 127–30
  experiment in 205–17
  and human action 36–7
decision principle 99
demand analysis 18–19
descriptive beliefs 167
Desi, G. 243
Diani, M. 3
dictionary, for player partitions 125–7
differentiated capabilities 28
differentiated learning 204
disembeddedness of economics 181
disorganization, commercial 24–5
diversity 250
division of knowledge 239
division of labour 19, 25, 239
Donzelli, F. 50
doubt, states of 6
Douglas, M. 191
Dubois, D. 146

Duguid, P. 240
Durieu, J. 102
Durkheim, É. 40, 159, 191
dynamic choice, and information 142–4
dynamic communities 262
dynamic competition model 62
dynamic consistency 141, 141–8
dynamic decision problems 139
dynamic equilibria
    eductive game theory 89–98
    evolutionist game theory 101–3

Economic Development, Theory of
    (Schumpeter) 30
economic man 19
economic problem, the 28
economics
    disembeddedness of 181
    experimental 203–4
    of innovation 216
    and mathematics 41
    of the mind 3–4
    and psychology 18–20, 217
Economics of Industry (Marshall) 24
economies of scale, and increasing
    returns 22
editing phase, decision making 127–30
eductive game theory
    dynamic equilibria 89–98
    equilibria 103–4
    vs evolutionist game theory 101
    static equilibria 84–9
eductive learning 75–6
eductive processes 2
egoism 164, 167, 176
elasticity, in organizations 22
electronic markets, consumer
    communities in 223–36
Ellison, G. 102
Ellsberg paradox 137–9, 147, 148, 151–3
emerging relations, knowledge creation
    255
empathic preferences 117
environment, influence on learning 215
epistemic communities 246–7
epistemic independence 97
epistemic learning 100
equilibrium
    belief equilibrium 87
    and co-ordination 64–6, 74–6

cognition 64–6
dynamic 89–98, 101–3
eductive game theory 89–98, 103–4
evolutionist game theory 98–103
game theory 1, 83
knowledge 23–5, 64–6
learning 74–6
multiplicity 63–7, 89, 184, 189, 253
partial 16–18, 30
probabilities 23
rational expectations 60–63
static 84–9, 101–3
stochastic 71–2
subgame perfect 94
sunspots 71–4
see also Arrow–Debreu general
    equilibrium model; general
    equilibrium theory; Walrasian
    equilibrium
equilibrium of prices, plans and price
    expectations (EPPPE) 62–7, 72
Euclid 13, 14
Euclideanity 85
evaluation phase, decision making
    127–30
evaluation principle 99
evaluative statements 165
evidential decision theory 92
evolutionary economics 216
evolutionary learning 74–5, 257
evolutionary processes 2
evolutionary psychology 14–15, 19,
    20, 21
evolutionary vision of competences
    244–5
evolutionist game theory 98–104, 117
exchange, sequential organization of
    62–3
expectations
    cognitive turning point 183–4
    and EPPPE model 63–7
    rational 183–4, 185–90
expected utility model (EUM)
    and beliefs 162–4
    vs general rational model (GRM)
        164, 166–74
    influence, reasons for 156–9
    rationality 155, 159–60, 163, 167
    shortcomings of 159–60
    weakness, sources of 162–4

expected utility theory 3, 128, 139, 141, 147, 150
experience goods 227
experience, learning from 203
experimental economics 203–4
experimentation, and knowledge growth 21
experiments in learning 205–17
exploitation behaviour 99, 100, 101
exploration behaviour 99, 100, 101

factual beliefs 4–5, 86
fairness games 121, 128–30
false consciousness 175
Faust, J. 73
feedback, positive 226, 255
Festré, A. 3
fictitious play (FP) model 100
firm
    analysis of 218
    communities in 239–41, 245–58
    corporate culture 256–61
    definition of 29
    hierarchy co-ordination mode 257, 258–61
    market co-ordination mode 257, 258–61
    theories of the 241–5
fixation of beliefs 6–7
Fleetwood, S. 43
focal principle 193
focusing message 90
forward markets 61
Foss, N. 257, 259
Foundation of Statistics (Savage) 123
framing
    of beliefs 162
    cognitive 160
    of games 110, 114, 121–31
    of problems 204
Fransman, M. 243
Frey's paradox 176
functional groups, in the firm 245–6
Fundamental Theorem of Welfare 262

game theory
    and beliefs 1–2, 86–7, 107–9
    eductive 84–98
    and equilibrium 1, 83
    evolutionist 98–104, 117
    rules 4, 109

game tree 93, 98
games
    definition of 109
    framing 110, 114, 121–31
    issues 109
    players' knowledge 109–21
    plays 110–112, 116
    rules 4, 109
    structures 109, 118–21
Garrouste, P. 45
Geanakoplos, J. 128
general equilibrium theory
    eductive learning 75–6
    and game theory 1
    heterogeneity, agent 2–3
    individual beliefs 4
    Marshall's view 16–18
    see also Arrow–Debreu general equilibrium model; Walrasian equilibrium
general explicit knowledge 43
general rational model (GRM) 164–6
    vs expected utility model (EUM) 166–74
    paradoxes explained 174–6
General Theory of Employment, Interest and Money (Keynes) 183
Gilbert, M. 5
Gilboa, I. 128, 139, 144, 149, 151
Gintis, H. 250, 262
global interactions 98
Gottardi, P. 69
governance, corporate 257–61
Grandmont, J.M. 67
Greenberg, J. 115, 121
Groenewegen, P. 13
group beliefs
    autonomy of 196–200
    concept of 184–5
    context 194–6
    definition of 190–192
    Schelling salience 192–4
    self-organized communities 228, 234
Growth of the Firm, Theory of the (Penrose) 29
Guesnerie, R. 2, 3, 4, 5, 62, 75

habits 51–2, 53
Hahn, F. 1, 3, 62
Hamel, G. 243, 244

Hammond, P. 139, 141, 150
Hardin, R. 159
Hargreaves Heap, S. 5, 6
Hayek, F.A. von
  Austrian tradition 35–6, 51, 53, 55
  knowledge 27, 39, 42–9, 56, 262
  logical circularity 2
Hens, T. 72
herd behaviour 224, 232
heterogeneity, agent 2–3
Hicks, J.R. 14, 17, 26
hierarchical groupings, in the firm
    245–6, 248, 250
hierarchy co-ordination mode 257,
    258–61
Hildebrand, W. 76
historical context 188, 195
History of Astronomy (Smith) 19
holism 40
Hollis, M. 156
horizontal co-ordination 242–3
human action 20, 36–8
*Human Action: A Treatise of
  Economics* (von Mises) 36
Hume, D. 14
Hume's theorem 166
hypothesis transformation function
    92

imagination, and knowledge 28, 30, 32
imitative behaviour 3, 53–4, 224, 225
imprecision, reduction of 149
incentives 248–9, 251
inclusion axiom 90
increasing return, law of 26
*Increasing Returns and Economic
  Progress* (Young) 25
increasing returns, law of 21
individual beliefs
  Austrian tradition 35–6
  collective beliefs 5–6, 35–6
  diffusion of 39–42
  general equilibrium theory 4
  human action 37–8
  inter-individual co-ordination 38–9
  and knowledge 44–5
  self-organized communities 227–8,
    234
  vs social beliefs 196–200
  social rules 6–7, 45–7, 48

individual cognition 185, 242
individual intentionality 5
individual rationality 234, 261
individual representations 182, 188–9
individualism 164, 167, 257
industrial districts 22–3
industrial organization 28–9
industry, specialization in 26
ineffectivity theorem 68
infinite horizon models 66–7
influence, in social interaction 224
information
  collective choice 201
  content 148–50
  dynamic choice 142–4
  negative value 151–3
Information and Communication
    Technology (ICT), consumer
    communities 223–36
information-dependant games 128
information goods 227
information principle 98–9
informational cascades 224–6
informational investment 99
informational mimesis 224–6
infra-classicality axiom 91
Inglehart, R. 167–8
initiative 22
innovation 53, 216, 240, 243, 245, 261
innovative behaviour 3
institutions 48
instrumental rationality
  vs axiological rationality 164–5, 166,
    171
  backward induction paradox 95
  vs cognitive rationality 44, 162–3,
    183–4, 186, 187–90
  and preferences 4, 6
insurance game 158
insurance, spot multiplicity 69
inter-individual co-ordination 38–9
interactions, between communities
    240, 252–3, 261
intercommunity mimesis 253
internal organization, of the firm 27
intertemporal calculation 41
intertemporal equilibrium multiplicity
    66–7
introspection 38, 84
issues, of games 109

Jaffray, J.Y. 62
Jeffrey, R.C. 123
justice 188

Kahneman, D. 156
Kajii, A. 69, 71
Kandori, M. 102
Kantian philosophy 37
Kehoe, T.J. 66
Keynes, J.M.
   diversity of beliefs 3
   probabilistic beliefs 137
   rational calculation 183, 184, 189
   typology of beliefs 5
   uncertainty 30
   unemployment 24, 188
Keynesian equilibrium 76
Khaneman, D. 127
Kirman, A. 224, 261
Knight, F. 27, 137
know-how 243, 247
knowledge
   assumptions about 108–9
   co-ordination in diffusion 240,
      242–3, 247–51, 256–61
   codifying 254, 255, 262
   cognition 44, 254
   collective 6
   common 4, 96
   communities 239
   communities of practice 246, 247
   definition of 43, 107
   division of 239
   emerging relations 255
   epistemic communities 246–7
   and equilibrium 23–5, 64–6
   firm, theories of the 241–5
   forms of 43
   games 109–21
   growth of 18–20
   Hayek's conception of 43–4
   and individual beliefs 44–5
   leadership 259
   Marshall's method 15–18
   Marshall's problem of 13–15
   and organization 21–3, 25–6, 29–30,
      250
   and routines 253
   social 44, 48–9
   stabilized relations 255–6
   see also learning

knowledge-based economies 3, 239–41,
   254
Kreps, D. 194, 252
Kuhn, T.S. 11
Kuran, T. 159, 163

Laffont, J.J. 72
Laidler, D. 188
Lamarckian mechanism 100
Langlois, R. 262
language, community communication
   248, 253, 254
Latour, B. 254
leadership 53–4, 259
learning
   from action 249, 263
   co-ordination 74–6
   context, influence of 215
   continuous 257
   definition of 204, 242
   differentiated 204
   environment, influence of 215
   equilibrium 74–6
   path-dependent 204
   process, experiment in 205–17
   role of 203–4
   studies of 78
   types of 148–50
   see also knowledge
Levine, D.K. 66
Lewis, D. 85, 91
Loasby, B.J. 3
local explicit knowledge 43
local interactions 98
logic, and beliefs 84–6, 89–92
logical circularity 2
logical omniscience 84–5

MacClennen, E. 151
McGregor, D. 27
Machina, M. 151
macroeconomics 187, 225
Malmgren, H.B. 259
management by communities 258–61
management by design 258–61
management vision, and competences
   244
Mansel, H. 13
March, J.G. 243, 244
Marengo, L. 242

marginal utility theory 17
market co-ordination mode 257,
    258–61
markets
    electronic 223–36
    forward 61
    as a process 40
Marshall, A.
    equilibrium 23–5
    knowledge, growth of 18–20
    knowledge, problem of 3, 13–15
    method of economic analysis 15–18
    organization 21–3
    post-Marshallians 25–31
Marxian analysis of investment 50
Mas-Colell, A. 69, 70
material rationality 94, 97
mathematics, and economics 41
mean field analysis 227
meetings 253
Mehta, J. 192
Menger, C. 35, 40
mental map 44
Merton, R. 189
metacode 255
methodological individualism 50
methodology of investigation 218
Mill, J.S. 14, 18
Mills, C.W. 161, 174
mimetic dynamics 234
Mintzberg, H. 252
Mises, L.E. von 35–42, 51, 53, 55, 56
Mithra cult 157
money, function of 41–2
mono-population games 98
monotony axiom 90
Moral Sentiments, Theory of (Smith)
    170
Morgenstern, O. 2, 110
motives
    economic 251
    individual 4, 50–51
    leaders 53
    unconscious 51–2
moves, sequences of 111
multi-population games 98
multiple prior beliefs 137
multiple prior model 139, 149, 151–3
multiplicity
    equilibria 63–7, 89, 184, 189, 253

expectations 188
    spot markets 67–71
Muth, J.F. 62, 183

Nash equilibrium
    dynamic equilibria 94
    players' knowledge 118–21
    players' rationality 115–18
    static equilibria 88–9, 102
Nashian regulator 83
Natural State 39
negative introspection 84
Nelson, R.R. 243, 244
neo-Darwinian belief 25
Neumann, J. von 110
new institutional economics 216
Newcomb's problem 92, 112
Ngo-Maï, S. 3, 4, 5
Nöldeke, G. 103
non-additive beliefs 137
non-Bayesian models 139, 150
non-consequential reasons for public
    opinion 170–174
non-contextual reasons for public
    opinion 172–4
non-cooperative games 109–10
non-empty communities, distribution
    of 227–33, 234–6
non-Euclidean geometry 14, 16
non-expected utility models 144
non-hierarchical communication 241
non-imitative agents 225
non-instrumental rationality 164–5
non-monotonic reasoning 91
Nonaka, I. 243, 259
normative beliefs 163–4, 167
normative mimesis 261
normative rules 48
normative statements 166
Novarese, M. 3, 6

Oberschall, A. 159
objectives, diversity of 242
opportunity cost 32
Organisation for Economic Co-
    operation and Development
    (OECD) 255
organization
    and disorganization 24–5
    industrial 28–9

internal 27
and knowledge 21–3, 25–6, 29–30,
    250
organizational structures 251
Orléan, A. 3, 4, 5, 224, 253
overreaction paradox 161
Oxford Economists' Research Group
    26–7
Oxford University 28

Paoli, M. 244
Pareto optimal equilibrium 47, 68, 71
parlour games 110–112, 114
partial equilibrium 16–18, 30
passive experimentation 99
path-dependent learning 204
Patry, M. 252
Pearce, D. 128
peer-reviewed publication 246
Peirce, C.S. 6
Penrose, E. 29–30, 243
perfect competition, equilibrium 17
perfect equilibrium 94–8
Philosophical Investigations
    (Wittgenstein) 7
players, framing of games 121–31
players' knowledge 109–21
plays, and games 110–112, 116
polarization, of communities 234
Porath, B. 96
positive beliefs 162–4
positive feedback 226
positive introspection 84
positivism 157
possibilistic decision model 146–8
possibility measures 146–7
post-Marshallians 25–31
power laws 225–6, 230, 232, 234
Prahalad, C.K. 243, 244
praxeology 37
preference system 4, 6, 17
preferences
    diversity 242
    empathic 117
    endogenously generated 155
    instrumental rationality 4, 6
    separability of 150
    strong dynamic consistency 142–5,
        150
    weak dynamic consistency 145–50
preferential attachment hypothesis 226

preservation axiom 90
preservation property 92, 94
prices
    expectations 59
    informational efficiency of 186–7
    short-run 24
    temporary equilibrium 24
    tool of action 41
principal–agent theory 28
Principe, A. 244
Principles of Economics (Marshall)
    16–17, 21, 24
privileged activities (core-competences)
    244
privileged learning platforms 253
probabilistic beliefs 5, 12, 87, 137–9
probabilities
    beliefs 5, 12, 87, 137–9
    equilibrium 23
    semantics 85
probability distribution, common prior
    88
problem-solution (Aumann) 107,
    109–15
problem solving 204, 242
project teams, in the firm 245–6, 253
promoters 39–40
prospect theory 127
psycho-neurobiological processes 204
psychological games 6, 121, 128–30
psychology
    cognitive 204
    and economics 18–20, 217
    evolutionary 14–15, 19, 20, 21
    individual beliefs 189
    Marshall's interest in 14
public opinion 167–74
punctual attractors 101
purchasing power 41–2
pure coordination games 120, 192
pure economics 181
purposeful behaviour 36

qualitative information 146–7
Quarterly Journal of Economics (1937)
    183
Quéré, M. 25

Rabin, M. 128
radical framing 121–2
radical subjectivism 36, 37

Radner, R. 3, 60, 62, 70
Radnitzy, G. 162–3
Raffaelli, T. 14, 16, 18
random network theory 225–6
rational action theory, *see* rational
    choice model (RCM)
rational beliefs 5
rational bubbles 182
rational choice model (RCM) 12, 22,
    156, 160
rational expectations 60–3, 183–4,
    185–90
rational expectations hypothesis 62
rational optimizer 19
rationalisable equilibrium 87–8
rationality
    axiological 164–5, 171, 175
    and beliefs 4–5
    cognitive 44, 95, 162–3, 165–6,
        183–4, 186, 187–90
    collective 261
    and conditional reasoning 93–4
    expected utility model (EUM) 155,
        159–60, 163, 167
    general rational model (GRM) 164,
        176
    hypothesis of 200–201
    individual 234, 261
    individual representations 189
    instrumental 4, 6, 44, 95, 162–5, 166,
        171, 183–4, 186, 187–90
    material 94, 97
    perfect equilibrium 94–8
    rules 115–18
    situated 185, 192, 257
    solution concepts 115–18
    substantive 94, 97
    weak 139
Raybaut, A. 3, 4, 5
reduction of imprecision 149
redundant assets 69–71
referential knowledge (basic
    knowledge) 122, 257
reflexivity axiom 85, 91
regularities, behavioural, experiment
    in 205–17
relational proximity 254
religious belief 13–14, 157
replicator model 101
representations
    co-ordination of 256–7

collective 182, 240
corporate culture 256
economic systems 11–12
individual 182, 188–9
of problems 204
Rescher, N. 164
resolution, of game players 96
resource allocation, and uncertainty
    27–8
revising message 89
Richardson, G.B. 27–9, 30, 243
Rizzello, S. 3, 6
Roman soldiers 157
Root, H.L. 158
Rousseau's political theory 158
routines
    co-ordination by communities 248,
        253
    creativity 22
    firm, theories of the 243, 244–5
    knowledge 253
    learning, experiment in 205–17
    unconscious motives 51–2
rules
    behavioural, experiment in 205–17
    collective 253
    communities 246–7
    consolidation of 216
    corporate culture 256
    game theory 4, 109
    general 47
    players' knowledge 118–21
    preferences, separation from 6
    rationality 115–18
    shared 7
    social 6–7, 45–9, 249
Ruse, M. 156

St John's College, Cambridge 13
sampling 148
Samuelson, L. 101, 103
Samuelson, P.A. 26, 66
satisfaction principle 98
satisfaction property 92, 94
Savage, L.J. 107, 121, 122–5, 137, 139,
    141–2
Savage's framework 122–5, 132
Scarf agency 64–5, 67–71, 74
Schelling salience 192–6
Schelling, T.C. 120, 184, 192, 250, 260

Schmeidler, D. 128, 139, 144, 149, 151
Schmidt, C. 4, 6
Schumpeter, J.A. 16, 24, 30, 35–6, 40, 50–55
scientific communities 239
scientific method of belief fixation 6
selection function 97–8
self-fulfilling prophecies 182, 200
self-interest, and social order 46
self-organized communities
    communities of practice 247
    definition of 226–7
    electronic markets 223–4
    group beliefs 228, 234
    individual beliefs 227–8, 234
    non-empty communities 227–33, 234–6
    research 224–6
self-referential mimesis 224
semantics 84–6, 90–92, 94, 121
Sensory Order, The (Hayek) 44
sequential hypothetical beliefs 97
sequential model (market organization) 61–2
sequential organization of exchange 62–3
Shackle, G. 30–31, 137, 146
shared beliefs 190
shared rules 7
Shell, K. 67, 68
Shiller, R. 195–6
short-run cost 24
short-run prices 24
signalling equilibria 182
Simon, H. 155, 218, 243, 244, 253
situated rationality 185, 192, 257
Smith, Adam 12, 19, 25, 170–172, 262
social beliefs
    autonomy of 196–200
    concept of 184–5
    context 194–6
    definition of 190–192
    vs individual beliefs 196–200
    Schelling salience 192–4
    self-organized communities 228, 234
social capital 262
social class 50–51, 54–5
'Social classes in an ethically homogenous environment' (Schumpeter) 50

social cognition 190–200
social contract 117
Social Contract (Rousseau) 158
social games 112–15
social knowledge 44, 48–9
social order, and self-interest 46
social rules
    co-ordination by communities 249
    collective beliefs 6–7, 47–9
    individual beliefs 6–7, 45–7, 48
Social Situations, Theory of (Greenberg) 121
Social State 39–42
social values 246
socialization 156–7
Solal, P. 102
solution concepts, rationality 115–18
sophisticated behaviour 151
specialization, in industry 26
Spencer, H. 20
spot markets
    Arrow–Debreu general equilibrium model 61
    insurance 69
    multiplicity 59, 67–71
    price multiplicity 63–7
    sunspots 72–4
stabilized relations, knowledge creation 255–6
Stachetti, E. 128
Stalk, G. 244
Stalnaker, R.C. 97
states of doubt 6
static competition model 62
static decision problems 138–9
static equilibria
    eductive game theory 84–9
    evolutionist game theory 101–3
stereotypical preference 193
stochastic equilibrium 71–2
stochastic fictitious play 100, 102
stock market crash (1987) 195–6
strategic beliefs 4–5, 86
strategic vision of competences 244
strong dynamic consistency of preference 142–5, 150
Strotz, R. 151
structural beliefs 4–5, 45, 86
structure, of games 109, 118–21
subgame perfect equilibrium 94

subjective opinion 175
subjectivism 36, 37
substantive rationality 94, 97
substitution, principle of 20
success axiom 90
Sugeno integral 147
sunk costs 240, 244, 248, 260
sunspots 67, 71–4, 182
sure-thing principle 137, 139, 144–6
symmetric games 98
syntax 84–6, 90–92

tacit (unconscious) knowledge 43, 47
Takeuchi, H. 243, 259
Tallon, J.-M. 3, 4
tâtonnement process 1
team thinking 5
Teece, D.J. 243
teleology, principle of 38
temporary equilibrium 24
tenacity, method of belief fixation 6
Tocqueville, A. de 158
traditions 48
transaction-cost theory 28, 241–3
transactional theory 241–3
transitivity 85
translation, in communication 254, 257
Treatise on Probability (Keynes) 5
trembling hand, of game players 96
Trieb (urges) 53
trust 249, 253
truth 188
Tuomela, R. 5
Tversky, A. 127, 156

ultimatum games 129, 160, 175–6
uncertainty
  decision making 122–5
  knowledge 29, 255
  Marshall, Alfred 16
  resource allocation 27–8
unconscious (tacit) knowledge 43, 47
uniqueness property 94
updating message 89–90
utilitarian criterion 171
utility maximization principle 92

Vanberg, V. 46, 47
variable universe games 121, 128–9
Varoufakis, Y. 5, 6
Vergnaud, J.-C. 3, 4
veridicity 84
vertical co-ordination 242–3
vicarious learning 203, 216
Vienna School 36
virtual communities 223–36, 239, 251, 262
vision, in the firm 244, 256–8
voting, paradox of 159, 175

Walliser, B. 2, 4–5, 45
Walras, M.E.L. 17
Walrasian auctioneer 64–5, 83
Walrasian equilibrium 16, 24, 60, 76, 83; *see also* Arrow–Debreu general equilibrium model; general equilibrium theory
wants, and knowledge growth 18–19
weak dynamic consistency of preference 145–50
weak rationality 139
weak sure-thing principle 146, 147, 149
Wealth of Nations (Smith) 170
Weber, M. 157, 159, 164, 166, 171
Weil, P. 189
White Collar: The American Middle Classes (Mills) 161
Wieser, F. von 35, 40, 50, 53, 54
Williamson, O. 242
Wilson, J.Q. 156
Winter, S. 243, 244
Wittgenstein, L. 6, 7
Wittgenstein's paradox 112
Wright Mills paradox 174

'Ye machine' (Marshall) 14–15, 19, 20, 21
Young, A. 25–6, 29
Young, H.P. 102

Zadeh, L. 146
Zhang, J. 101